THE SECOND FRONT

KEN CONBOY

THE SECOND FRONT

Inside Asia's Most Dangerous Terrorist Network

EQUINOX
PUBLISHING
JAKARTA SINGAPORE

Equinox Publishing (Asia) Pte. Ltd.
Menara Gracia 6/F
Jl. HR Rasuna Said Kav C-17
Jakarta 12940
Indonesia

www.EquinoxPublishing.com

ISBN 979-3780-09-6

The Second Front:
Inside Asia's Most Dangerous Terrorist Network

©2006 Ken Conboy

First Equinox Edition 2006

1 3 5 7 9 10 8 6 4 2

Printed in the United States.

C O N T E N T S

PREFACE

O n Saturday evening, 1 October 2005, a trio of young men strolled into three popular restaurants on the Indonesian resort island of Bali. Making a beeline for the areas most crowded by diners, each paused long enough to set off explosives stored inside Tupperware containers stuffed into their backpacks. Ball bearings encrusting the devices sliced across the dining halls, killing nearly two dozen and wounding more than 100.

At the top of the shortlist of suspects was Jemaah Islamiyah, the shadowy terrorist organization responsible for hundreds of deaths during its decade-long campaign to found an Islamic super-state across Southeast Asia. If true, the attack was in some ways a new departure for the group. After all, Jemaah Islamiyah's annual attacks since 2002 centered around spectacular car bombs, and common wisdom pointed at a continuation of this formula. Indeed, warnings issued by Indonesian President Susilo Bambang Yudhoyono the previous month urged vigilance toward another vehicle-borne device, probably targeted against the capital of Jakarta.

But while some saw this change in tactics as a sign of dwindling ability, writing Jemaah Islamiyah's epitaph is a bit premature. After all, some of its most dangerous members are still on the loose and appear to be having little trouble sourcing explosives – often from mines and rock quarries – and foot soldiers willing to seek martyrdom. Worse, though the United Nations has officially vilified Jemaah Islamiyah as a terrorist organization, and international efforts have been enacted to close off its sources of outside monies, there are recent indications of foreign funding again making its way into their coffers.

What follows is the history of Jemaah Islamiyah, from its origins as an offshoot of the Darul Islam movement through its deadly campaign against Western interests and the secular authorities of Southeast Asia. It is important that the story be told for several reasons. First, Islamic extremism is not new to Southeast Asia and, as it colors the current generation of radicals, its past history should be explored in an objective light.

Second, extremism remains a sad fact of current-day Southeast Asia. Given the strategic importance of this part of the world – its location astride sea lanes, its natural resources – it is important that the threat posed by extremism be properly analyzed and placed in context.

Third, and most important, extremism in Southeast Asia – and especially Indonesia – may go into remission in the coming years, but it is almost certain to return in the future under different names. The radical threat, after all, has been predictably cyclic: the current crop of terrorist leaders can be killed, captured, or rehabilitated, but the seeds have already been planted for the next generation. By learning what they have done to date, one can better anticipate the chapters that have yet to be written.

This book is based on both written sources from several countries, as well as interviews. To the extent possible, sources have been identified in footnotes. Some of the best sources, especially serving intelligence officers in the Indonesian State Intelligence Agency (*Badan Intelijen Negara*, or BIN) and National Police, must remain anonymous. Special thanks go to General A.M. Hendropriyono, who was extremely generous with his time and extraordinary support. I also extend my sincere gratitude to Nasir Abas, Ken Brownrigg, Noor Huda Ismail, Gary Laing, John MacDougall, the late Bram Mandagi, Len Medieros, Soeharjono, Veera Star, and Jason Tedjasukmana. Strong thanks, too, to Mark Hanusz and John Hanusz for their usual outstanding work in editing and producing this volume.

A note on spelling is in order. Spelling in Bahasa Indonesia is often an inexact science, especially since grammatical changes instituted in 1972 have not always been implemented for personal names. Further complicating matters, transliterations from Arabic to Bahasa Indonesia have spawned further spelling variants. The Malaysian language, too, has its variants: for example Azhari is often spelled Azahari. In many cases, these variants are addressed in the pages that follow.

One other point deserves mention. The reaction among those linked to Jemaah Islamiyah varies greatly. Some, such as Amrozi and Imam Samudera, are unapologetic for their acts of violence. Others, such as Ali Imron, are repentant. Still others, such as Abu Bakar Ba'asyir and his son Abdul Rahim, vehemently deny any connection to terrorist activities. Such denials are duly noted.

Although all books are a collaborative effort, the author takes responsibility for everything in these pages. Any errors in fact or interpretation are my own.

Ken Conboy
Jakarta, October 2005

CHAPTER ONE

THE REBEL

The six-man military firing squad took positions in the sand along a beach in a desolate corner of the Thousand Islands, the name given to the arc of idyllic islets off the coast of the Indonesian capital of Jakarta. Per army regulations, five of their rifles held blanks; just one chambered a real bullet. Their target, ten meters before them, was a stoic, elderly man at pains to battle a stoop brought on by his advanced years. It was difficult to believe this had been Indonesia's top fugitive for more than a decade.

But for those who knew Sekarmadji Maridjan Kartosuwirjo, his defiant end was consistent with a lifetime of rebellion. Born to an opium seller in Cepu, Central Java, five years into the twentieth century, Kartosuwirjo had come of age just as the Dutch were opening up their school system to select colonial subjects. Through family connections, he landed a berth at the local Dutch-run school; there he excelled in the secular sciences.

Upon graduation, Kartosuwirjo entered a society in the midst of profound social change. Unlike some of the earlier anti-colonial protests that had sporadically flared across the archipelago the previous century, a new sense of Indonesian nationalism was slowly taking shape. Spearheading this movement was *Sarekat Islam* – the Islamic League – a grassroots organization that had started as a protection society to shield Javanese traders from the sharp competition offered by ethnic Chinese counterparts.

Drawn toward Sarekat Islam, Kartosuwirjo found the league had radically departed from its original mandate. Under the leadership of the charismatic

Oemar Said Tjokroaminoto, the organization was busy hammering out a political role for Islam. Part intellectual, part businessman, part magnetic orator, Tjokroaminoto had also ditched his initial loyalty to the colonial government and was now talking up independence.

Spellbound by Tjokroaminoto's rebellious leanings, Kartosuwirjo became the diligent protégé. By his early twenties, he had been handpicked as his mentor's private secretary. In this role, however, he had competition for Tjokroaminoto's attention. Four years Kartosuwirjo's senior, a firebrand named Sukarno had taken Sarekat Islam by storm. An accomplished orator in his own right, Sukarno was bright and dashing. He was also family: Tjokroaminoto had bequeathed Sukarno his teenaged daughter.

As rivals, Sukarno and Kartosuwirjo quickly came to differ on substantive matters. Sukarno favored a synthesis of nationalism, communism, and Islam as the basis for an independence movement. Kartosuwirjo, by contrast, detested the atheistic underpinnings of communism; Russian communists, he felt, deserved much of the blame for destroying the Ottoman caliphate.

The Ottomans provided another dividing line for the two. For Sukarno, Mustafa Kemal Ataturk, father of Turkey's modern secular state, was someone worthy of emulation. But for Kartosuwirjo, Ataturk had done little other than preside over the funeral for what had once been a formidable Islamic empire; modern-day Turkey, he felt, was little more than an anemic vestige.

In time, the two parted ways. Forfeiting his role as Tjokroaminoto's heir apparent, Sukarno split with Sarekat Islam in 1927 to form the Indonesian National Party. There he went from strength to strength, his blend of quasi-socialist populism resonating among the Javanese masses. Kartosuwirjo, by contrast, remained a league loyalist, then became a founding member when it was transformed into a political party.

But even among colleagues, Kartosuwirjo began to show an unwillingness to cooperate or compromise. By 1936, a year before he was elected his party's vice president, he started promoting the idea of Indonesia as an independent Islamic state. This course set him at odds with Sukarno and the nationalist mainstream, which was heading in a decidedly secular direction.

Kartosuwirjo's musings might not have gone anywhere had it not been for World War II. As the Imperial Japanese pushed their way across the Indonesian archipelago, they initially persecuted indigenous nationalists. But as the Allies made advances, Tokyo pragmatically reversed itself and encouraged the growth of religious organizations and independence movements – even to the point of training indigenous armies – as a means of currying local favor and frustrating attempts by the Allies to reassert colonial domination in Asia.

Wearing religious and political hats, Kartosuwirjo appealed to the Japanese on both counts. Stoking his activism, the Japanese allowed him to set up a four-hectare training camp in West Java for a fledgling Islamic youth militia known as *Hizbullah* (Arabic for "God's Army").

West Java, it turned out, was perfect for Kartosuwirjo's purposes. Though cramped onto a single island, the ethnic Sundanese that populated West Java were worlds apart from the Javanese that dominated the remaining two-thirds. Culturally and linguistically, the Sundanese for centuries had chafed in the shadows of the more powerful Javanese kingdoms further east. Eager to differentiate themselves, they came to shun the heavily stratified, Hindu-influenced societies – and resulting class conflicts – favored by the Javanese.

All of this had a direct impact on the direction of Indonesian nationalism. Already too familiar with class stratification, the Javanese rural masses were receptive to the liberating precepts of communism. The secular ideological brew of Sukarno and his ilk, therefore, struck a chord. But among the Sundanese in West Java, where class conflict was historically less pronounced, many embraced Islamic piety both as a means of differentiating themselves from the Javanese and expressing an Indonesian national identity. Kartosuwirjo, even though he was himself Javanese, found his non-secular message had powerful traction among the Sundanese.

Taking full advantage of the Japanese push, Kartosuwirjo began rotating classes through his paramilitary camp. By the time World War II ended, and renewed hostilities against the Dutch looked set to begin, Hizbullah had a significant armed presence across the Sundanese heartland.

During the war of independence that followed, Kartosuwirjo took it upon himself in July 1947 to declare *jihad* – a holy war – against the returning Dutch colonialists. In doing so, he and his partisans formed a loose alliance with the nationalist guerrillas that had also taken up arms across Java. Neither faction lost sight of the fact that theirs was a marriage of convenience: whereas the nationalists were fighting for a secular state, Kartosuwirjo's religious warriors made no secret that they envisioned a non-secular Indonesia.[1]

Midway through the war, Kartosuwirjo caught a lucky break. When the Dutch agreed to a ceasefire in January 1948, they stipulated that the 35,000 nationalist guerrillas operating in West Java were required to regroup near Sukarno's headquarters in Central Java. Doing as instructed, the nationalists conducted a long march to the east. But Kartosuwirjo, who was not party to the ceasefire, felt no compunction to abide by its letter or spirit. In mid-February, he formally established the Indonesian Islamic Army (*Tentara Islam Indonesia*, or TII) in West Java consisting of four battalions of his former Hizbullah and other Islamic partisans. Later that same month, they had their first clash with the Dutch.[2]

Perhaps predictably, the ceasefire collapsed toward year's end. Having never laid down arms, Kartosuwirjo sought to re-double the efforts of the TII in December by again declaring jihad. This time, however, he did not have his sights solely fixed on the Dutch. As nationalist guerrillas filtered back toward West Java, they discovered the TII had expanded its area of operations during the interim. Kartosuwirjo mocked the returnees as cowards, noting his partisans alone had carried on the armed struggle against the Dutch for almost a year. With the nationalists crying foul, the two sides in January 1949 experienced their first firefight.

Switching to the political arena, Kartosuwirjo ratcheted up his struggle to the next level. Having spent as much time promoting independence as his nationalist rivals, he saw no reason why he had to subjugate his vision to theirs. In August, he formally proclaimed himself head of the Indonesian Islamic State (*Negara Islam Indonesia*, or NII). The areas of West Java under the control of his partisans became known as *Darul Islam*. Derived from the Arabic words *Dar Al Islam*, it literally translated as "House of Islam" or "Realm of the Faith," but

---

[1] Early in the independence struggle, Kartosuwirjo participated in the debate over the wording of the 1945 constitution being championed by the nationalists under Sukarno and Mohammad Hatta. Kartosuwirjo and his top followers eventually gave tacit support to a secular state as set forth in the constitution; however, they continued to harbor the conviction that Indonesia would become an Islamic state after the withdrawal of the Dutch.

[2] Prior to the formal establishment of the TII, the Islamic partisans in West Java often operated as autonomous district-level bands and sometimes used names other than Hizbullah. In the Tegal area, for example, they were known as *Mujahidin* (Arabic for "Warriors of Jihad"). Others, known as *Sabillillah* (Arabic for "In God's Path"), tended to consist of more senior personnel than the Hizbullah youth militia. The term *mujahidin* is often transliterated as *mujahideen* in the English-language press.

more broadly referred to a state or zone ruled according to Islamic law.

More bad blood was to come. When the Dutch finally granted independence in December 1949, the nationalists naturally snubbed the rebellious Darul Islam partisans when they began selecting guerrillas for integration into the downsized post-independence armed forces. This only convinced Darul Islam not to lay down their arms.

At the same time, however, the nationalists could offer only a limited response to the Darul Islam challenge. First, they were more urgently needed to counter a Dutch-inspired uprising near Bandung in January 1950. Next, there was a need to export Java-based troops to confront a secessionist rebellion in the Maluku islands.[3] As a result, when Sukarno formally announced the formation of a republican government in Jakarta that August, Kartosuwirjo again felt sufficiently confident to reject the secularists' right to rule.

He had good reason for his confidence. Over the ensuing years, the TII had mirrored the territorial structure of the republican guerrillas in West Java down to the village level. Its fledgling officer corps, with a rank structure that extended to general, oversaw a division in West Java consisting of three regiments. In neighboring Central Java, the TII had established the framework for a second division.

By the following year, Darul Islam had made West Java a province aflame. It effectively displaced the government across much of rural West Java and was not above inflicting bloodshed in the countryside. During the last three months of 1951, Islamic guerrillas were accused of killing over 400 and burning more than 4,000 houses.[4]

This put the government in a fix. Compared with previous threats – most notably the secessionist rebellion in the Malukus – Darul Islam was a far more serious affront to the fledgling republic. Not only was it operating close to the center of power in Jakarta, but combating such a guerrilla insurgency required a non-conventional campaign – something the Indonesian military (despite its guerrilla origins) was ill equipped to conduct. "Our armed forces had replaced the Dutch as a conventional military," one Indonesian general would later ob-

---

[3]   In 1964, the Indonesian government claimed that Darul Islam had conspired with the Dutch to conduct the 1950 uprising around Bandung. See Pinardi, *Sekarmadji Maridjan Kartosuwirjo* (Djakarta: PT Badan Penerbit Aryaguna, 1964), p. 122.

[4]   During the first three months of 1952, Darul Islam partisans were accused of killing 428 persons and burning 3,052 houses. *Sejarah TNI*, Jilid II (Jakarta: Markas Besar Tentara Nasional Indonesia, 2000), p. 82.

serve, "and Darul Islam had replaced us as a guerrilla army." In one Darul Islam cache, the army even found notes about guerrilla warfare by army chief-of-staff A.H. Nasution – lessons that the Indonesian armed forces had already forgotten.[5]

For the next two years, Darul Islam increased in strength. As of late 1953, it fielded some 6,700 partisans with over 2,500 firearms in West Java. "After three o'clock in the afternoon," noted one Indonesian officer, "the countryside belonged to them."[6] And in Central Java, it now held sway over the western periphery of that province. Playing off their village contacts and superior knowledge of the local terrain, the religious partisans in West Java would invariably melt into the jungle just ahead of patrolling troops. Worse, Darul Islam was becoming a countrywide phenomenon.

By the mid-fifties, several small but vibrant Darul Islam chapters had sprung up across the archipelago. While all attempted to define their struggle as a battle between secularists and non-secularists, that was only a small part of the story. In general, their religious proclamations were extremely rudimentary and came across as little more than convenient rallying cries. This was understandable: partially because illiteracy rates in the countryside were high, and partially because their ability to publish and disseminate religious writings was limited, Darul Islam's leaders were not prone to advancing their thoughts in writing. And given they were operating as insurgents, their ability to openly proselytize to the masses was equally limited. Their non-secular vision, therefore, amounted to little more than support for the implementation of Islamic law, but even that was never presented in any great detail.

Rather that purely religious motivation, the partisans were more often driven by intense dissatisfaction over perceived social and cultural inequalities; theirs was a prolonged, angry reaction at the Java-centric nationalists wresting away the right to rule and for having their contribution to the war of independence largely overlooked.

On the island of Kalimantan, for example, the motivation for Darul Islam had to do with prolonged indifference from the Jakarta government. Because of its physical distance from Java, and its relatively scant population, Kalimantan

---

[5]   Interview with Himawan Sutanto, 22 August 2005.

[6]   *Ibid.*

had never ranked high as a priority for the central authorities. The feeling was reciprocated: during the war of independence, revolutionary fervor in Kalimantan was often muted. This benign neglect eventually provided fertile ground for Darul Islam to establish a foothold in South Kalimantan.

In South Sulawesi, the reason was more personal. After the war of independence was over, the government had neither the budget nor the need to maintain the hundreds of thousands of guerrillas that had taken up arms across the archipelago. But while they were being demobilized, there were hard feelings all around due to the impression that Javanese were being favored for retention. In July 1950, a former South Sulawesi revolutionary leader named Kahar Muzakkar entered the jungle near Makassar in an attempt to mediate a settlement with local guerrillas who were irate at not having been integrated into the national army.

But instead of making peace, Muzakkar – who had expected a prominent army post – joined the rebels as their commander. For the next two years, Muzakkar kept the authorities at bay. But perhaps realizing that he needed to seek allies in order to give his movement momentum, by January 1952 he took on a more pronounced Islamic slant and announced a merger with Darul Islam.[7]

In Aceh, the reasons were equally personal. The Acehnese (who long cultivated an image as some of the more pious Muslims in the archipelago) had proved difficult subjects for anyone trying to impose their will from afar. Though they had fought alongside the nationalists during the war of independence, their links with Jakarta quickly cooled. The reason: Daud Beureueh, the self-appointed governor of Aceh during the revolution, had expected to maintain this lofty title. But to his chagrin, the central government in August 1950 opted to rule Aceh as a district within the larger province of North Sumatra. In a further perceived slight, the powerful military commander for North Sumatra was a Christian.

---

[7]   Muzakkar became Darul Islam's deputy defense minister, commander of the movement's Fourth Military Zone in Sulawesi, and military commander of its so-called Fourth Division on the same island. Muzakkar also claimed his Darul Islam chapter was part of the Indonesian Islamic Republic (*Republik Islam Indonesia*), though the rest of Darul Islam never used this nomenclature.

Unable to reach an accommodation, the Acehnese revolted in September 1953, declaring their home districts loosely aligned with Darul Islam.[8] While the national army quickly retook key towns in the vicinity, the Aceh countryside remained in rebel control.

With these alliances, Darul Islam now had affiliated movements on the islands of Java, Kalimantan, Sulawesi, and Sumatra. In addition, there was growing dissatisfaction across the nation with the chaotic political and economic policies being pushed by Sukarno. This was especially pronounced in the outer islands, with several key provinces in Sumatra and Sulawesi demanding greater economic autonomy. And just as with many of the Darul Islam adherents, much of their dissatisfaction could be traced to the dominance of ethnic Javanese in the central government at the expense of regional representation.

By 1957, opposition to the central government was reaching the breaking point. During that year, local military leaders across Sumatra and Sulawesi gave ultimatums to Jakarta. Most of their demands revolved around greater economic freedoms. Unfortunately for them, Sukarno was not in a negotiating mood. Calling their bluff, he refused to compromise. Backed into a corner, the rebels on Sumatra and Sulawesi effectively ceded from Jakarta in February 1958 and announced the formation of a revolutionary government (*Permerintah Revolusioner Republik Indonesia*, or PRRI). In doing so, they declared a loose coalition with the Darul Islam chapters across the country.

From the start, the PRRI and Darul Islam were strange bedfellows. They were united in their opposition to Javanese chauvinism, but little else. In fact, the core of the PRRI consisted of senior military officers staunchly opposed to religious fundamentalism and committed to a secular state. Many were Christians, and some had even played key roles in battling the Darul Islam insurgents.

Now they were in an alliance with these same religious extremists, which did not sit well with either side. The result, predictably, was a lack of coordination and a healthy dose of mutual suspicion. Example: when rebel Christian

---

[8] Daud Beureueh was already well on his way to starting a revolt when Darul Islam "Colonel" Abdul Fatah Wirananggapati was dispatched from Jakarta to convince the Acehnese to join the NII. According to Wirananggapati, the Darul Islam leaders in West Java courted Aceh because they wanted to use it as a staging point for launching diplomatic forays into Malaya. As they both had common cause to form an Islamic state, Beureueh agreed. Widjiono Wasis, *Geger Talangsari* (Jakarta: Balai Pustaka, 2001), p. 183.

troops and Acehnese guerrillas were supposed to launch a pincer attack against the North Sumatran capital of Medan in March 1958, the promised Acehnese prong never materialized.

In the end, the national army defeated the main PRRI strongholds within four short months. Although the rebels melted into the jungle and carried out guerrilla attacks for another three years, the PRRI's epitaph was not a matter of if but when.

Darul Islam was to eventually meet the same fate. This was true for several reasons. First, Darul Islam was never a coordinated movement. Rather, it was an umbrella for disparate chapters that generally sympathized with each other, but never synchronized their operations. Kartosuwirjo, though titular head, held no real sway over the Darul Islam entities outside of West Java.

Second, Darul Islam never gained significant external support. This was not for lack of trying. One Darul Islam sympathizer – a former Dutch conscript – wrote dozens of letters seeking foreign help; not a single nation answered the call. At one point, the U.S. Central Intelligence Agency briefly contemplated supplying the Acehnese and Sundanese Darul Islam chapters in early 1958 as part of its covert support to the PRRI; this never materialized. Without external aid, Darul Islam never had sufficient weaponry to seriously challenge the national army.[9]

Third, the Acehnese proved to be opportunistic. Even before the PRRI was declared fully defeated, the Acehnese were already well on their way to negotiating a truce with the government. After extracting several concessions over years of slow negotiations, a separate settlement was reached with the Acehnese in 1962.[10]

Fourth, Darul Islam never gained widespread appeal in Central Java. By 1955, the Darul Islam foothold in Central Java was effectively countered. This was due to a prompt and effective military response, and the fact that Darul Islam's underlying opposition to Javanese chauvinism rang hollow in the Javanese heartland.

---

[9] In 1957, Darul Islam units in West Java were regrouped into two divisions. In reality, it numbered just five battalions, with sufficient weaponry for only four.

[10] A key compromise came in December 1956, when the central government promised to administratively remove Aceh from North Sumatra (it was subsequently given special status in mid-1959).

But perhaps most important, the national army had grown more competent. During the campaign against the PRRI, Indonesia's armed forces proved surprisingly adept. Gathering much confidence in the process, they refocused their attention against the Darul Islam pockets around the country. Special attention went to the Darul Islam heartland in West Java. There the army literally planned a march from the west to the east, cleansing districts as they went. By the time it reached some of the most infested areas in 1961, it initiated a plan known as *Pagar Betis* ("Gate of Calves"). Explained one officer:

> We would isolate Darul Islam to a specific mountain stronghold. Then we would empower the villagers around the mountain to form a human chain, such that any Darul Islam guerrillas would literally see a wall of human legs and not be able to escape. We would then send in a couple of army battalions to sweep the mountain and eliminate the Darul Islam pocket.[11]

By that time, Kartosuwirjo was quickly running out of alternatives. Two factors proved his final undoing. First, the government in early 1962 began a series of amnesty campaigns. Tired after more than a decade fighting in the hills, even some of Kartosuwirjo's closet lieutenants – Adah Djaelani, for example, one of the original Darul Islam battalion commanders – opted to lay down their arms.

Second, the government dispatched one of its best units – the 328th Raider Battalion – to extend their Gate of Calves against Darul Islam's last holdouts. On 31 May 1962, acting on information that Kartosuwirjo's wife was in the forests near Bandung, the raiders began relentless patrolling. Two days later, further reports indicated that half a dozen guerrillas were camped in the same vicinity.

Acting on this fresh intelligence, on the evening of 3 June a platoon of raiders led by a Lieutenant Suhanda approached the reported campsite. Finding evidence indicating it had been freshly abandoned, the soldiers bivouacked for the night. At first light on 4 June, they picked up the trail and traced it to an adjacent riverbank. As scouts caught sight of a fleeing guerrilla, the platoon gave chase.

---

[11]   Interview with Alwin Nurdin, 22 August 2005.

The rebels, in turned out, were in little mood for a fight. One stood his ground, hands raised in surrender. The raiders approached cautiously, carbines at the ready. Their prisoner proved to be an important catch: Aceng Kurnia, Kartosuwirjo's bodyguard.

Interrogated by the raiders, Kurnia revealed there were almost two dozen guerrillas in his group. Using Kurnia as an intermediary, Lieutenant Suhanda opened negotiations for their surrender. Messages passed back and forth from the bush until, finally, Suhanda was beckoned forward. There, under a primitive lean-to, he found an elderly man sapped by age, exhaustion, and a myriad of jungle ailments. With unkempt hair and a bushy moustache, he looked every bit the Indonesian version of Albert Einstein. Quietly, without fanfare, Kartosuwirjo was taken into custody. [12]

For the next two months, Indonesia was fixated on the aging rebel. Everything he did – getting a haircut, visiting with senior military officials – was carefully orchestrated and photographed for propaganda value. Finally, on 13 August, he hobbled with a cane before a military tribunal. Three days later, Kartosuwirjo and four of his colleagues were sentenced to death by firing squad. On 12 September, without offering any details as to exactly where or when, the government announced the sentence had been carried out.

With the capture of Kartosuwirjo, leadership of Darul Islam ostensibly shifted to Kahar Muzakkar in South Sulawesi. But with the exception of that chapter, the rest of the Darul Islam movement looked set to atrophy.

---

[12]   Accounts of Kartosuwirjo's capture can be found in several official Indonesian military histories. The best is the classified volume detailing the activities of the 17th Airborne Brigade, *Sebelas Tahun Karya Juang Brigif Linud 17 Kujang* (no publisher listed, 1977).

CHAPTER TWO

KOMANDO JIHAD

I f anyone had a chance of keeping the Darul Islam cause alive, it was Kahar
Muzakkar. Born in 1921 in Luwu district, South Sulawesi, his Islamic credentials were beyond reproach: after attending the Muhammadiyah School
for Islamic Teachers in Surabaya during 1937, he taught at a Muhammadiyah
school in Luwu until World War II. He also had strong military credentials:
during the war of independence, he had once been a bodyguard of Sukarno and,
rising to the rank of lieutenant colonel, served as a deputy brigade commander
for the nationalist guerrillas in East Java.

But despite this impressive resume, Muzakkar was not of the preferred ethnic pedigree and met a glass ceiling after the war of independence. Deprived of
an expected prominent army post, in 1950 he linked up with guerrillas in his
native South Sulawesi – who were also dissatisfied after not being hired into the
post-independence military – and began a festering insurgency. But perhaps
realizing that he needed allies in order to give his movement momentum, by
January 1952 he took on a more pronounced Islamic slant and announced a
merger with Darul Islam.[13]

For the remainder of that decade, the latter part of which he was allied with
the PRRI rebellion, Muzakkar kept up his sniping from the jungle. And well

---

[13] In 1953, Muzakkar padded his resume with the first in a series of titles. After announcing that Sulawesi
was part of the *Republik Islam Indonesia* – the Indonesian Islamic Republic – he took for himself the title
of deputy defense minister. He later called himself the republic's caliph.

before Che Guevara embodied the image of the suave revolutionary, Muzakkar was building a similar romantic persona among locals. His reputation was also tinged with the supernatural. A legend popular in Luwu claimed Muzakkar's father had once left his young son unattended to pick jackfruit. When he descended the tree, he found his son accompanied by an identical twin. Shortly thereafter, the real son died; the mystical twin, gifted with immortality, grew up in his place.

Legends aside, by the early sixties the tide was slowly turning against Muzakkar and his South Sulawesi rebels. The government amnesty program in early 1962, which resulted in large numbers of defections among the Darul Islam insurgents in West Java, took an equally heavy toll on their Sulawesi compatriots. Even two of Muzakkar's own wives took up the offer and left the jungle. By the third quarter of that year, with Kartosuwirjo heading for a firing squad, a shrinking, exhausted band of Muzakkar's guerrillas was all that remained of the Darul Islam network.

In mid-1964, the government decided to get serious about rooting out these diehard holdouts. That August, the 330th Airborne Battalion got orders to head into the hills near Tanah Toraja to find Muzakkar, dead or alive, by month's end. Soon after arriving, however, they received word that the rebel chieftain had shifted east to the mountains near Lake Towuti.

With paratroopers on his tail, Muzakkar managed to evade the government dragnet through year's end. In January 1965, however, he had been pushed to the hills of southeastern Sulawesi. Finally, on 3 February, he was cornered in a village and felled in a hail of bullets. Photographs of his corpse were widely circulated, though the location of his grave was never revealed in order to prevent it from becoming a rallying point for his sympathizers.

With the death of Muzakkar, Darul Islam went into full remission. All that remained were a handful of members from Kartosuwirjo's high command (mostly from West Java) languishing in prison. Their predicament was not unlike the PRRI movement with which they had once been loosely aligned: most of the grassroots PRRI supporters had been given amnesty, but its top commanders were occupying jail cells.

Dramatic events in the second half of 1965 would quickly change the collective fortunes of these incarcerated leaders. In circumstances that are still not fully clear, senior cadre from the Indonesian Communist Party (*Partai Komunis Indonesia*, or PKI) and a handful of disillusioned military officers conspired to cripple the army and seize control of the country. At the time, the PKI was by far the most powerful political institution in the nation, with a grassroots membership that was rivaled only by China among Asian communist parties.

These conspirators looked to deal a decisive blow against army rivals by targeting several key generals. Although they succeeded in killing half a dozen important officers, they neglected others – General Suharto among them – who maneuvered for a counterstrike. While an accurate casualty count has never been produced – estimates range from 50,000 to two million – reciprocal attacks over the following months resulted in the bloody elimination of the PKI. The end result: Suharto effectively seized power from Sukarno the next year, and was officially elevated to president in 1968.

In its decisive fight against the PKI, the military pulled no punches in demonizing the communists. Staunch anti-communism, as a result, would become the nation's mantra for the next three decades. This had an effect on the jailed leaders of both the PRRI and Darul Islam. In the case of the PRRI, its upper echelon had been preaching anti-communism long before it became fashionable in the military (until September 1965 the military was best described as non-communist, not anti-communist). Still in prison, the PRRI veterans defiantly noted that they had been prophetic in their beliefs. Within a few short weeks after the military began moving against the PKI, Suharto's troubleshooter, Lieutenant Colonel Ali Moertopo, visited the PRRI rebels. They were released shortly afterward, with some taking jobs as intelligence officials in Moertopo's special operations unit.

The Suharto regime – dubbed the "New Order" – also sought a fresh start with Islamic groups. In eliminating the PKI, Suharto received crucial support from moderate grassroots Muslim organizations in both Central and East Java. These Muslim organizations saw common cause with the military in fighting atheistic communists; in addition, they were irate at the PKI because the latter had been an irritating rival for grassroots appeal in the Javanese countryside.

The military's attitude toward Darul Islam was slightly more complicated. Many in the military had earlier demonized Darul Islam as much as the PKI, and most of the army's senior leadership had participated in the hard-fought campaign against these violent extremists.

But showing pragmatism, Ali Moertopo and members of his special operations unit visited many of the jailed fundamentalists at the same time he was calling on the PRRI leaders. In short order, several of Darul Islam's top figures had their sentences commuted and were set free.

With a reputation for unorthodox thinking, Moertopo was quick to explore synergy with the former religious radicals. By 1965, an assistant from his office had established ties with Danu Mohammad Hasan, a top Darul Islam commander who had accepted the earlier amnesty offer. Proving amenable to cooperation, Danu and a small group of his followers were soon combing Jakarta to track down officials from the Sukarno regime that had gone into hiding.

The remainder of Darul Islam's first generation was suitably contrite, at least initially. Having already spent many years battling in the jungle, and several more sitting in prison, none showed any immediate interest in resorting to violence to press their beliefs.

But by 1968, veterans from the movement were growing restless. That year, Kartosuwirjo's son, Dodo Mohammad Darda bin Kartosuwirjo, presided over a secret meeting attended by many of his father's former Sundanese lieutenants. Behind closed doors, they declared their intention of resurrecting the Darul Islam vision of a non-secular Indonesia ruled according to Islamic law.

For its first year, the reborn Darul Islam was nothing more than a talk shop. It did not attempt to publicly proselytize to a wider audience, much less conduct any paramilitary activities. Adah Djaelani, Kartosuwirjo's onetime protégé, emerged as the overall head. Under him – on paper – Indonesia was divided into seven area commands that mimicked the former Darul Islam organizational chart. Of the seven, the only one of substance was the command covering West Java – Darul Islam's old stomping grounds – which was to be commanded by Moertopo's informant, Danu.

It was through Danu that the government quickly received news of the initial Darul Islam trysts. But while the New Order normally was notoriously thin-skinned toward dissent, this time it saw opportunity in a revived religious right. This was because Moertopo was already looking to identify constituent blocs that would stump for Golkar – the New Order's political machine – ahead of the 1971 national polls. In the hope that the top figures in Darul Islam might be able to deliver the votes of their sympathizers, beginning in 1969 they were discreetly courted by offering them kerosene distribution rights for parts of Java.

Two top Darul Islam members were quick to jump on the Golkar band-wagon. The first, Danu, had already been proving cooperative for most of the decade. The second, Ateng Djaelani (no relation to Adah), showed strong en-trepreneurial skills and was ultimately placed in charge of the kerosene network allocated by Moertopo.

When elections were held on 3 July 1971, Golkar – predictably – emerged victorious. The efforts to woo Darul Islam, however, had only been partially suc-cessful. Said one government case officer on the project: "Of the twenty-six core leaders in the movement, only about a third were cooperative."[14]

Although the vote had concluded, the government's lobbying of Darul Is-lam continued. During a string of secret meetings in 1972 and 1973, all at-tended by a representative of Moertopo, the movement's leadership mapped out efforts to realize chapters outside of West Java. In Central and East Java, they achieved some initial success in attracting adherents among a younger gen-eration of Islamic activists. In Aceh, contact was reestablished with the former Darul Islam chief in that region, Daud Beureueh. Representatives were also dispatched to South Sulawesi and Kalimantan. Despite this push, however, no presence of any substance ever took root outside of Java – in part because ex-tremists on the outer islands were irate that Ateng Djaelani was not generous with his kerosene concessions.

Meantime, efforts by the government to co-opt Darul Islam were growing more difficult by the year. During a 1974 restructuring, informant Danu was promoted to commander for all of Java. But Haji Ismail Pranoto (better known as Hispran) and Dodo Mohammad Darda bin Kartosuwirjo, both hard-liners that had rebuffed government entreaties, were chosen as deputy commander and chief of staff, respectively.[15]

Of equal concern to the government were the activities of an Islamic ex-tremist cell roaming Sumatra. That seven-man band, calling itself *Momok Rev-olusioner* ("Revolutionary Ghost"), hailed from a younger generation that de-veloped outside of the original Java-centric Darul Islam. It was violent, setting

---

[14] Interview with Pitut Soeharto, 9 May 2003.

[15] According to a 1974 classified report prepared by Indonesia's State Intelligence Coordination Agency, sev-eral Darul Islam leaders – including Ules Sudjai, Abdul Salam Hasanuddin, Adah Djaelani, and Aceng Kurnia – were involved in the anti-Japanese riots (known as the Malari Affair) that rocked Jakarta in January 1974. How or exactly when they participated is not detailed. Bakin Report, "Gerakan Subversi Mahasiswa," 20 April 1974, p. 41.

off a string of explosions at theaters, bars, and churches in Medan, as well as a Baptist church and a mosque in West Sumatra. Worse, from the government's perspective: some of the pamphlets left behind by the group were rife with communist rhetoric.[16]

Given that the 1977 national elections were fast approaching, the government was especially sensitive to such threats. This time around, the New Order had reduced the number of recognized political parties to just three: the government's own political machine, Golkar; the Muslim-oriented United Development Party (*Partai Persatuan Pembangunan*, PPP); and the secular catch-all Indonesian Democratic Party (*Partai Demokrasi Indonesia*, PDI). Suharto was determined to receive – or orchestrate, if need be – an overwhelming mandate via Golkar.

Just as Moertopo had done prior to the 1971 polls, his men again tried to mobilize Darul Islam votes. This time around, the Darul Islam members had adopted the new moniker of *Komando Jihad* ("Holy War Command").[17] And this time around, not all of the Komando Jihad votes would be going to Golkar. Longtime Golkar informant Danu, for one, hinted he would throw his weight behind the PPP. While that would not contribute to a Golkar landslide, the fact that he was favoring elections, rather than violence, was welcomed by Moertopo's case officers.

This strategy was not without its detractors. Among the upper echelon of the military, many questioned Moertopo's dealings with, if not encouragement of, Komando Jihad. One of them was Major General Himawan Soetanto, the commander of the military region covering West Java. Himawan, who took over the command in January 1975, had first been informed about Komando Jihad "from the top" – Jakarta – rather than information percolating up from the military's territorial intelligence network. Growing increasingly concerned by their presence, in late 1976 he beckoned Ateng Djaelani to his headquarters in Bandung. What happened next shocked him:

---

[16] In 1975, Gaos Taufik, an ethnic Sundanese who had been fighting alongside the Daud Beureueh's Darul Islam chapter since the mid-fifties, convened a secret meeting in Medan to discuss the formation of a community that would be ruled according to Islamic law. While this tryst was attended by members from Momok Revolusioner, there were strains over politics. "They were leftists," said Gaos, "because its members were young, and such politics were fashionable among students." Interview with Gaos Taufik, 23 July 2003.

[17] The meaning of the Arabic term *jihad* (literally, "striving") is open to interpretation. Moderates see jihad

I had expected only a few, but at least one hundred Komando Jihad members, including Ateng Djaelani and Hispran, assembled in the ceremonial field in front of my office. They were extremely well organized; some of them claimed they were company commanders. I told them to remember their pledge to renounce violence back in 1962. They told me that they were a front against the spread of communism in Southeast Asia.[18]

A few months later, in March 1977, Himawan and the other military region commanders from Java confronted Moertopo on the sidelines of a military anniversary in Jakarta. Said Himawan:

We were all concerned about his acquiescence to let Komando Jihad grow unchecked in our regions. Ali Moertopo told us not to worry. He said that he was letting them think they were a bulwark against communism, but was really using them for votes. Komando Jihad, meanwhile, was telling Ali Moertopo that they would guard against communism, but they were really using the opportunity to organize themselves. He was overly confident and assured us he could control them. It came down to a game of who was playing whom.[19]

But even with Ali Moertopo's considerable clout, there were limits to the New Order's patience. In early 1977, just ahead of the May polls, hypersensitive security officials went on the offensive and eventually detained 185 Komando Jihad members by mid-year. All these arrests took place on Java: 105 were in Jakarta, 38 in West Java, 19 in Central Java, and 23 in East Java.[20] A separate series of

as a call to achieve higher moral standards, with violence not necessarily implied. A more extreme – and commonly held – interpretation, however, defines jihad as an injunction for military action by the pious against non-believers and all others not sharing in their militancy. There is controversy as to whether the term Komando Jihad was used by the participants themselves, or if this was an inflammatory term coined by the Indonesian government. According to Pitut Soeharto, the government's case officer who attended many of the Darul Islam meetings beginning in 1969, the name was used by the movement's members. Gaos Taufik, a Darul Islam member based in North Sumatra, also says that the name was commonly used within the movement. Pitut Soeharto, Gaos Taufik interviews.

[18] Himawan Soetanto interview.

[19] *Ibid.*

[20] Those arrested in East Java referred to themselves as *Barisan Jihad* ("Jihad Front"). This group had been almost fully penetrated by government informants. Pitut Soeharto interview.

raids in Sumatra netted the Momok Revolusioner cell over the next two years. Although a handful of extremists were still on the lam (including informant Danu), Komando Jihad as an organized movement was no more.[21]

⊰❧⊱

By the close of the seventies, the government's crackdown had left most of those who claimed inspiration from Darul Islam ducking for cover. Yet there were still some religious hard-liners that persisted with the goal of overthrowing the Indonesian government. Arguably the most bizarre flirtation with this concept took its inspiration from events half a world away. In February 1979, the Iranian government imploded and was replaced by an Islamic revolutionary regime under the Ayatollah Khomeini. This was the first successful Islamic revolution in modern times and, although the Iranians were Shiite Muslims (as opposed to Indonesians, who are overwhelmingly Sunni), the rise of Khomeini had ripples across the Indonesian archipelago.

One of those who felt inspired was Imran bin Zein. Born in 1950 in West Sumatra, Imran at twenty-two had been a stowaway to Saudi Arabia in an attempt to pursue a religious education. But unable to gain university admission, he stayed in the kingdom working as a servant and at other menial jobs.[22]

Imran also found time to dabble in activism. In 1976, he befriended several fellow Indonesians living in Saudi Arabia and talked up forming a *jemaah*

---

[21] Danu was not arrested until 1981. During his trial, he claimed that he had been recruited by Indonesian intelligence officers in 1971 and hinted that Komando Jihad was little more than a government sting meant to lure the religious right into the open. This theme was repeated in a 2002 report by the International Crisis Group, which claimed that Ali Moertopo "reactivated Darul Islam to preempt the possibility of a large [Muslim opposition party] vote during the 1977 elections." (ICG Indonesia Briefing, "Al-Qaeda in Southeast Asia: The Case of the Ngruki Network in Indonesia," 8 August 2002, pp. 5, 11n.) This is wrong on several counts. First, while it is true that Indonesian intelligence eventually penetrated Komando Jihad, its formation predates government contact. Second, the government was not afraid of a large Muslim opposition vote; in fact, according to intelligence officer Pitut Soeharto, who spearheaded the government's penetration of the militants, many Komando Jihad members were openly encouraged to join the PPP ahead of the 1977 election. Third, some of the persons identified in the ICG report as government recruits, such as Adah Djaelani, were in fact staunchly resistant to government entreaties.

[22] Originally born with the single name Harmon, he changed his name to Imran bin Zein while living in Saudi Arabia. B. Wiwoho, *Operasi Woyla* (Jakarta: PT Menara Gading Nusantara, 1981), p. 175. Details of Imran's group were largely gleaned from two publications: *Imran: Imam Jamaah* (Solo: CV Masyasari, 1982), and Emron Pangkapi, *Hukuman Mati Untuk Imam Imran* (Bandung: Alumni, 1982).

– a community – in which its members would live according to a pure form of Islam. Adding a touch of the fanciful, that August they approached the Libyan embassy in Saudi Arabia in an unsuccessful bid to obtain weaponry. It was never made clear what exactly they intended to do with the firearms.[23]

Not until 1977 did Imran return to his native Sumatra. Shifting to Jakarta late the next year in search of better employment, he could only eke out a living as a street vendor. It was while shopping for more lucrative job prospects that Imran chanced upon other members from his Saudi jemaah. During that same period, he ventured to the West Java town of Cimahi and befriended Azhar Zulkarnaen, the son of a retired army lieutenant colonel who had formed his own community of young Islamic puritans.[24]

By 1979, Imran had an epiphany. Despite the fact that his formal religious education was suspect, he highlighted his extended stint in Saudi Arabia and began extolling the conservative, intolerant strain of Islam common in the kingdom. Just as had been the case with Darul Islam, he vaguely preached the need to replace the secular New Order with a theocratic state. Also like Darul Islam, Imran never articulated key details, such as exactly what Islamic law meant to him or how it would be implemented. Still, he won a quick pledge of loyalty by members of his former Saudi jemaah. Pledging loyalty, too, was Azhar and his Cimahi group. And unlike Darul Islam, which tended to cater to rural, lesser-educated recruits, Imran would eventually tap into the discontent among students around Bandung and gain a small but significant university following.

By that time, the Iranian revolution had rocked the Islamic world. Sensing that Iran might be sympathetic to his fundamentalist slant, in December 1979 Imran and his followers penned a letter and posted it to the Iranian embassy in Jakarta. In the letter, they referred to themselves as the Indonesian Islamic Revolutionary Council; they further claimed to have branch offices in Medan and Jakarta. Imran used the letters to repeat his bromide that he wanted a pure form of Islam in Indonesia, and added that he wanted to accomplish this via an Iranian-style upheaval.

Not receiving any response to the first, Imran composed a second letter in

---

[23] In 1975, after gathering evidence that Libya had started giving paramilitary training to Indonesian students the previous year, the Indonesian government forced Libya to close its embassy in Jakarta.

[24] Imran and Azhar had briefly met in Saudi Arabia in 1973. Zulkarnaen's father had earlier been a rebel officer in the PRRI movement.

March 1980. This one was personally addressed to the Ayatollah Khomeini and carried to Tehran by Mahrizal, a top Imran acolyte heading to the Middle East on business. Again they were dismissed: far from gaining an audience with the Ayatollah, Mahrizal was given a stack of books lauding the Iranian revolution and sent on his way.

Undeterred, Imran ratcheted up his revolutionary fervor. In December 1980, he composed a third letter and, taking it to the Iranian embassy, sought a meeting with the chargé. Sitting with the diplomat, Imran boldly said he wanted six pistols, a grenade, and US$1,500 to jumpstart his revolution. As a sign of good faith, he offered to kidnap the Iraqi oil minister (the Iran-Iraq War was in full swing at the time) during an oil seminar set to convene later that month in Bali. Thinking this a provocation, the chargé showed his unwanted guest the door.[25]

Despite the Iranian rebuff, Imran's stint as a militant preacher was showing dividends. In Bandung and neighboring Cimahi, he had nurtured sizeable congregations; smaller groups were taking shape in Surabaya and Jakarta. And perhaps not surprising given that Bandung and Cimahi hosted a large number of military installations, no less than five members came from military families. One was an army corporal; another was the son of a brigadier general.

During that same time frame, Imran began to authorize acts of violence. In January and February 1981, his members twice tried to stab to death Muslim community leaders in Bandung (apparently because they dared question his religious credentials). On both occasions, their targets managed to fend off their assailants. They also tried – again unsuccessfully – to kill one of their own members who had left the group.

After these botched assassinations, Imran realized his struggle was handicapped by a lack of firearms. Looking to rectify this shortcoming, one of his members in February snuck into the military transportation school in Cimahi

---

[25] The Indonesian government remained extremely sensitive to any attempts by the Iranian revolutionary regime to spread propaganda in Indonesia. During 1981, a 20-year-old student activist named Irfan Suryahardy Awwas began publishing two militant newsletters that contained quotes from Khomeini, interviews with former Darul Islam leaders, and critiques of the New Order. Predictably, Irfan's publishing ventures eventually invited a harsh response from the government. In 1983, his office was raided and both bulletins banned. During his trial, the government claimed Irfan – like Imran – had seen the Iranian revolution as a model for Indonesia. As proof, it claimed Irfan had in his possession newsletters from the Iranian embassy and had received overseas funding (the source was not specified).

and made off with an aging Garand rifle. Another member lifted a pistol from his father, an army colonel.

Seeking more weaponry, the group turned deadly serious on 11 March. That night, fifteen of Imran's followers – one of them dressed like an army commando and armed with the Garand – overwhelmed a small police outpost outside Bandung. Finding two Colt revolvers, they bundled the four resident police officers into a holding cell, then shot them all. Three succumbed to their wounds, while the fourth was seriously wounded but survived.

The government's reaction to the Bandung raid was swift. On 14 March, twenty-nine persons were arrested in a massive dragnet. By the following week, another two dozen were in detention.[26]

Though on the run, Imran was far from conceding defeat. During the second half of the month, he hatched plans to hijack a Garuda airliner and swap the hostages for his jailed colleagues. Five were handpicked to carry out the hijacking: an Indonesian of mixed Arab parentage Imran knew from his Saudi days, two from North Sumatra, one from West Sumatra, and one from Jogjakarta. Some of the members from military families, meanwhile, were able to discreetly obtain an automatic pistol, a grenade, and a stick of dynamite.[27]

Three days before the end of March, the five put their quixotic plan into effect. Commandeering a Garuda DC-9 on its way from Palembang to Medan, they forced the pilot to fly to Bangkok. Once on Thai soil, the hijackers issued a series of demands. Highest on their list was the release of some eighty religious extremists. This number included those detained for the Bandung raid, as well as several leading radicals caught up in the arrests of the late seventies. Among the latter was the head of Momok Revolusioner in Sumatra, as well as Abdullah Sungkar, a fiery preacher from Solo who had urged his followers to boycott the 1977 elections.

Initially, the government was at a loss to identify the hijackers. *Bernama*, the Malaysian news agency, issued an early but erroneous wire report claiming they were from Komando Jihad. In conversation with some of the hostages, the

---

[26] Bakin Case File, "Cicendo."

[27] The fact that several members of Imran's group came from military families was an embarrassment for the government. Even more embarrassing was the fact that some of their weaponry had indirectly come from government sources. During Imran's subsequent trial, the public prosecutors noticeably glossed over this aspect of the case. Even within classified Bakin files, many of these details were redacted. Bakin Case File, "Pembajakan Garuda."

hijackers themselves were vague and only claimed that they sought the overthrow of the Suharto regime because it was not in keeping with the true tenets of Islam.[28]

Whatever the hijackers' affiliation, the government was in no mood to negotiate. During the early morning hours on the last day of the month, a crack Indonesian commando team successfully stormed the plane. All five hijackers were killed, two of them apparently at the hands of interrogators during the flight back to Jakarta.

Still unfazed, Imran immediately began plotting his next move. On 2 April, he gathered his remaining followers and planned the killing of the army lieutenant colonel who had led the commando detachment to Bangkok. Two days later, they conducted a reconnaissance of the colonel's house on the southern outskirts of Jakarta. Before they could enact their revenge, however, the authorities caught up. By week's end, Imran was in shackles. He, along with his top followers, met firing squads the next year.[29]

---

[28] Memorandum from a counterpart organization dated 29 April 1981, "Observations of American Passengers Aboard Recently Hijacked Garuda Flight 206," found in Bakin Case File, "Pembajakan Garuda."

[29] In the weeks following the hijacking, conspiracy theories abounded. Given Ali Moertopo's earlier courtship of Komando Jihad, many suspected he had penetrated, if not manipulated, Imran's clique. However, no compelling evidence was ever uncovered that Imran himself had links to the government. To the contrary, Imran on 27 March 1981 ordered one of his members – who later turned out to be an army corporal – murdered following suspicions he was a government informant. At his trial, Imran also spoke of an earlier plot to assassinate Ali Moertopo. See *Indonesia: Muslims on Trial* (London: Tapol, 1987), p. 35.

CHAPTER THREE

THE DUUMVIRATE

In hindsight, Indonesia's Islamic extremism of the seventies barely rated as a serious security threat. This was due to several factors. First, proponents were exceedingly small in number, probably never exceeding a few hundred. Second, with notable exceptions like the Imran group, they rarely chose to match their intolerant rhetoric with violence. Third, the extremists made government vilification all the easier after a small number resorted to criminal activity. The name most closely associated with this was Musa Warman, a shadowy figure who had first come to the attention of the authorities in the early seventies when he moved from his native Java to Lampung province in the southern end of neighboring Sumatra. Because of its relatively sparse population and easy access from crowded Java, Lampung for decades had been a favored destination for Javanese migrants seeking better economic prospects. Lampung eventually became home to dozens of communities almost entirely comprised of recent arrivals from Central and East Java. Common, too, were instances of Javanese escaping checkered pasts by starting anew in southern Sumatra.

Warman was in the latter category. But rather than shunning attention, he soon made a name for himself among fellow migrants as a critic of the government. In 1971, he came to the attention of the authorities while urging a boycott of that year's national elections. Though such calls begged arrest, Warman remained on the move and used at least four aliases as he moved between Sumatra and Java for the next half-decade.

During that period, Warman became progressively more extreme in his religious beliefs. Initially limiting himself to distributing pamphlets that lamented Indonesia's alleged "Christianization," he eventually began to call on sympathizers to resort to violence in the name of Islam.[30]

His message struck a chord among fringe circles. By about 1978, Warman had been able to assemble a few dozen committed followers. And much as would be the case with Imran in Bandung, the diverse ethnic composition of Warman's group was noteworthy. Whereas the original Darul Islam and Komando Jihad had relative ethnic cohesion in their various cells, Warman's band was an ethnic blend of Sumatrans, Javanese, and even a Papuan. One of them, Abdullah Umar, was a religious teacher who had attended a 1975 meeting of Momok Revolusioner in Medan; he had fled to Solo after the authorities began to arrest the Medan attendees in 1977.

By January 1979, Warman's gang turned deadly. Initially at least, its motive appears to have been revenge tinged with fundamentalism. During that month, for example, its members murdered an assistant principal at a Solo university; it had been rumored that this individual assisted the authorities with the arrest of two fiery clerics in Solo. After that, Warman conspired to kill the judge and prosecutor that had sent Hispran – Komando Jihad's deputy commander – to prison in 1978. Although neither of these assassinations was carried out, it is noteworthy that Warman was trying to cloak his criminality by portraying himself as the champion of more widely recognized militants.

His group also staged several strikes against religious targets. Warman's members, for example, were accused of hurling a grenade at a Koran reading competition in North Sumatra and detonating an explosive at a mosque in Padang. They also burned several churches. While the motivation for targeting the churches is obvious, it was never clear why the Muslim sites were chosen.

Finally, the gang became best known for committing criminal acts ostensibly aimed at raising funds to perpetuate their campaign. Between January and April 1979, three robberies were attempted, one each in Magelang, Jogjakarta, and Malang. During the Jogjakarta heist, the gangsters succeeded in stealing the salaries for the faculty at the State Islamic Institute. Warman justified these crimes by claiming it was permissible to attack the enemies of Islam – ironic given that two of the robberies were against Islamic centers of learning, and

---

[30] The charge of "Christianization" no doubt stemmed from Suharto's increasingly close affiliation with powerful Chinese (Christian) businessmen.

several of Warman's members had attended these institutes.

On 4 April, the authorities finally caught up with the gang in Malang. Three key members were captured, including Warman and Abdullah Umar. After a four-month campaign, the so-called *Teror Warman* was no more.[31]

⋘⟡⋙

But perhaps the biggest reason why religious extremists were not developing into a major security threat was due to demographics. The upper echelon of Komando Jihad was dominated by the same aging militants that had filled Darul Islam's ranks two decades earlier. Rather than replenishing their numbers with fresh blood, beginning in 1978 these graying chieftains spent their time to dueling among each other over who would formally inherit Kartosuwirjo's title.[32]

There was a significant exception, however. In Central Java, a new generation of Islamic activists was taking shape under the guidance of two clerics of Yemeni descent. The first, Abdullah Achmad bin Sungkar, had been born in 1937 in Solo, Central Java.

A keen intellect, Sungkar had taught himself how to speak Arabic and English at an early age. By the fifties, while the Darul Islam insurgency raged across the border in West Java, he busied himself in Muslim youth movements and briefly dabbled in politics. Remaining in Solo to try his hand as an itinerant preacher, he began proselytizing before paltry crowds on university campuses and even at a dormitory for the blind. But his energetic oratory skills, propensity to speak in provocative terms, and Middle Eastern ethnicity eventually combined to attract far bigger audiences.[33] Sungkar was especially prone to denouncing President Sukarno, a dangerous practice that nevertheless enhanced his standing.

In 1963, Sungkar met a kindred spirit in Abu Bakar Ba'asyir. The two were born only a year apart and both were of Yemeni descent. The more academic of

---

[31] Warman later escaped from prison in 1980, but was shot dead near Bandung in July 1981. Abdullah Umar was executed in 1989.

[32] In July 1979, Adah Djaelani was named head of Darul Islam/Komando Jihad after having a top rival killed off.

[33] Many Indonesians reflexively pay added respect to local preachers of Arab ethnic origin. Most ethnic Arabs that have settled in Indonesia trace their origins back to seafaring traders from the Hadramaut region in Yemen.

the pair, Ba'asyir had studied at Pondok Gontor, a prestigious Islamic boarding school (*pesantren*) in East Java that, based on the model of Christian missionary schools, offered a reformist-oriented, modern curriculum. He then studied and taught at the al-Irsyad al-Islamiyah school in Solo.

Though less overtly political than Sungkar, Ba'asyir shared an interest in forceful preaching. Pooling their talents, in 1967 they rented a modest Solo cottage, obtained a small transmitter, and founded the Islamic Proselytizing Radio of Solo (*Radio Dakwah Islamiyah Surakarta*, or Radis).

Radis was a bold departure from the norm. The station broadcasted Malay songs and a variety of segments with Islamic themes, including fiery speeches by Sungkar. As the only non-profit radio station in Solo, it competed with dozens of commercial stations. Still, it was able to support itself – even thrive – only from private donations.

What came next was even more significant. During 1971-2, the pair founded the al-Mukmin pesantren, which included a junior high school annex, in the southern part of Solo. After outgrowing that location within a year, both the school and Radis moved to a more spacious site at Ngruki, a hamlet in the eastern outskirts of Solo near the city bus terminal.[34]

Al-Mukmin from the start was an enigma. On the one hand, students at Ngruki faced long hours often immersed in a decidedly puritan curriculum. One daily routine[35] was as follows:

0700-1300	Islamic code of conduct and law; Koranic study; Arab language lessons
1300-1700	Lunch; afternoon prayers; rest; prayer at dusk
1700-1900	Exercise
1900-2030	Koran study groups

But like Ba'asyir's alma mater, the modernist Gontor, attendees at Al-Mukmin were given heavy doses of Arabic- and English-language training. Moreover, in a reflection of the school's two founders, students were imbibed with a rebel-

---

[34] Al-Mukmin, Arabic for "The Faithful," is also transliterated as al-Mu'min.

[35] This schedule, as followed by student Ahmad Faisal Iman Sarijan during the first half of the nineties, was little different from that practiced since Ngruki's inception. See *Badan Intelijen Negara* [hereafter "BIN"] document, "Percakapan Deni Ofresio," January 2004, p. 9.

lious streak and – unlike the learning by rote favored at traditional pesantren – often encouraged to mold their beliefs by questioning authority, religious or otherwise. All of this was done against a backdrop of strict discipline. Example: if students did not perform any of the five ritual daily prayers, they had their hands whipped ten times.[36]

For their own part, Ngruki's founders were growing more belligerent. Long one to speak his mind, Sungkar heaped criticism on the New Order. By international standards, much of what he said was relatively tame. For example, he claimed that saluting the flag ran against Muslim beliefs. More provocative were his calls to disregard the country's constitution and refuse to pay taxes.

Ba'asyir, too, pulled few punches. One of his more colorful tirades:

> We Indonesians live as if we are riding an air-conditioned bus. It's all cool and comfortable but we are actually heading towards Hell. And the driver is…Suharto![37]

After listening to such brickbats being thrown over the airwaves for eight years, the government finally intervened in 1975 and ordered Radis closed.

Apart from the radio, silencing Sungkar was another matter. In his sermons, he began urging his audiences not to vote in the coming 1977 national polls. Behind the scenes, in 1976 he invited Ba'asyir and Hispran – the Komando Jihad deputy commander – to his house in Solo. There they discussed forming a *jemaah Islamiyah*, a fairly innocuous term meaning simply "Islamic community." In this planned community, they would shun secular norms in order to live strictly according to the tenets of the Koran and Sunna (traditions associated with the Prophet Mohammad).

Getting wind of Sungkar's call for an election boycott, the government responded in 1977 by throwing the cleric in a jail cell. Though released after six weeks, he, along with Ba'asyir, was re-arrested in November 1978. By this time, the authorities had already captured and interrogated Hispran, from whom they learned about the meeting at Sungkar's home in 1976. They also heard of the plan to form a jemaah Islamiyah.

---

[36] "The Travails of Ngruki Two," *Tempo*, 4 November 2002, p. 19.
[37] *Ibid.*

For government prosecutors, Hispran's admissions were courthouse gold. Both clerics were accused by government prosecutors of meeting Hispran, a charge which they readily conceded was true. Building on this, the authorities accused the pair of giving *bayat* – an oath of allegiance – to Hispran.[38] They further charged that Sungkar had been installed as the Darul Islam military governor of Central Java during a second meeting with Hispran.

Perhaps most significant about the government charges was the intentional blurring of designations. The government was now referring to Darul Islam and Komando Jihad interchangeably – not unreasonable, since the latter was a direct progeny of the former. But the government also started equating Komando Jihad with Jemaah Islamiyah – both words capitalized – the concept broached during the 1976 meeting with Hispran. By this way of reasoning, Sungkar, in talking up Jemaah Islamiyah with Hispran, was a member of Komando Jihad, which in turn meant he was Darul Islam.[39]

With these charges hanging over their heads, the two clerics cooled their heels in prison for the next four years pending trial. Ironically, rather than driving them into obscurity, the government's incarceration only served to enhance their reputations: once a minor nuisance with a local following around Solo, Sungkar, in particular, was now elevated into a national figure. It was not by accident that the Imran group, when issuing hostage demands in Bangkok, mentioned Sungkar by name as someone they wanted freed.

Finally, in 1982, Sungkar and Ba'asyir had their day in court. Both used this opportunity to put a different spin on their ties to Hispran. With they admitted discussing the possibility of forming a Jemaah Islamiyah, they repeated the bromide that it was merely intended as a religious bulwark against the spread of atheistic communism from mainland Southeast Asia.

Playing the anti-communist card was a savvy move. Anti-communism, after all, was the mantra of the New Order, and any effort to turn back the spread of communism might be expected to win government sympathy. Their gamble ultimately paid off, to an extent. Although both preachers were found guilty of subversion and sentenced to nine years in prison, but these sentences were

---

[38] Sungkar and Ba'asyir openly sympathized with Darul Islam's aims, but repeatedly denied ever having been officially inducted into the organization. Still, rumors would persist among radical circles that Sungkar had given an oath of allegiance to Hispran. During interrogations in 2003, Hambali stated his belief that the oath had taken place.

[39] ICG Briefing, p. 7.

almost immediately reduced on appeal to time served. By year's end, both were free men.

Interpreting the government's waffle as a moral victory, neither man showed any sign of remorse or repentance. Making their way back to Ngruki, they found their school had continued to turn out students in their absence – many of them with a decidedly militant outlook. It is difficult to generalize about the motivation of these Ngruki alumni. Some genuinely wanted the Darul Islam goal of an Islamic state, or at least Islamic law being made mandatory for Muslim citizens.

But others were most troubled by Indonesia's domestic repression and lack of political participation. This became acute after President Suharto in mid-1982 insisted on *Pancasila* – a mostly secular creed that, among other things, called on belief in a singular Deity – as the sole ideological basis for all Indonesians.[40] They also saw as immoral the government's family planning blitz that had earned Suharto kudos from the United Nations. Militancy in the name of Islam, therefore, was as much a reaction against the heavy-handed nature of the New Order as it was a clamoring for religious conservatism.

It was this sentiment that greeted Sungkar and Ba'asyir in Ngruki. Picking up where they left off, both preachers urged followers to avoid all secular social organizations, such as schools and courts. Anything other than Islamic law, they said, was to be ignored.

But rather than saying so from a soapbox, this time the clerics were somewhat more discreet. Their newfound approach borrowed heavily from the teachings of Egyptian Hasan al-Banna, founder of *Ikhwan al-Muslimin* ("Muslim Brotherhood"). Born in 1906, al-Banna had grown up in an Egypt, whose once proud history of pharaohs and pyramids had been fully eclipsed by the embarrassment of British colonial domination. Groping for meaning in this, he concluded that Muslims had folded to European domination because they had deviated from "true" Islam.

Al-Banna had a ready remedy. First, he called for a return to the Koran and Sunna, the implementation of Islamic law, and the eventual founding of a worldwide Islamic caliphate. Second, he called for fascist-style discipline. Third,

---

[40] *Pancasila*, which is based on five principles spelled out in the preamble to Indonesia's 1945 constitution, is an exceedingly tolerant creed. But precisely because of its tolerance toward other monotheistic religions, some Muslim hard-liners took offense.

he preached a mixed line against the West. On the one hand, he pragmatically welcomed selective learning from the colonial powers. But on the other hand, he chided the moral laxity of secular Europe and was especially critical of Egypt's Westernized elites.

Initially, al-Banna set his sights on liberating Egypt from colonialism by forming a defensive mass movement. But not stopping with that country's independence, he soon expanded his opposition to capitalism and liberalism across the Arab world. In particular, he ditched an earlier alliance with Egypt's secular authorities and was soon accused of being the intellectual mastermind behind many of the government's ills.

Outlawed in 1954, al-Banna's Muslim Brotherhood was forced underground. To protect themselves, members formed compartmentalized cells that would shield members from mass arrest. As branches mushroomed across the Arab world, which had similarly intolerant governments, this cell structure was replicated.

The New Order government in Indonesia, Sungkar and Ba'asyir found, was not all that different from the one-party systems prevalent in the Middle East. Taking their cue from al-Banna, they organized a compartmentalized Islamic study cell at Ngruki known as *usroh*. This was the Javanese version of the Arabic word *usrah*, meaning "family" in the broader sense of a close-knit group.

Very quickly, the Ngruki usroh became the hub of a series of like-minded grassroots study groups dispersed across Java. This was spurred by a significant demographic shift in Indonesia. During the eighties, Indonesia's impressive annual economic gains were luring villagers into urban areas at exponential rates. Linked to this, attendance at universities was also fast on the rise, yet job opportunities for college graduates were not keeping pace. The result: a burgeoning number of urbanized unemployed, underemployed, and otherwise disaffected Indonesians.

It was this anti-New Order sentiment that the two clerics tapped at university-based mosques in Central Java and Jogjakarta. Other study groups took root in the heavily-populated southern reaches of Central Java; ironically, this region in the sixties had been the locus of Indonesia's communist movement.

In large part, these study groups devoted themselves to the relatively tame goal of building networks and relationships. Indeed, most met weekly to merely talk about their desire to live according to the Koran and Sunna. Although they took inspiration from Darul Islam, there were major differences. First, the sizable percentage of university members in the usroh cells meant they tended to be more cerebral than Darul Islam, which had primarily catered to a rural, often uneducated crowd. Second, although they romanticized the Darul Islam vision as a righteous struggle over the secular authorities, usroh completely ditched Darul Islam's ethnic dimension as a Sundanese backlash against Javanese chauvinism; indeed, the usroh network was a movement largely grounded in Central Java. And third, though their message was often one of religious intolerance, the usroh members tried not to repeat the mistakes of previous movements by jumping headlong into acts of violence or outspoken calls for the overthrow of the government.

Still, the government saw sinister motives behind usroh. Prosecutors claimed that Ba'asyir, the alleged founder of the movement, had members swear oaths of allegiance to him. In addition, they pointed out that both Sungkar and Ba'asyir had circulated a book at Ngruki that reportedly urged Muslims to go to war against anybody opposing the implementation of Islamic law. At least in writing, said the authorities, these ideological successors to Darul Islam were hinting at a return to violence.

Mobilizing against this perceived threat, the authorities over three years beginning in 1983 detained forty usroh members on charges of subversion. Specifically, they were said to be planning a three-stage revolt against the secular government, one of which involved the creation of a Jemaah Islamiyah. One of the detained, from Gadjah Mada University in Jogjakarta, was said to have run an usroh training course that counseled members not to obey Indonesian law if it did not correspond to the Koran.

For their part, Sungkar and Ba'asyir sensed that their own arrests were just a matter of time. Already, state prosecutors had appealed their reduced sentences and in February 1985, the Supreme Court summoned them for a hearing. By that time, military intelligence officers were keeping Ngruki under close surveillance. To escape, Sungkar did the unexpected, uncharacteristically dressing in a sarong and driving a motorcycle through the front gate to the Solo bus station. Making his way to Jakarta via Semarang, he briefly sought sanctuary with sympathizers in the capital before heading for Lampung during April and finally crossing into Malaysia and taking up residence in Kuala Pilah district, Negeri Sembilan state.

On 1 April, Ba'asyir and seven other senior Ngruki members followed in Sungkar's wake. In Lampung, Ba'asyir obtained a false identity card in the name of Abdus Samad bin Abud.[41] Continuing to Medan, the group took a speedboat across the strait to Malaysia's Selangor state. The Malaysian government, which effectively had an open-door policy toward foreign Muslim activists, offered no obstacles as Ba'asyir made his way to Negeri Sembilan and rented a village house near a scenic nature preserve in Jempol district.[42]

From their Malaysian sanctuary, Sungkar and Ba'asyir sent word back to select followers at Ngruki that they had conducted a *hijrah*. Arabic for "emigration," hijrah referred to the Prophet Mohammad's flight from Mecca to Medina to escape enemies of Islam. While this might have put a more respectable spin on their escape, they had left their usroh followers in a lurch. Irate that the Ngruki clerics had slipped their surveillance, the government initiated a crackdown. The first usroh member – a 22-year-old from Jogjakarta – went on trial in February 1986 and received a six-year sentence. More trials followed in quick succession; among them, a goldsmith from Solo received eleven years for subversion in July.[43]

By August 1985, after less than six months in Malaysia, Sungkar and Ba'asyir called a series of meetings to salvage their movement and chart its future. Several key decisions were made over the course of those trysts. First, they agreed to beckon select Ngruki members from Solo to work in Malaysia and turn over twenty percent of their salaries to the two clerics.

---

[41] Abdus Samad was the name of a well-known Solo cleric; Ba'asyir had once been his student. Abud was the name of Ba'asyir's father.

[42] BIN document, "Gambaran Pena Abu Bakar Ba'asyir," p. 5.

[43] Correctly fearing a government backlash, members of the Ngruki usroh assumed low profiles for the next several years. Three of them eventually made their way to Lampung province in Sumatra, where they joined an Islamic commune led by a itinerant preacher named Warsidi. In late 1988, members of that commune, who had embraced the earlier Ngruki philosophy of opposing the secular authorities, confronted the local hamlet chief. Several more confrontations ensued, culminating in a February 1989 clash in which commune members killed a regional military officer in a frenzied arrow and machete attack. A subsequent government counterattack resulted in at least two dozen deaths, many of them after the commune members apparently set fire to their own longhouses rather than surrender. A detailed account of the clash can be found in Wasis, *Geser Talangsari*.

Second, they erected a courier network to shuttle directives between Malaysia and their former Ngruki base. This would allow them to maintain contact with the splintered remnants of their usroh network.

Third, Sungkar and Ba'asyir made the decision to venture to Saudi Arabia. Their reason for this was twofold. For one thing, they wanted to meet potential Saudi benefactors who might be enticed into providing much-needed funds to keep alive their movement in exile. For another thing, their trip was grounded in ideology. It was not by coincidence that Sungkar had settled in Kuala Pilah, a district that hosted a congregation led by the popular Wahhabi preacher Hashim bin Abdul Gani.

Wahhabism arguably ranks as the most puritanical strain of Islam. It traces back to the eighteenth century, when an Arabian cleric named Mohammad bin Abdul Wahhab traveled the Middle East before eventually coming full circle to his home village in the desolate sand flats of Hejaz. There he pondered what he felt was the deteriorating spiritual state of his fellow Muslims; he was especially incensed by the rise of the Ottoman Empire, which had enabled a Turk – rather than an Arab – to proclaim himself the universal caliph for all Muslims.

Brooding over this, Wahhab concluded that the decline of Muslims was because they had strayed from God's divine plan. To reverse this, he turned to the Hambali school of jurisprudence, the most conservative and intolerant of the four primary schools of thought in Islam. This had been founded by Ahmad bin Hambali, a Baghdad-born theologian from the first century who advocated a "back to basics" pristine form of Islam practiced by the earliest Muslim community. A later Hambali disciple, Ibn Taymiyya, used this approach to shape the Salafiyyah reformist movement which shirked rational interpretation and instead relied solely on a direct, textual understanding of Islamic scriptures.

Building on these precepts, Wahhab exponentially ratcheted up the level of intolerance. First, he underscored the need to use force to press home his aggressive proselytizing. Second, he made no secret of being a xenophobe: only Arabic culture and language, he insisted, were the prisms through which one could correctly live out his literal interpretation of the Islamic scriptures. Third, Wahhab was as seething toward non-Muslims as he was toward Muslims that did not share his fundamentalist bent. Fourth, he aimed for a backward-looking utopia bereft of most forms of modernity. This was taken to ridiculous extremes: adherents, for instance, were forbidden from such practices as drawing human figures, smoking, or drinking coffee.

Wahhab's take on Islam quickly proved controversial, even among a home crowd. Roundly condemned, for a time he was forced into exile. But showing a pragmatic streak, he joined forces with a promising local chieftain named Muhammad Ibn Sa'ud. In exchange for unquestioned religious authority, he lent religious legitimacy to the House of Sa'ud as it expanded its authority across the Arabian peninsula. This is the same Saudi kingdom, and the same synergy between political and religious leaders, that continues through the present day.

Not surprisingly, a handful of Indonesian visitors to Saudi Arabia over the centuries were exposed to, and smitten by, the potent Wahhabi revolutionary spirit. Among the first to import it back to the Indonesian archipelago was a *haj* pilgrim from West Sumatra in the early nineteenth century. Later that same century, another pilgrim introduced the tenets to a small congregation in Banten. But all of these persons had remained marginal puritanical figures; Wahhabism, as a result, never extended beyond the most inconsequential of footholds.

In the second half of 1985, Abdullah Sungkar and Abu Bakar Ba'asyir were set to change all that. First, however, they had pressing matters in the shadow of the Hindu Kush.

CHAPTER FOUR

AFGHANISTAN

The Soviet Union's elite *Spetsnaz* commandos had known from the start that Tadzh-Bek palace would be a formidable target. Located on a terraced rise in the southern outskirts of the Afghan capital of Kabul, it could only be approached along a single road that meandered up its slope. Strategically deployed along that route and on an adjacent hill was the bulk of an Afghan army brigade, including nearly a dozen dug-in tanks. Worse, movement was impeded by waist-deep snow.

The palace itself was a hulking three-story structure, its massive walls impervious to small arms and machine gun fire. Inside was the Afghan president's fiercely loyal personal bodyguards, all drawn from his own tribe.

But preparations for the assault on Tadzh-Bek had been long in coming. Back in the first half of 1978, soon after Soviet-trained Afghan military officers had conducted a military coup to bring communist power to their country, Soviet military and intelligence advisors had been introduced across the Afghan order-of-battle down to the battalion level.

During the first quarter of 1979, Moscow moved beyond the advisory stage. At that time, the Soviets began a gradual build-up of helicopters, transport aircraft, and paratroopers at Bagram airbase, north of Kabul. These were sent ostensibly to support Afghan President Nur Taraki.

Such support was desperately needed. Immediately after the 1978 coup, a substantial portion of the Afghan armed forces had mutinied to join a rural resistance movement led by tribesmen who had taken exception to the egalitarian ideals being pushed by Kabul's new communist rulers. Particularly antagonizing, for example, was an early 1979 compulsory literacy campaign for all women – a seemingly innocent concept which ran directly counter to Afghan tradition.

The presence of the Soviets, however, had little positive effect. As Afghanistan descended further into chaos, in September 1979 Taraki's prime minister, Hafizullah Amin, seized power and secretly executed Taraki. But Amin, it soon became apparent, was no more successful in stabilizing the situation. With the resistance gaining strength, the Soviets toward year's end decided to decisively intervene in the Afghan quagmire. Key to that intervention: they intended to overthrow Amin and replace him with a hand-picked and theoretically more dependable successor, Babrak Karmal.

To achieve its objective, Moscow in November dispatched Spetsnaz elements to Afghanistan. The initial unit, nicknamed the "Muslim battalion," was under the control of the GRU, the Soviet military intelligence organization. It received this moniker because it consisted exclusively of ethnics from the traditionally Islamic areas of the Soviet central republics; many spoke the dialects of Afghanistan. Much of the battalion, in fact, was outfitted in Afghan uniforms and attached to the security forces that stood watch around Amin's Tadzh-Bek residence.

Early the following month, Moscow readied more Spetsnaz for Kabul. Unlike the Muslim battalion, the two thirty-man assault groups in this contingent were under the control of the KGB, the Soviet civilian intelligence service. The first of these, codenamed Thunder, consisted of commandos who, to disguise their movement during foreign assignments, often masqueraded as professional athletes. The second, called Zenith, was the KGB's special reserve unit.

At 1500 hours on Christmas Day 1979, the Soviet high command issued word for a massive intervention task force to begin closing on Afghanistan by land and air. Less than two hours later, the first planes packed with paratroopers touched down at Bagram. There they laid in wait for further orders from Moscow.

That same day, the Muslim battalion invited the commanders of the Afghan security brigade for a festive reception. Vodka and cognac – poured from teapots to assuage Islamic sensitivities – flowed freely. The occasion allowed the commandos to make a final, detailed reconnaissance of the palace.

Clueless to what was actually unfolding, President Amin on the afternoon of 27 December presided over a garish banquet at Tadzh-Bek to commemorate the founding of the Afghan communist party. Having been informed of the recent Soviet military arrivals at Bagram, and believing they had come to help prop up his regime, Amin could not conceal his delight.

Such glee, of course, was completely misplaced. As dusk approached, Soviet cooks at Tadzh-Bek put the final touches on the president's dinner. Conspiring with the KGB, they spiked the food in hopes of eliminating Amin with poison. Initially, the plan seemed to be working: the president, his children, and many of the guests quickly fell ill. Eyes rolled back, Amin fell unconscious.

At that point, things began to go wrong. Because the assassination plot against Amin was highly compartmentalized, Soviet physicians assigned to the palace had not been informed. When they rushed to the comatose Amin's side, the president barely had a pulse. Placing intravenous tubes in both his arms, they began pumping in medicine. By 1800 hours, the Afghan leader's condition had stabilized.

Realizing that Amin would need to be eliminated by more aggressive means, the Spetsnaz commandos were given orders to proceed with a frontal assault against Tadzh-Bek. Plans called for the Muslim battalion to focus against the security forces immediately surrounding the palace, especially the dug-in tanks. Meanwhile, the Zenith assault group, riding four armored vehicles, was to approach Tadzh-Bek from the west, then circle to the front to link up with Thunder, riding aboard five vehicles. Both groups would then enter the palace and – their superiors in Moscow emphasized – leave no witnesses.

As scheduled, the commandos converged on the presidential residence at 1930 hours. But with the Afghan security forces on heightened alert following the poisoning, they came under withering fire from the opening minute. Bullets kicking up geysers of snow, both KGB assault groups dismounted and slogged up the hill with their assault ladders. Converging at the front entrance, the bloodied Spetsnaz began to squeeze through a ground-floor window as Amin's bodyguards took them in their sights from inside.

Pushing back the bodyguards with return fire, the commando column split in two. One group began to methodically clear the ground floor, while the second charged up the central staircase. As they approached the first rooms, grenades were thrown inside. Waiting for the concussion blasts to stifle any resistance, they then raked the interiors with automatic weapons.

At the end of the hall, Amin had been pacing the room in shorts and an Adidas t-shirt. With intravenous tubes in tow, the dazed president was muttering aloud. Initially in denial that his patrons could have betrayed him, he eventually accepted the obvious. His spirit broken, he laid down on a wooden counter as KGB commandos kicked in the door. One burst of gunfire later, Amin became the late president of Afghanistan.

The operation had been costly for the Soviets. Five KGB Spetsnaz commandos were killed, including the assault commander. Five others had died in the Muslim battalion. Virtually every other commando was wounded. One of the Soviet doctors tending to Amin had also perished in the crossfire.

But the Afghans had it far worse. The presidential security brigade, the bulk of which was led away at gunpoint, was effectively removed from the order-of-battle. Of Amin's personal bodyguards, half were captured and the other half killed, wounded, or missing. Amidst the mayhem inside the palace, even Amin's two young sons had been among the dead.

In hindsight, the siege of Tadzh-Bek marked the opening scene in the final act of the Cold War. The Soviet intervention of December 1979 not only provided a rally cry for the Afghan resistance, but also won the attention of both the West – which was eager to bleed Moscow white – and Muslims the world over. But while much of the Muslim world initially gave little more than moral support to the Afghan guerrillas, there was one significant exception.

That exception, Abdullah Azzam, had been born in 1941 to a humble Palestinian family on the West Bank. Part charismatic activist (he was a leader within his local chapter of the Muslim Brotherhood) and part academic, Azzam had just taken up a teaching berth at a Jordanian college when he experienced a defining moment in his life. Over the course of just six days in July 1967, the Israeli army humbled the combined militaries of its Arab neighbors. The West Bank – including Azzam's hometown – suddenly became Israeli-controlled territory.

Azzam was incensed. Taking to the pulpit, he became an outspoken proponent of jihad against Israel. But dissatisfied with the Palestinian guerrillas that were continuing the struggle to retake their homeland – in particular, he condemned the Palestinian Liberation Organization as too secular – Azzam opted to spend much of the next six years studying Islamic law in Egypt. By 1973, with a doctoral degree in hand, he accepted a teaching stint at a university in Jeddah, Saudi Arabia.

Azzam's time in Jeddah hardened his already rigid views on jihad. With the Israelis winning yet another war against the Arab states in 1973, the increasingly frustrated scholar became convinced that dialogue and negotiation were useless. He instead preached the need – indeed, the obligation – to use force of arms to return an Islamic caliphate to all lands that were once ruled by Muslims. This he defined in exceedingly broad terms: even Spain, he insisted, was among the territory in need of liberation. But the destruction of Israel, he emphasized, was a necessary first step.

Azzam's uncompromising views found a ready audience among his students. Among those particularly influenced was Osama bin Laden, the lanky scion of a Yemeni construction magnate who had made his fortune in the Saudi kingdom. Though the end of the decade, however, both mentor and pupil could offer their cause little more than lip service.

The December 1979 Soviet invasion of Afghanistan changed all that. With tales leaking across the Pakistani border of primitive tribesmen holding their own against the godless Soviets, Azzam saw in them a mujahideen worthy of foreign assistance. Deciding to lead by example, he left Saudi Arabia (where he had already overstayed his welcome among the Saudi authorities due to his incessant activism) and took up a teaching post in Islamabad in order to be closer to the front.

Azzam's thoughts never strayed far from the West Bank. Afghanistan, he reasoned, could act as a jihad training ground to prepare Muslim militants for battles elsewhere – especially in Palestine. He popularized this theme in books and booklets that were translated into numerous languages and disseminated across the Muslim world. He would also put his captivating oratory skills into play, crisscrossing the globe to make fiery recruitment pitches on behalf of the Afghan cause. Eventually, this self-styled "Godfather of Jihad" would visit some fifty American cities to shill for the mujahideen.

From early on, his call found willing recruits. Among the first arrivals in Pakistan was his former student, Osama bin Laden, who turned up at the start of the eighties with a couple of dozen Arabs in tow. They were motivated by a variety of reasons: some were seeking adventure, others genuinely believed doing battle against the Soviet invaders would place them on the fast-track to

Paradise, and still others were certifiable psychopaths. Later in the war, several Arab nations – notably Egypt – quietly emptied their prisons of homegrown delinquents and sent them packing to the Afghan jihad in the hope they might not return.[44]

For his part, bin Laden initially focused his energies – and deep pockets – on construction projects: building orphanages and homes for widows, as well as roads and bunker complexes for the mujahideen along the Afghan border.

The Arabs, however, itched to take part in combat. By 1984, with about 200 non-Afghan jihadists on hand, Azzam and bin Laden joined forces in the Pakistani city of Peshawar to create a coordinating body to handle the burgeoning legion of foreign volunteers eager to fight in Afghanistan. Known simply as the Services Bureau (*Maktab al-Khidmat*, or MAK), it administered their training at paramilitary camps straddling the Afghan frontier. Azzam appointed himself *emir* – leader – for the bureau; bin Laden was his deputy.

In reality, the foreign jihadists channeled through MAK were superfluous. The idea that Afghans somehow needed fighters from outside their country, one senior CIA officer would later observe, ignored basic historical and cultural facts. Indeed, virtually all of the Afghan mujahideen leaders generally saw them as nuisances, only slightly less bothersome than the Soviets.[45]

But there was one mujahideen commander who felt differently. Abdul Rassul Sayyaf was an Afghan intellectual whose academic career closely paralleled that of Azzam: after earning a graduate degree in Egypt, he had also spent considerable time studying in Saudi Arabia. It was there that he became a committed Wahhabi, which set his beliefs apart from the more tolerant brand of Islam practiced by most Afghans. His radical views eventually earned him a long jail sentence in Kabul during the seventies, but he had gotten his freedom on the eve of the Soviet invasion and quickly made his way across the border.

In Pakistan, Sayyaf rendezvoused with the growing number of mujahideen commanders congregating in Peshawar. To coordinate their efforts against the Soviets, they agreed to form a resistance umbrella known as the Islamic Union for the Liberation of Afghanistan. But in keeping with his Wahhabi creed, Sayyaf remained outspokenly anti-West, and especially anti-American. Almost

---

[44] Milton Beardon, "Afghanistan, Graveyard of Empires," *Foreign Affairs* (November/December 2001). Beardon was the CIA Station Chief in Pakistan from 1986 to 1989.

[45] *Ibid.*

immediately, this clashed with the views of the other militia commanders, who were doing their best to court support from Washington. Due to subsequent internal squabbling, the front dissolved and Sayyaf struck out on his own.

Alone, Sayyaf faced hardships. His radical recruitment pitch barely resonated among the Afghan refugees pouring into Pakistan; within Afghanistan, too, he commanded little support.

But Sayyaf held one advantage his mujahideen peers did not. Due to his Saudi connections, he had captured the attention of Azzam, bin Laden, and the foreign jihadists. Synergy between them made sense: Sayyaf needed funds and combatants; the Arabs needed a willing conduit for their volunteers. Not surprisingly, vast sums of Arab money, and weapons purchased with Arab cash, soon began to flow his way. His coffers flush, Sayyaf used this as a lure to attract members for his anemic *Ittihad-e Islami* militia.

Arab largesse was most apparent in Kurram Agency, one of the semi-autonomous tribal zones along Pakistan's frontier with Afghanistan. Straddling a traditional smuggling route, Kurram was shaped like a peninsula jutting toward Kabul, just 90 kilometers away. Both on account of its easy access to Afghanistan, and its Wild West reputation, Sayyaf and his MAK patrons saw the agency as an ideal staging and training locale. Very quickly, they began building a sprawling paramilitary complex near the town of Sadda for Ittihad-e Islami and the foreign jihadists.

⁂

Inside Afghanistan, meanwhile, an increasingly frustrated Soviet war machine during the first half of 1985 ratcheted up its counter-insurgency campaign. This fueled a vicious cycle, with the Saudis increasing their financing for the jihad, which in turn fueled heightened recruitment across the Muslim world.

By that time, it was not merely Arabs answering the call to jihad. As early as 1982, a handful of Southeast Asians – primarily Filipinos – had offered their services to various mujahideen commanders along the border. The conflict had also attracted the attention of Abdul Wahid Kadungga, the son-in-law of the late Darul Islam chieftain Kahar Muzakkar.

Like Muzakkar, Kadungga was a career rebel. After spending his teenage years rubbing shoulders with the top guerrillas of Darul Islam's South Sulawesi chapter, he had departed Indonesia in the early seventies to study in Europe. There he helped found the All-Europe Muslim Youth Association (*Persatuan Pemuda Muslim se-Europe*, or PPME), and later visited some of the Middle East's more radical regimes – Libya and Syria – on its behalf.

With this worldly outlook, Kadungga in 1975 ventured back to his homeland. There he spent much of his time working with the Indonesian Islamic Propagation Council (*Dewan Dakwah Islamiyah Indonesia*), a non-governmental organization concerned with missionary work. But showing his rebellious streak, he could not resist the temptation to begin railing against the New Order regime. Specifically, he vented over the country's draft marriage law, a secular document that offered few restrictions against registering couples of different religions. Predictably, his public criticism invited harassment by the thin-skinned authorities.

Under pressure, Kadungga moved back to Europe in 1980 and settled in the Netherlands. Perhaps in an attempt to gain political asylum, he grew ever more outspoken in his condemnation of Suharto. He also sought to politicize the PPME, which ultimately led to his expulsion from the mainstream organization and his subsequent creation of a splinter group known as PPME-Rotterdam.

Despite his incessant sniping against the New Order, in mid-1985 Kadungga wanted to risk a return to his homeland. But having heard the stories of foreign jihadists making their way to the Afghan front, he first felt the urge to make a short diversion to Pakistan. There he made his way to Peshawar, where he visited the MAK office and met with Abdullah Azzam.

Sold on the Afghan jihad, Kadungga departed Pakistan for Southeast Asia. But he again opted for another short diversion, this time to Malaysia. There he headed for Kuala Lumpur, where he used the opportunity to introduce himself to the freshly-exiled Ngruki leadership.[46] Talking up the MAK and its efforts along the Pakistani border, Kadungga found he was singing to the choir: Abdullah Sungkar and Abu Bakar Ba'asyir, who had already heard of Azzam's efforts, saw merit in sending Indonesians to fight alongside the Afghans and Arabs. Not only would it fulfill a perceived holy duty, but on a more pragmatic level would

---

[46] BIN report, "Abdul Wahid Kadungga," 16 June 2003, p. 3.

be a good opportunity to give fledgling Indonesian militants practical training in guerrilla tactics.[47]

During the fourth quarter of 1985, the Indonesian clerics in Malaysia readied an initial contingent for travel to Pakistan. Showing foresight, the idea was for this first group to be trained as instructors for later waves. This meant that candidates would need to be of a sufficiently high intellectual and physical caliber in order to be effective understudies.

Twelve candidates made the cut. Of these, Sungkar chose eleven; the Jakarta-based leadership of the Islamic Youth Movement (*Gerakan Pemuda Islam*, or GPI) picked the twelfth.[48] Of this first group, two persons stood out. The first, Aris Sumarsono, was a 24-year-old native of the outskirts of Solo who appeared a most unlikely jihadist. Slight in build, he struck most as quiet to the point of being unsociable. Too, he had a soft soul: a colleague would later recount how he often broke into tears when reading the Koran or when somebody would relate their misfortunes.

Sumarsono was also somewhat bookish. Attending Ngruki for six years through the end of high school, he graduated among the top five in his class. During that time, he had become reasonably proficient in Arabic. He had then headed in a secular direction, majoring in biology at Gadjah Mada University in Jogjakarta.[49]

But in Sumarsono, Sungkar saw only strengths. Not only did he display good academic instincts, but his ability in Arabic was vital: those in the first contingent would need to translate training materials from Arabic and master subjects from Arabic-speaking instructors. When the offer reached Sumarsono in Jogjakarta, he quickly booked a flight to Pakistan.

The other standout in the first class was Laode Agus Salim. At 23 years-old, Laode was everything Sumarsono was not: gregarious, entrepreneurial, and

---

[47] From Malaysia, Kadungga took a speedboat to Sumatra for a brief, discreet visit to Indonesia. In 2002, the International Crisis Group (ICG) claimed that Kadungga was a key figure in introducing Jemaah Islamiyah leaders to militants linked to al-Qaeda ("*The Case of the 'Ngruki Network' in Indonesia*," 8 August 2002, p. 16). These claims were later retracted by ICG on 10 January 2003.

[48] GPI, earlier known as the Indonesian Islamic Youth Movement (*Gerakan Pemuda Islam Indonesia*, or GPII), was a youth organization created during the Indonesian independence struggle and affiliated with the conservative Masyumi political party. Both Sungkar and Ba'asyir had been student leaders in the GPII during the fifties.

[49] "Jenderal Laskar Istimata," *Tempo*, 19 October 2003.

athletic. Though he had not gone to Ngruki, the Makassar-born Laode had attended Abu Bakar Ba'asyir's alma mater, the Gontor pesantren, and was a standout in the GPI. The son of a Darul Islam member, Laode himself had earlier pledged fealty to Sanusi Daris, the Darul Islam "minister of defense" under Kahar Muzakkar in the early sixties.

Arriving in Peshawar, the Indonesians were escorted by MAK to Kurram Agency. Featuring the occasional lush valley, Kurram was set to a backdrop of picturesque snow-capped mountains. In more peaceful times, tourism might have been a major draw.

Pushing west, they approached within six kilometers of the town of Sadda. Fourteen kilometers from the Afghan frontier, Sadda was a miniature version of Peshawar – raucous bazaar, terraced fields, scenic mountains. The surrounding hills had once been brimming with poppies, though most of those plots had recently been eradicated as part of a Pakistani government anti-drug campaign.

It was to the east of the main road leading into Sadda that Sayyaf, with MAK funds, had built a sprawling training complex. The heart of the complex was a semi-circle of six "faculties." These faculties, each consisting of a small cluster of stone buildings, acted as separate schools that taught such subjects as engineering (a euphemism for demolitions), infantry, cavalry, communications, logistics, and artillery. Positioned on three surrounding peaks were anti-aircraft guns to guard against the possibility – however remote – of a Soviet airstrike.

Teaching at the faculties was an eclectic mix of Afghan, Pakistani, and Arab instructors.[50] Reflecting the MAK's Saudi sponsorship, Camp Sadda also featured a strong dose of conservative religious indoctrination. The cadre relied heavily on the texts of Ibn Taymiyya, the Hambali disciple whose views had shaped the Salafiyyah reformist movement which relied solely on a direct, textual understanding of the scriptures.

Arriving at Camp Sadda, the first order of business for the Indonesians was to pick a *kunya*, Arabic for alias. Aris Sumarsono took the regal title of Zulkarnaen, the name of a king in the Koran thought to be a historical refer-

---

[50] Among the instructors was Mohammad Showki al-Islambuli. His brother, Khalid al-Istambuli, was one of the extremists who killed Egyptian President Anwar Sadat in 1981. Mohammad Showki al-Islambuli was later sentenced to death in absentia by the Egyptian government for a failed assassination attempt against President Hosni Mubarak in 1995; he is now a leading member of al-Qaeda.

ence to Alexander the Great. Laode Agus Salim from that point forward became Syawal.[51]

Plunging into their coursework, most of the twelve excelled. Plans called for the foreign jihadists to attend the Sadda "academy" for three years. The Afghan recruits – who comprised the bulk of the student body with 360 at any given time – stayed at one faculty for the entire three years and emerged as specialists in that particular field. The first Indonesian contingent, by contrast, was to train intensively for only a year in order for them to be on hand to assist future cycles. Not unexpected given his academic background, Zulkarnaen emerged as the best in demolitions training; the athletic Syawal was rated the best in paramilitary tactics. Four others washed out for a variety of reasons and returned home early.[52]

Even before the first eight graduated, a second Indonesian contingent arrived during the first quarter of 1986. This cycle consisted of thirty persons, many of them Ngruki alum and all vetted by Sungkar. From this group, the intention was to retain some as camp instructors. Others, meanwhile, devoted their time to building guesthouses and dormitories. All would have their food provided by Sayyaf with MAK funds; travel expenses, however, would be borne by the Indonesians.

While this second group was still in the midst of instruction, Sungkar in November 1986 readied yet another contingent of Southeast Asian jihadists. Like the second cycle, this would consist of thirty volunteers. Of the coveted slots, one went to a rotund, taciturn Indonesian named Nurjaman bin Isamuddin. Born in April 1964 in the sleepy West Java town of Cianjur, Nurjaman – known to friends and family by the nickname Encep – faced a difficult childhood. He was the second oldest among a dozen children born across a span of more than two decades; the youngest sibling, a brother, was twenty-one years his junior. Not surprisingly, Encep's father, who eked out a modest existence as a teacher, could barely make ends meet in their cramped, single-story home.

Growing up, Encep was remarkable for being thoroughly unremarkable. An introvert, he attended elementary and junior high school at a neighborhood

---

[51] Syawal would eventually amass more kunyas than virtually any other extremist in Indonesia. Among his other aliases: Salim, Yasin, Abu Seta, Muhammad Mubarok (spelling variant, Mubarak), Mahmud, Syawaluddin Kalla, and Laode Ida.

[52] BIN document, "Afghan Alumni," October 2003.

Islamic school (*madrasah*) founded by his grandfather's brother, a mullah. He went on to complete three years of senior high school in his hometown, where he was known as a quiet, average student.

Upon graduation, prospects for Encep were not good. No one from his family had attended college, and he had insufficient funds to be the first. (An application for a scholarship at one of Malaysia's top Islamic schools had been denied.) Worse, jobs around Cianjur were difficult to be had. Of all his siblings, only his older sister, who had married the owner of a vegetable stall, had an independent source of income.

Jobless for six months, in the summer of 1982 Encep made a desperate decision. In the hope of finding better employment prospects in Malaysia, he took a boat out of Indonesia with no travel documents, no funds, and no leads. Looking to make a fresh start, he took the new name Riduan Isamuddin.

His gamble worked. Taking up residence in Klang district, Selangor state, he sold chickens in the market each morning, then hawked Muslim caps and religious book at the port by night. From this, he earned enough to support himself and occasionally repatriate money back to his family in Cianjur.[53]

But predictably, Riduan grew homesick. In search of a father figure, he soon found a surrogate. In mid-1985, word had quickly spread among Indonesians expatriates in Malaysia about the arrival of the charismatic Abdullah Sungkar. By late that year, Riduan was making monthly trips to Kuala Pilah to attend the cleric's energetic sermons.

Sungkar lit a spark within Riduan. Midway through the following year, the impressionable Indonesian also began attending sermons by the fiery Malaysian preacher Abd al-Zukar. Talking up the Afghan jihad, al-Zukar repeatedly spoke of Asian volunteers making their way to Sayyaf's Camp Sadda.

Listening to these tales, Riduan was mesmerized. Placing a call to his family, he told them of his desire to fight in the Afghan jihad. The family, however, was anything but supportive. Although Cianjur was once square in the heartland of Darul Islam, it was hardly a hotbed of radicalism as of 1986. His uncle – a strong supporter of President Suharto – was especially outspoken in his opposition to his nephew's plans.

Undeterred, Riduan appealed to Sungkar. By that time, the cleric had grown familiar with the 22-year-old Indonesian who made monthly treks to his

---

[53] Undated BIN document, "Ambaran Pena – Riduan Isamuddin," p. 5.

prayer meetings. Too, Sungkar was increasingly willing to accept any suitable volunteer to fill the growing number of training berths being allocated by MAK. The preacher offered his quick approval, with a catch: he would assist Riduan in acquiring travel documents, but Riduan would have to pay for his own airfare to Pakistan.

At year's end, Riduan scrounged up enough cash for a one-way ticket to Karachi. Two other prospective Indonesian jihadists joined him on the journey. Arriving on Pakistani soil, they were met by a *masul*, or group leader. A Pakistani under the employ of MAK, the masul took them to an economy hotel for the night.

The next morning, the three Indonesians were awakened early and placed on a train bound for Peshawar. Once at their destination, they were taken to a local guesthouse managed by Sayyaf's Ittihad-e Islami. There they waited as the rest of the third training contingent arrived on subsequent flights from Southeast Asia.

Unfortunately for Riduan and his fellow prospective trainees, the winter of 1986-87 was particularly harsh. With heavy snows and frigid temperatures bringing the fighting inside Afghanistan to a standstill, and training at Camp Sadda an impossibility, the Indonesians spent the next two months virtual prisoners inside the Peshawar guesthouse.

Not all was lost, however. Over those two months, Riduan used the time to bond with Zulkarnaen. Three years Riduan's senior, Zulkarnaen was accorded considerable respect as Indonesia's most accomplished Sadda graduate to that point. In recognition of this, he had been appointed by Sungkar as masul for all Indonesians and Malaysians cycling through Kurram Agency.

Not until February 1987 had the snows sufficiently melted for Riduan and his compatriots to continue their journey. Boarding buses, they wound their way through Kurram before reaching Sadda. There they found a sprawling training complex divided into segregated ethnic clusters. One of them, for example, hosted Arabs and used Arabic as the medium of instruction. Another, supervised by Zulkarnaen, was for Indonesians and Malaysians; Indonesian and English were the tongues spoken there.

As with the previous groups, each of the new arrivals chose a kunya to be used during their tenure along the border. Looking for something with meaning, Riduan dubbed himself Hambali, the name of the conservative first-century theologian whose revivalist ideology was the basis for the Salafiyya and Wahhabi movements.

By that time, the Sadda academy had been fine-tuned for its varied students. Remembered one Malaysian instructor:

> All of the Indonesians and Malaysians were taught in the mosque in the center of the camp. Almost all of them specialized in either infantry or engineering classes for their entire three years. Only a few specialized in artillery or communications; none went to logistics or cavalry school.[54]

For the next eight weeks, Hambali familiarized himself with a wide range of weaponry. This included everything from the AK-47 assault rifle, to pistols, mortars, and rocket-propelled grenades. In theory, he was to continue this tutelage for at least a full twelve months.[55]

The realities of the battlefield inside Afghanistan dictated otherwise. Since the previous year, MAK's deputy emir, Osama bin Laden, had been living and working from a two-story villa in the outskirts of Peshawar. While he had accomplished much in terms of training and construction, his Arabs had barely participated in the actual jihad. Looking to rectify that, bin Laden had decided to build a base inside Afghanistan where they could pick a fight with the Soviets.

The location for that base was chosen carefully. Just across the Afghan border in Paktia province, the village of Jaji sat astride an infiltration route favored by the mujahideen. Overlooking the village was a towering mountain range, which in turn was honeycombed with caves. Significantly, heavy snow and ice made an assault on those caves all but impossible during the winter months.

Selecting one set of caves in this vicinity, bin Laden brought in some of his construction equipment. A reinforced command bunker soon took shape, along with some storage bunkers, an anti-aircraft position, and even a kitchen. With a flair for the dramatic, the Arabs called their new base *al-Massadaat al-Ansar* – the Lion's Den.

---

[54] Interview with Nasir Abas, 23 August 2005.
[55] In theory, students at the Sadda military "academy" would stay for three years. In reality, many Indonesians stayed for half that time or less.

As expected, it did not take the Soviets long to note the activity in the mountains over Jaji. As part of a larger sweep to eliminate mujahideen staging areas and supply dumps across Paktia, they began to plan for a spring offensive after the snows had started to melt.

On 17 April 1987, the Soviet assault began. Blending tactical airstrikes and heliborne commando raids, they began inching their way across the mountains. What took place next was a defining moment for MAK. In part because the airstrikes made it prohibitive to leave their shelters, and in part because snowdrifts still covering the upper slopes made movement difficult, bin Laden and about fifty other Arabs in the Lion's Den had little choice but to make a stand. For the next two weeks, they hunkered down in their reinforced caves and waited out the bombs that rained over their heads. Some two dozen reportedly did not make it out alive.

By the beginning of May, the snows had sufficiently melted for bin Laden to lead a withdrawal back toward Pakistan. In the overall context of the Afghan jihad, their two-week defensive action near Jaji hardly rated as a major engagement. But on a symbolic level, it was pivotal. For the first and only time, the Arabs had engaged a large number of Soviets and – though they ultimately retreated – had performed well. Bin Laden was no longer merely a generous patron, but was now lauded as a heroic combat leader. As his legend began to grow, the recruitment of Arab jihadists skyrocketed.

While the Jaji battle was still raging, word had quickly filtered back to Camp Sadda. The Indonesian trainees were burning to participate, and at least some of them joined a reinforcement column of Afghan mujahideen that headed north for the front. Hambali and Zulkarnaen were among them, though they and their fellow Afghan guerrillas did not get far across the border before they were bogged well down short of the Lion's Den. Waiting in the mountains to ambush the Soviets, they ended up returning to Pakistan without firing a shot.[56]

---

[56]   Several Indonesians have claimed they participated in combat inside Afghanistan against Soviet forces, though there is reason to treat their stories with a heavy dose of skepticism. For example, Mukhlas (alias Ali Gufron), a member of the second Indonesian training contingent at Sadda, has improbably claimed he was among bin Laden's Arab contingent at Jaji. More amusing is the case of Ja'far Umar Thalib, who boasted – with considerable hyperbole – that he shot down five Soviet helicopters with a single rocket-propelled grenade circa 1988. See "His Afghan Boast: Five Soviet Copters Shot Down With A Single Rocket," *Straits Times*, 30 March 2002. Nasir Abas, a Sadda instructor, notes that Indonesian students made shallow forays during the late nineties into Afghanistan for field exercises, but never came into contact with Soviet forces. It was not until

Once back at Sadda, the Indonesians resumed training alongside a growing number of Southeast Asians. By that time, a separate Filipino contingent with its own masul had been formed. Even Thai Muslims had reached critical mass, forming a small unit led by a masul named Abdul Fatah. Zulkarnaen remained in charge of the Indonesians and Malaysians.

Besides absorbing the basics of guerrilla warfare, Hambali also used his time in Kurram Agency to grow closer with Abu Bakar Ba'asyir. Both Ba'asyir and Sungkar had ventured to Pakistan during early 1988 to tour the border and meet the MAK leadership. Although Hambali had already become acquainted with Sungkar, the more reserved Ba'asyir was still largely a stranger. Seeking to rectify this, Hambali made a concerted effort to befriend Ba'asyir. The preacher proved amicable, and revealed that he had sent his son – a precocious preteen named Abdul Rahim – to live in a Kurram guesthouse; Zulkarnaen, among his other duties, was named Rahim's guardian.

Not until April 1988 did Hambali prepare to return home. Intelligence officials would later calculate that some sixty percent of those three initial cycles at Sadda would seamlessly re-enter Indonesian society and lead unremarkable, law-abiding lives.[57]

Hambali, history would prove, was not one of them.

1990, following the departure of the Soviet army, that Indonesian jihadists ventured deeper into Afghanistan to attack positions held by the communist Najibullah regime. At least two Indonesians were killed during these operations. Nasir Abas, *Membongkar Jamaah* [sic] *Islamiyah* (Jakarta: Grafindo, 2005), p. 57.

[57] BIN report, "Afghan Alumni."

CHAPTER FIVE

ESTRANGEMENT

Hambali returned to Malaysia on a high. After all, it had been a heady experience stepping away from the conformity of Southeast Asian society to take up arms in a holy struggle. Now prone to wearing *shalwar khameez* – baggy Pakistani clothes – and a *kullah* – the rolled cap popular along the Afghan frontier – to advertise his Sadda stint, the erstwhile stall vendor found that his tales of near-jihad struck awe among his Malaysian colleagues. And steeped in Wahhabi ideology, he came away convinced about the righteousness of his newfound beliefs and, conversely, the mandate to confront those that did not adhere to the same intolerant path.

But the Southeast Asia that greeted Hambali was hardly primed for fundamental social change, let along the backward-looking utopia championed by Wahhabists. Indeed, the six member states of the Association of Southeast Asian Nations – which included Malaysia and Indonesia – had given a full embrace to the secular trappings of modernity. In 1987, the association had even kicked off a campaign for regional tourist promotion looking to substantially increase the number of Western tourist arrivals – a move certain to rub Islamic conservatives like Sungkar raw.

Among all its neighbors, Indonesia was perhaps the least likely setting for change. Arguably the most stable, predictable nation in Southeast Asia, Suharto had been in power more than two decades and showed no sign of leaving any decade soon. In what was dubbed "Indonesian-style democracy," the former general helmed what was effectively an uncontested national election every five years. Pundits, thirsty for an angle to report, were left to speculate on his choice of vice president – not that it mattered, given that Suharto ceded little authority to his understudy.

Such a scene was disheartening for the Afghan alumni. Sinking back into a familiar, boring routine, Hambali resettled in Selangor to peddle kebabs and honey at the Klang market.[58] His only reprieve from this tedium came once a month, when he took a bus to Negeri Sembilan to attend Sungkar's sermons. These marathon sessions often lasted from sundown to sunrise the following morning, during which time Hambali could meet with budding adherents cut from the same theological cloth.[59]

During this period, Sungkar resurrected a practice that dated back to the Darul Islam days. Taking aside promising prospects, he had them repeat an oath of loyalty in the Arabic language. Translated, it came across as a rather tame pledge: "I offer my allegiance to you to listen to and obey the orders of God and His messenger to the best of my ability."[60] Still, it remained a powerful compliance mechanism for relatively young, impressionable Indonesian expatriates, many of whom shared the exclusivity of their Sadda training.

Though hardly part of Sungkar's inner circle, Hambali was among those given the opportunity to pledge fealty to the cleric. Initiated in this manner, for the next two years he continued his monthly jaunts to Negeri Sembilan.

Not until 1990 did Hambali get a chance to escape the monotony of Selangor. That year, Sungkar offered him the opportunity to venture to Tawi-Tawi – the chain of islands extending across the southernmost Philippines – for missionary work. Specifically, he was to replace another Sadda veteran who had been teaching children how to read the Koran. To offset expenses, he would live with a Muslim family and receive a stipend from Sungkar. Though hardly as exciting as paramilitary training, it promised to be a welcome, eight-month reprieve from Klang.

---

[58] In November 1989, Hambali received his permanent residency card from Malaysian immigration authorities.

[59] The clerics did not have it easy, either. When not preaching, for example, Abu Bakar Ba'asyir made money from selling clothes and raising chickens.

[60] BIN document, "Surat Pernyataan: Faiz bin Abu Bakar Bafana," 22 October 2002, p. 2. The exact wording of the oath varied slightly over the years. In addition, the oath was sometimes given by senior followers of Sungkar on his behalf. For example, in 1992, Zulkarnaen administered the oath to a candidate in Afghanistan. See "Berkas Perkara (Pemeriksaan Tambahan) Tindak Pindana Terorisme, Thoriquddin als Abu Rusydan als Hamzah," September 2003, p. 3.

The work in Tawi-Tawi, it turned out, was not all about the scriptures. In between classes, Hambali befriended a fellow Indonesian and Sadda graduate named Arqom (spelling variant Arkam, alias Syamsuddin). Forty years old with a stringy goatee, the skittish Arqom, who counted himself as a follower of Darul Islam chieftain Ajengan Masduki, was the first Indonesian militant to regularly visit Muslim separatists in the southern Philippines. (Following the mass arrest of Komando Jihad members in the late seventies, the name "Darul Islam" came back in vogue among the resilient cadres that once more took root beginning in the eighties.) As proof of his travel history, he displayed a comfortable fluency in both English and Tagalog. Sensing a fellow hardcore rebel in Hambali, Arqom offered him a chance to join him on a secret trip to Mindanao.

He did not have to ask Hambali twice. Late that year, the two boarded a ferry for Mindanao. En route, Arqom offered a primer on the nuances of Islamic militancy in the Philippines. Moro Muslims dominated the country from Mindanao southward, and for generations they had bristled at being incorporated into a single nation with the Catholic majority which populated the rest of the Philippines. Beginning in the seventies, this opposition had exploded into full-scale rebellion. Pioneering the insurgency was the Moro National Liberation Front (MNLF), a secular organization that packaged its opposition toward Manila in cultural and ethnic rather than solely religious terms.

Dissatisfied with the MNLF's lack of religious emphasis, a splinter organization inevitably took shape. Known as the Moro Islamic Liberation Front (MILF), this group made no secret of its desire to split from the Philippines and abide by a strict religious code. In 1981, the MILF had established its first paramilitary training site in the jungles of Mindanao. Known as Camp Abu Bakar al-Siddique – after the first successor to the Prophet Mohammad – it was much more than a training complex: by the end of that decade it covered 5,000 hectares and was a sprawling 40 kilometers long covering parts of seven towns.

Hambali, it turned out, was already roughly familiar with the MILF. At Sadda, virtually all of his Moro co-trainees had come from that organization. Now eager to view their struggle firsthand, he and Arqom made their way to Cotabato City, then took a bus to Matanog. From there, they hired a *skylab*, the local name for a motorcycle jockey. Already, signs of Islamic piety were starting to show: Hambali noted that female passengers were not allowed to touch male jockeys, so young children were hired to sit in between as a physical buffer against direct contact.

Passing through a series of roadblocks manned by the MILF's semi-conventional army, they eventually arrived at the front's headquarters. Over the next three days, Arqom brokered introductions with the MILF's leadership, including their chairman and fellow Sadda alum, Slamet Hashim.

Reinvigorated by these encounters, Hambali returned to Tawi-Tawi. But rather than heading straight back to Selangor when he finished his proselytizing tour in 1991, he instead took up another Arqom offer to make a short detour into Malaysia's Sabah state. There he befriended a small group of self-exiled Indonesian radicals who, like Arqom, claimed affiliation with Darul Islam cells on Java.

Hambali made another important acquaintance in Sabah. Noralwizah Lee binti Abdullah was the 21-year-old daughter of a Chinese father and Malay mother. Like Hambali, she had endured a poor upbringing – worsened by her father's alcoholism and philandering. To escape pressures at home, she had followed the lead of her older sister and converted from Buddhism to Islam while in high school, then headed to a religious school in Johor.

While in Johor, Noralwizah had a fateful encounter during 1990.[61] By that time, Sungkar had raised a small corps of female adherents whose role was to make the rounds among the wives of Sungkar's followers, offering lectures on such topics as "characteristics of a good wife," and "the role of jihad." In Noralwizah, they found an eager new recruit; by late that year, she was a full-fledged member of their community.

To Hambali's way of thinking, Noralwizah was ideal on a number of counts. For one thing, she shared his conservative religious outlook. For example, she agreed with his belief that jihad was a necessity and not an option. In addition, because she had originally come from a Buddhist background, Hambali felt he could take some credit for "saving" her soul. After only a single meeting, he proposed marriage. She accepted.

Newly engaged, the couple moved back to Selangor. After a simple wedding ceremony within the budget of a small-time stall operator, Hambali returned to the Klang market and once again sold such varied items as religious books and

---

[61] Like Hambali, Noralwizah would eventually be known by several aliases. These included Lee Yen Lan, Awie, and Acang.

vegetables. He also resumed his earlier schedule of monthly attendance at the Kuala Pilah trysts to study the Koran and discuss activities to prepare for jihad. By his own admission, however, he was still a "nobody" in the eyes of Sungkar.

❧

Worlds away, major changes were taking place in Afghanistan. During the same month that Hambali had left Sadda for Malaysia – April 1988 – the Soviets had declared they would withdraw in order to escape the growing costs of a deadlock. Elated, Azzam and bin Laden quickly began contemplating a post-Afghanistan world and agreed not to dismantle the jihadi capabilities being coordinated by the MAK. In its place, bin Laden proposed a foundation or base – known in Arabic as *al-Qaeda* – that would serve as a headquarters for managing future jihad in other theaters.

By August 1988, the structure of al-Qaeda had been mapped out on paper. With a wider geographic scope than the MAK, it included an intelligence component and military, financial, political, and media affairs committees. It also included an advisory council, or *shura*, that would review key decisions from a Koranic perspective. Significantly, all leadership positions were monopolized by bin Laden and his closest Egyptian allies within the MAK.[62]

Half a year later, in February 1989, the commanding general of Soviet forces in Afghanistan crossed into Uzbekistan and brought nine years of Soviet occupation to a humiliating end. This had immediate, and destabilizing, consequences inside Afghanistan. Deprived of a common foreign enemy, the various mujahideen commanders began sniping at each other as they poured into their homeland to carve out spheres of influence.

For most of the Arab jihadists, the Soviet withdrawal was the end of an era. The majority returned to their homelands and blended back into civilian life. But for those charged with terrorism in their home countries, a homecom-

---

[62] With the Afghan jihad fast winding down, bin Laden and his Egyptian colleagues looked to wage their next jihad against Egypt's Mubarak regime. To their consternation, however, Azzam insisted that they would instead focus their energies against Palestine and expressly forbid MAK assets from being used in any other theater. In the no-holds-barred world of jihad, Azzam eventually suffered a deadly vote of no confidence. During November 1989, a powerful car bomb on the Pakistani frontier tore apart the jihadist chieftain and his two sons. Though never proven with certainty, the assassins were assumed to be his Egyptian rivals. With bin Laden left in undisputed control of the MAK, he folded its assets into al-Qaeda.

ing carried the unwelcome prospect of a jail sentence or worse. Complicating matters, Egypt and Algeria had launched formal complaints with the Pakistani government, accusing Islamabad of harboring wanted criminals. The Pakistanis, already impatient with the Arabs, began pressuring the MAK to vacate its soil.

With little choice, the MAK phased out its Peshawar office and Sadda camp before moving across the frontier into Afghanistan. Reaching agreement with various mujahideen warlords for land use, they opened a string of six training camps – most of them little more than a simple collection of tents and stone huts – to continue churning out foreign jihadists.

For the Indonesian instructor cadre at Sadda, still led by stalwarts Zulkarnaen and Syawal, a shift was also in order. By 1991, most of their time was spent at a new exclusively Indonesian camp established at Torkum (spelling variant Towrkham), just inside the Afghan border.[63] A handful of trainees also ventured to a MAK camp established near the eastern Afghan city of Jalalabad, and another set up at Khaldan outside the city of Khost.[64]

Among the camps' Arab patrons, more changes were in store. As of 1991, the MAK had quietly folded and its assets – in theory – were merged into bin Laden's al-Qaeda. Bin Laden himself had returned to Saudi Arabia a hero, but just as quickly wore out his welcome when he lashed out at the Saudi authorities for allowing a U.S.-led coalition to liberate Kuwait from Saudi soil. Even though his passport was seized, he stole out of the kingdom in April 1991 and headed for Sudan, where he had an open invitation from that country's hard-line Islamic government.

In Khartoum, bin Laden was permitted to build his al-Qaeda network provided that he did reveal his presence in Sudan. This was easier said than done. At that early point, al-Qaeda was little more than a theoretical umbrella for like-minded extremist groups; it had clear operational control over very little. Even bin Laden's ties to key colleagues were informal. Case in point was Abu Zubaydah, a Palestinian militant who ran the Khaldan training camp near Khost:

---

[63] According to al-Qaeda member Umar Faruq, after the Indonesians departed Torkum circa 1995, the site primarily became a Kurdish training camp with Turkish instructors.

[64] "Surat Pernyataan: Faiz bin Abu Bakar Bafana," pp. 2-3. Umar Faruq, who was later rendered from Indonesia in 2002, met Syawal at Khaldan in 1991. Based on extensive interviews with Afghan alumni, BIN believes that a total of 197 Indonesians were "full-time" paramilitary students at the Afghan "military academy" (either Camp Sadda or, after 1991, one of the camps inside Afghanistan) between 1985 and 1994. Although the academy was theoretically three years in length, some stayed for as little as one month.

while an openly sympathetic peer of bin Laden, he did not yet count himself as a subordinate.

All members of bin Laden's emerging network, however, were tied by a growing hatred of the United States. This was in part born out of frustration by their inability to topple targeted regimes in the Middle East, especially in Egypt. Part, too, followed from bin Laden's own indignation at having U.S. troops still stationed in the Saudi kingdom a year after the liberation of Kuwait. This second factor had prompted bin Laden to issue an early 1992 fatwa – even though his religious credentials were hardly authoritative – calling for a jihad against the so-called Western occupation of Islamic lands. Al-Qaeda, at least in rhetoric, had declared war.

Beginning in this period, bin Laden started to show heightened interest in a different part of the world: Southeast Asia. This had first become apparent in 1988, when he dispatched his brother-in-law, Muhammad Jamal Khalifa, to the Philippines. A Saudi national of Jordanian origin, Khalifa was ostensibly an Islamic missionary and philanthropist. As a cover for his operations, one of Khalifa's first assignments was to set up a front company in Manila to export rattan. A series of charitable and educational organizations, all funded by bin Laden, followed. Some nine different organizations were founded between 1989 and 1994, all of them eventually incorporated under the International Relations and Information Center (IRIC), a company established by Khalifa in June 1994. Khalifa also subverted the Philippines branch of the Saudi-based Islamic International Relief Organization (IIRO), a legitimate charity with worldwide offices.[65]

As would later become common practice within al-Qaeda, Khalifa's charities at times performed legitimate charity work, albeit to win sympathy and support. But much of their work involved channeling paramilitary assistance to Muslim rebels. As early as October 1991, Filipino officials tracked financial transactions between Khalifa and two armed Islamic separatist organizations, the MILF and another extremist organization called the Abu Sayyaf Group

---

[65]   As director of the Manila branch of the IIRO, Khalifa also oversaw programs in neighboring countries such as Indonesia, Taiwan, and Thailand.

(ASG).[66] Some of this involved organizing volunteers, through the IIRO, to train in Afghanistan. By the mid-nineties, it is also believed that Khalifa was sponsoring the paramilitary training of foreign mujahideen at the MILF's Camp Abu Bakar.

While Khalifa was busy with these ventures, the Philippines took on relevance for a different set of bin Laden sympathizers. In 1993, a group of freelance Islamic radicals led by Kuwaiti national Ramzi Ahmed Yousef attempted to topple New York's twin towers by placing a car bomb in the basement; six died and a hundred were injured in the resulting explosion, but the towers stood.

After that bombing, Yousef escaped a U.S. dragnet and fled to Manila. This was not new territory for him. During a 1991 training stint in Afghanistan, he had been introduced to the Filipino founder of the ASG. Later, at bin Laden's request, he had ventured to the Philippines from December 1991 to May 1992 to train ASG rebels in bomb-making techniques. With Yousef during that period were fellow Afghan alumni Abdul Hakim Murad (a Kuwaiti-born Pakistani) and Wali Khan Amin Shah (an Uzbeki).

Arriving in the Philippines after the New York bombing, Yousef remained there through mid-1994. At that point, he was joined by his uncle and Afghan veteran, Khalid Sheikh Mohammad. Over the next half year, the two led double lives. On the one hand, they frequented seedy Manila bars and enjoyed a bevy of Filipina girlfriends.[67]

Almost immediately, they began brainstorming more apocalyptic terrorist plots against Western, and especially American, targets. Eager to help, both Murad and Shah returned to the Philippines and joined the conspiracy.

Before they could continue with their plans, the group looked to establish a commercial front in order to give them the means for shifting funds around the region. In need of local faces to process the paperwork, they turned to the Afghan jihadi network. This immediately led them to Abdullah Sungkar, who had vetted the hundreds of Southeast Asians who passed through Camp Sadda during the previous decade. Appealing to Sungkar, they requested a local partner who could help open a business without asking questions. When the cleric looked among his congregation for a discreet follower who could legally establish a company in Malaysia, Hambali was at the top of his shortlist.

---

[66] ASG was created in 1991 with US$6 million from bin Laden and Libya.

[67] Maria Ressa, *Seeds of Terror* (New York: Free Press, 2003), pp. 21-23.

For the previous year, Hambali had been juggling more parochial concerns. With a new wife and limited income, he had scrambled to save money on housing. On the advice of Mohammad Iqbal bin Abdul Rahman, a fellow Sungkar follower who had been in his same Sadda training cycle, he learned of a low-income neighborhood favored by Indonesian migrant workers in Sungai Manggis, a village in Selangor's Banting district. There he rented a simple plywood house; in the nearby night market he sold traditional medicines, carpets, and honey, and occasionally drove two hours to Kuala Lumpur to peddle *batik* cloth. His wife, meanwhile, taught the Koran to children at their house.

Hambali also found time to remain one of about ten regulars at Sungkar's sermons. By that time, he was making the trek to Kuala Pilah on a weekly basis. The cleric had taken note of his dedication; in a first, he pulled aside Hambali and asked a favor. Conjuring a cover story, Sungkar said that one of their Arab brothers wanted to import *zam zam* – water from a sacred well in Mecca – into Malaysia, but he needed a Malaysian national as a silent business partner.

Hambali did not disappoint his mentor. On 2 June 1994, he and his wife ventured to the newly-opened office of the import company, Konsojaya Senderian Berhad, and signed their names to legal papers making them board members. They briefly met Mihannad, one of the Arab businessmen investing in the company; much later, Hambali would learn that Mihannad was an Afghan veteran.

As a legitimate business, Konsojaya would prove a bust. The Malaysian government ended up giving the zam zam concession to another company, so Mihannad had his license revoked almost from the start. Showing dexterity, he then declared Konsojaya would export Malaysian palm oil to Pakistan. But there is no evidence that Konsojaya ever orchestrated any exports, and Hambali never heard of any profits being generated.

As a front, however, Konsojaya was a success. First, it provided Wali Khan Amin Shah, listed as a company director, with an alibi for traveling throughout the region. Second, it served as a coordination hub: telephone taps by the Philippines police later showed frequent calls between the Konsojaya office in Malaysia and Khalifa's IRIC in Manila. There is also evidence of funds being channeled from Konsojaya to the Philippines.[68]

---

[68]   Singaporean authorities claim to have evidence that Konsojaya funds were used to send nine Singaporean Muslims for paramilitary training in Pakistan and Afghanistan.

The reason for these transfers became apparent in December 1994. During that month, Ramzi Yousef smuggled a bomb aboard a Philippine Airlines jet bound for Japan. The bomb exploded en route, killing a Japanese businessman but failing to bring down the plane.[69]

As it turned out, the December 1994 bomb was intended as a trial run for a terrorist operation the likes of which the world had never seen. Looking to simultaneously blow up twelve U.S.-bound jetliners while airborne over Asia – resulting in perhaps 4,000 deaths – the plot was codenamed *Bojinka*, the Serbo-Croatian word for "explosion."

But even for terrorists, Murphy's Law is often alive and well. Yousef, Murad, and Shah were mixing chemicals in Yousef's apartment during January 1995 when the mix accidentally caught fire. Police came on the scene, arresting Murad and Shah (though the latter escaped in a matter of hours). Yousef managed to flee the city and made his way to Pakistan. Its patrons behind bars or on the run, the Bojinka operation was stillborn.[70]

Hambali claims to have been an ignorant of Konsojaya's ulterior role. There is good reason, however, to believe he was not a complete innocent. It was Hambali, after all, who provided cash and cover for Shah when he fled the Philippines for Malaysia and hid out at a Langkawi resort. Hambali, moreover, began flaunting several cellular phones and in March 1995 reportedly threw a lavish Idul Adha feast; the source of his newfound wealth was never made clear.

Indeed, Hambali appears to have been one of the few touched by Konsojaya to have benefited from a windfall. In December 1995, Malaysian authorities tracked Shah down and quickly extradited him to the U.S. Pakistani officials, meanwhile, caught up with Yousef in Islamabad and also sent him packing to an American prison. And in 1996, Khalifa was arrested on a warrant issued by a Jordanian court in connection with a bomb blast in Jordan.

---

[69] Yousef later called media outlets and claimed responsibility for the bombing in the name of the ASG.

[70] Members of the extremist cell in Manila were planning three other terrorist operations during the same period. The first was the assassination of Pope John Paul II, who was scheduled to visit the Philippines in 1995. The second was the assassination of U.S. President Bill Clinton. The third was a plan to hijack a commercial airliner and kamikaze the aircraft into the CIA headquarters in McLean, Virginia; Murad, a licensed commercial pilot who trained in flight schools in the U.S., was to be in the cockpit. In late 2002, it was learned that other Middle Eastern radicals, including Umar Faruq, had ventured to the Philippines in 1995 to an attempt to get flying lessons so they could conduct suicide flights.

After these arrests, U.S. interest in Southeast Asian terrorist operations waned. Investigations into local accomplices – namely Hambali – were never pursued. In return, Hambali did not try to tempt fate. Following Shah's arrest, he laid low for a time and focused on his odd jobs and networking among the Kuala Pilah congregation.

⊷

As head of that congregation, Abdullah Sungkar had been overseeing a fundamental shift in its outlook and goals. During the initial years of exile, many of the Kuala Pilah diaspora – Sungkar included – had retroactively proclaimed lineage with the historical Darul Islam movement.[71] In particular, Sungkar for most of the eighties had remained deferential to the handful of aging Darul Islam leaders that had still eluded a prison cell back in Indonesia. Topping that list was Ajengan Masduki, a rebellious octogenarian from West Java who in late 1987 was chosen as acting head of the movement. During occasional medical visits to Malaysia, Masduki would usually visit his exiled countrymen in Kuala Pilah.

But by the close of the decade, ties with the residual Darul Islam leadership inside Indonesia had grown strained. There were several reasons for this. First, Sungkar for years had been advocating a more academic direction in developing his Islamic community. Whereas Masduki's Darul Islam still saw itself as a true grassroots organization, usually catering to society's lowest common denominator, Sungkar sought to work through select cadres imbibed with conservative doctrine from hard-line Islamic boarding schools like Ngruki. This had given Sungkar a far more organized, often more educated network of supporters than was afforded the Darul Islam network in Indonesia.

Second, Sungkar had embraced a more militant view of jihad brought about by his association with Afghanistan. By contrast, his Darul Islam contemporaries in Indonesia had backed away from armed conflict and settled on a more passive, defensive version of jihad, even suggesting that it could be waged through prayer.

This difference of opinion grew personal as the increasingly dogmatic Sungkar began leveling accusations against patriarch Masduki. Specifically, Masduki was accused of joining the Sufic *tarikat* movement, which advocated non-vio-

---

[71]   Hambali did not see himself as a member of Darul Islam, but rather as a disciple of Sungkar.

lence and religious tolerance. Just as Abdullah Azzam had fallen out with the less flexible elements of the MAK, Masduki's alleged deviations were deemed nothing less than heresy by Sungkar.[72]

Finally, there was a financial element to their rift. While it was assumed that money from Middle Eastern benefactors was helping to underwrite the dispatch of jihadists to Pakistan, a lack of transparency in the use of those funds led to suspicion and jealousy among the Darul Islam adherents inside Indonesia. Sungkar, some charged, was benefiting personally.[73]

By 1991, their rift had grown apparent to the followers in Malaysia. Not until 1 January 1993, however, did Sungkar move to formally sever ties.[74] Asking his congregation to renew its vow of loyalty, Sungkar quickly received pledges of obedience from Hambali and the rest of the expatriate congregation. In particular, virtually all of the Sadda alumni, which owed their training opportunities to Sungkar's acquiescence, fell in line behind the Kuala Pilah cleric. Significantly, this included a sizable number of Malaysian and Singaporean nationals that had been among later cycles passing through MAK training.[75]

That June, Sungkar began to flesh out his estranged faction. Using Arabic terminology, he split his followers into *mantiqi*, or regional chapters. Mantiqi 1 (in Arabic, *Mantiqi Ula*), which covered Malaysia and Singapore, was placed under the leadership of longtime deputy Abu Bakar Ba'asyir. Mantiqi 2 (*Mantiqi Tsani*), covering Indonesia, was given to Abu Fatih, a member of Sungkar's exile community since 1986. On paper, each mantiqi controlled up to four sub-regional branches (*wakalah*), and each branch controlled one or more compartmentalized cells (*fiah*). Appropriately, Sungkar named himself emir (spelling variant *amir*).[76]

---

[72] "The Travails of Ngruki Two," *Tempo*, 4 November 1992, p. 19.

[73] Gaos Taufik interview; "Ambaran Pena – Riduan Isamuddin," p. 8.

[74] The 1 January 1993 date for the formal split with Masduki comes from the testimony of Achmad Roichan, a member of the first Indonesian contingent to Camp Sadda. See Testimony of Achmad Roichan (p. 6) in "Berkas Perkara, No. Pol. BP/16/VII/2003/Dit-1, Thoriquddin als Abu Rusydan als Hamzah," 5 August 2003.

[75] Sungkar required all of the Indonesian students still training in Afghanistan and Pakistan to renew their oaths. Most of the pledges were administered by Zulkarnaen on behalf of Sungkar. For example, Mustopha swore allegiance via Zulkarnaen in Peshawar during 1993. See Mustopha testimony (p. 3) in "Berkas Perkara, No. Pol. BP/16/VII/2003/Dit-1, Thoriquddin als Abu Rusydan als Hamzah," 5 August 2003.

[76] Jemaah Islamiyah envisioned a military structure – at least on paper – which included *saroyah* (akin to a battalion) under the wakalah level. Each saroyah had three *katibah* (equivalent to a company), which in turn were comprised of three *kirdas* (platoons), each of which contained three fiah of between six and ten operatives. Nasir Abas, p. 122. In reality, fiah members reported direct to their wakalah leaders.

This rather ambitious wire diagram was matched by equally ambitious organizational goals. According to Sungkar, Muslims in Southeast Asia represented a formidable bloc: almost 270 million people, exporting more than US$330 billion per annum, producing a sizable percentage of the world's oil supply.[77] Too, he had rubbed shoulders with like-minded radicals from across Asia for the past decade. Both these factors led Sungkar by 1995 to no longer set his sights merely on implementing Islamic rule in Indonesia. Rather, he began contemplating a regional Islamic super-state – *Daulah Islamiah Raya* – that would encompass Indonesia, Malaysia, Singapore, and parts of the Philippines and Thailand.

With this broadened goal, Sungkar looked to make a clean break from Darul Islam by adopting a different organizational moniker. Taking a page from the early eighties, by 1995 he had resurrected Jemaah Islamiyah – "Islamic Community" – as the group's new name.[78] But unlike the earlier manifestation – when there had been debate as to whether it was a tangible group or merely a collection of like-minded radicals – this time Jemaah Islamiyah had organizational substance with defined positions. Sungkar himself said as much in an interview with Sydney-based Islamic magazine *Nida'ul Islam* ("Call of Islam"). In it, he identified himself as leader of Jemaah Islamiyah – both words capitalized – and said that his group's aims were to "establish the supremacy of Islam [in Indonesia] by the strategies of preaching, strategic evasion, and Jihad."

Elsewhere in the interview, Sungkar drew attention to his regional vision when he spoke of "the obligation of Jihad within the framework of [establishing] an Islamic state of southern Thailand, Malaysia, Indonesia, and the southern Philippines." He added that "cooperative movements," such as Islamic political parties, could not succeed in accomplishing his goal, but "non-cooperative" movements (which did not seek to cooperate with government authorities) could emerge victorious. For this, he concluded that *Quwwatul Musallaha* – military strength – was essential.[79]

---

[77] BIN document, "Gambaran Pena – Abu Bakar Ba'asyir," 11 September 2001, p. 7.

[78] According to Bafana, Sungkar initially named the organization *Jamiatul Minal Mulimin* (spelling variant, *Jemaah Minal Mulimin*), though it soon became commonly known as *Jemaah Islamiyah* (spelling variant, *Jamaah Islamiyah*). "Surat Pernyataan: Faiz bin Abu Bakar Bafana,"p. 3.

[79] Portions of this interview, which were published in early 1997, are found at http://www.atimes.com/ se-asia/DB06Aeo1.html. Jemaah Islamiyah had already codified these teachings in an internal manual for its senior members entitled "Guidebook for the Jemaah Islamiyah Struggle" (*Buku Pedoman Umum Perjuangan al-Jamaah al-Islamiyah*, or PUJPI), which was compiled over a series of ten meetings in 1994. "Gambaran Pena – Abu Bakar Ba'asyir," p. 13.

When Sungkar had this epiphany, his timing was not the best. Indonesia – and indeed most of Southeast Asia – was running at full economic speed. Much of Indonesian society, as a result, was satiated during the boom. With no end in sight, the radicals based in Malaysia, armed with little more than tough talk, seemed destined to network among little more than the disillusioned fringe.

CHAPTER SIX

FIRST BLOOD

Aside from talking up jihad, Sungkar's Jemaah Islamiyah offered little more than harsh rhetoric during its first five years of existence. Venting from the sanctuary of Malaysia, it hardly constituted a credible threat to the Suharto regime, much less any other regional government.

During those same years, much the same could be said for al-Qaeda. While bin Laden was equally inflammatory in his proclamations, and there was no denying that thousands of jihadists had been preened in Afghanistan, his organization had yet to plan and carry out a single terrorist operation. Rather, acts like the 1993 New York bombing had been conjured and conducted by independent, albeit sympathetic, operators like Ramzi Yousef.

Beneath the surface, however, significant developments were starting to place in both organizations. For its part, Jemaah Islamiyah instituted five major changes. First, with no apparent end to their Malaysian exile, Sungkar and Ba'asyir established a modest Malaysia-based Ngruki clone, the Luqmanul Haqiem pesantren, in Johor state. In this way, they could continue turning out impressionable, hard-line adherents for as long as Ngruki was operating under less than optimal conditions.

Second, Jemaah Islamiyah mimicked the structure of al-Qaeda by codifying a headquarters element – known by the Arabic word *markaz* – and a shura council that would look at issues from a Koranic perspective. As of mid-1997, the markaz reportedly included Sungkar, Ba'asyir, and longtime paramilitary instructor Zulkarnaen. Also named to the ruling clique were Abu Rusdan, a Central Javanese cleric who had graduated at the top of the second Sadda cycle, and Ali Gufron (alias Mukhlas[80]). An East Java native, the intense Mukhlas had been near the top of his class at the Ngruki pesantren. A Sadda alum and long-time Malaysia exile, he had been chosen to head the Johor wakalah. These same five Jemaah Islamiyah members also comprised its shura council.

Third, Jemaah Islamiyah – at least on paper – registered exponential growth. Within Mantiqi 2, for example, the number of wakalah jumped from four to nine by 1997. Even more significant, that same year a Mantiqi 3 – in Arabic, *Mantiqi Tsalits* – was created to coordinate operations across eastern Indonesia, Malaysia's Sabah state, and Mindanao. Mantiqi 2, its jurisdiction reduced, now covered only Java, Sumatra, and West Kalimantan.

Fourth, Jemaah Islamiyah turned in a big way toward the Philippines for its paramilitary training needs. This move had been necessitated by the loss of Saudi subsidies, which from the mid-eighties until 1995 had been underwriting the training of Southeast Asian jihadists in Pakistan and Afghanistan. With insufficient funds in its own coffers to pay for trainees to venture to Afghanistan, Sungkar had shopped around for cheaper, local alternatives.

As it turned out, the MILF's Abu Bakar facilities were attractive on a number of counts. First, the cost of sending Indonesians to neighboring Mindanao via sea was a fraction of the airfare to Pakistan. Second, the southern Philippines was easily accessible to Indonesians and Malaysians without proper documentation: for generations, Indonesian traders and smugglers had been illegally plying routes between Sulawesi and Mindanao without passports or visas. Third, the MILF was amenable to offering brotherly assistance to a fellow radical organization. Indeed, Darul Islam member Arqom, who had escorted Hambali to Mindanao in 1991, had built his own house in Camp Abu Bakar and had been dispatching a small but steady trickle of followers through the site since the early nineties.

To map out formalized cooperation with the MILF, Jemaah Islamiyah sent an operative to Mindanao in late 1996 on a fact-finding mission. That operative, 25-year-old Fathur Rahman al-Ghozi, was a good pick. Born in Madiun, East Java, he was a second generation radical: his father, a Komando Jihad activist, was jailed in 1982 during the government crackdown in the wake of the Woyla aircraft hijacking. No doubt influenced by his father's leanings, and profoundly impacted by his father's arrest, he opted to receive his high school education at Ngruki.

---

[80] Mukhlas is Arabic for "To be pure."

Immediately upon graduation in 1989, al-Ghozi headed west to Pakistan. Part of a 25-person Southeast Asian contingent that received MAK training beginning in 1990, he lingered in Afghanistan through 1995 and would be one of the last Indonesians to depart Afghan soil before the military "academy" was closed down that same year.[81] Returning to Southeast Asia via Malaysia – where he spent time with the leaders of Jemaah Islamiyah – he was back in East Java by 1996.[82]

The reprieve did not last long. At the end of that year, al-Ghozi received orders from Malaysia to make a month-long assessment of the MILF's training facilities. Sungkar had singled him out for the job due to the fact he had grown particularly close to two MILF co-trainees during his time in Afghanistan. Departing Indonesia via North Sulawesi, he was greeted in Mindanao by both of these MILF colleagues. With them brokering introductions, he spent the next four weeks absorbing events at Camp Abu Bakar and brushing up on rudimentary Tagalog.

The MILF, it turned out, was at a turning point. Earlier that year, its secular rivals, the MNLF, had accepted the terms of a government peace deal and laid down its weapons. As part of that deal, the MNLF's top leader was named governor of Mindanao. This was a double-edged sword for the MILF. On the one hand, it received a windfall in the form of MNLF defectors irate at the peace accord. On the other hand, the government could now focus counter-insurgency efforts against the MILF.

With a showdown looming, al-Ghozi toured Camp Abu Bakar. Foreign jihadists, he found, were already being trained by the MILF. Aside from a handful of Indonesians (Arqom's Darul Islam cell, for example), there was also a group of thirty-five Arabs who had recently arrived for paramilitary instruction.

The arrangement between the Arabs and the MILF, learned al-Ghozi, was far from ideal. First, although the MILF had theoretically pledged to cover the training costs for the Arabs during their stay in the Philippines (in return for the considerable donations it received from Arab sheikhs), in reality the Filipinos balked. The Arabs, as a result, were forced to collect money among themselves to buy food and weapons.

---

[81] While most Indonesian alumni of jihadist training in Pakistan and Afghanistan proudly advertised this fact, al-Ghozi consistently lied about his past and claimed he was studying at a university in Lahore between 1990 and 1995. See "Travel Notes of a 'Terrorist,'" *Tempo*, 25 February 2002, p. 17.

[82] In Malaysia, al-Ghozi had been given a job at the construction company owned by fellow Jemaah Islamiyah member Faiz bin Abu Bakar Bafana. Ressa, *Seeds of Terror*, p. 78.

Second, the MILF was deeply sensitive to government charges that it was harboring foreign terrorists. As a result, MILF chairman Slamet Hashim refused Arab entreaties to participate in combat with the Philippine army; instead, he kept them sequestered in a remote corner of Camp Abu Bakar.

Third, the Arabs moaned about cultural differences. According to one Arab veteran, they found the proclivity of Filipino males to affectionately smack each other on the backside as particularly offensive.

Fourth, the curriculum at Camp Abu Bakar was long on talk and short on action. On an average day, the Arabs would wake before dawn and go for a walk prior to morning prayer. Then came individual religious reflection, roll call, calisthenics, and breakfast. After that, they would talk about military theory until noon. Finally, there were more prayers, another session on military theory, a late afternoon lecture about religion, and dinner. At no point did they drill with automatic weapons, much less train with explosives.

As it turned out, al-Ghozi was not the only Jemaah Islamiyah representative reviewing these arrangements at Camp Abu Bakar. In early 1997, he was reportedly joined by Mantiqi 1 leader Abu Bakar Ba'asyir. Later still, Hambali arrived to spend a month on site. Based on their findings, two key decisions resulted. First, it was decreed that any Jemaah Islamiyah members who wanted to participate in jihad could go to the MILF frontlines. Second, Jemaah Islamiyah found the MILF cause sufficiently worthy to merit funding.

Almost immediately, Jemaah Islamiyah ratcheted up the relationship. By mid-1997, it had received MILF acquiescence to send members for paramilitary training in Mindanao. But rather than repeat the lackluster results experienced by the Arabs, Jemaah Islamiyah members sought to create their own segregated training site within Camp Abu Bakar. There they would attempt to replicate their Afghan training academy in terms of size, curriculum, and staff.

Before training could start, funding had to be tackled. With annual operating costs estimated at US$25,000, the Jemaah Islamiyah markaz gave each mantiqi a funding target. The mantiqi, in turn, assigned quotas to each wakalah. Mantiqi 1, which covered the more affluent countries of Singapore and Malaysia, was able to collect US$10,000 in individual donations within just two weeks.

Using couriers, these funds were channeled to Jemaah Islamiyah's military chieftain, Zulkarnaen. With them, he bankrolled construction of a simple camp – living quarters, a mosque, an obstacle course, and a playing field – a mere forty-minute walk up a mountainside adjacent to the MILF headquarters. Dubbed Camp Hudaibiyah, its name was derived from the location on the outskirts of Mecca where the Prophet Mohammad had once signed a peace treaty with a band of marauding pagans.

By the close of 1997, Hudaibiyah was ready to open its doors. A Jemaah Islamiyah operative named Mustopa, who had been part of the second Sadda training cycle, was named the first commander of Mantiqi 3 and subsequently given jurisdiction over the operation of the camp. He quickly made plans for an Indonesian training staff, heavy on Afghan alumni, to rotate through Mindanao for a semester at a time.

As had been the case in Afghanistan, Jemaah Islamiyah wanted to create in Mindanao a comprehensive military academy for carefully-screened candidates. In the case of Afghanistan, the academy theoretically lasted three years. At Hudaibiyah, the camp's cadre penned a "long course" that covered three semesters totaling eighteen months. Mantiqi leaders were allowed to nominate prospective trainees that fit rigid requirements: they had to be young, fit, unmarried, high school graduates, and good in math and physics. Showing a bias, the markaz ultimately decided to limit entrants to Indonesians from Mantiqi 2.

At the same time, Hudaibiyah would offer "short courses" of between one and two months. The requirements for attending these abbreviated blocs of instruction were far less stringent: anybody who had pledged allegiance to Sungkar at least a year earlier, and had a letter of recommendation from his wakalah commander, could attend. He also had to have sufficient family funds to pay for his own transportation. Short courses were opened to all mantiqi; early cycles included several Malaysians and Singaporeans.

Although Camp Hudaibiyah was built and funded by Jemaah Islamiyah, the group ultimately proved accommodating to like-minded extremists. More than a few MILF students, for example, trained at the site. In addition, two smaller sub-camps were opened within its perimeter. One of these, dubbed the Sulawesi camp, was headed by longtime Sadda instructor Syawal and largely catered to Sulawesi trainees who were not necessarily Jemaah Islamiyah members. The second, nicknamed the Banten camp, primarily hosted West Javanese candidates who were also not on the Jemaah Islamiyah roster.[83]

<hr />

[83] In 1998, Camp Hudaibiyah even hosted four of the Arabs who were going stir-crazy at Camp Abu Bakar.

Perhaps the greatest development within Jemaah Islamiyah during this period was the emergence of Hambali as a significant player. In many respects, his rise to prominence was rather odd. After all, he was not of the preferred pedigree: he had not graduated from Ngruki, he had never excelled in school, and he was hardly a charismatic orator. Physically, he cut a rather slovenly figure and had barely passed the more grueling elements of his Camp Sadda training. And he was unimpressive in matters of business – after a decade in Malaysia, he was still selling from a stall and living in the local equivalent of a ghetto.

But Hambali held one advantage that made him stand out. Since 1985, he had been unwavering in his slavish devotion to Sungkar. Rarely had he missed one of the monthly, and later, weekly, sermons. Sungkar had noted Hambali's loyalty, and had been quietly drawing him closer over the years. In 1994, there had been the request to discreetly facilitate the legal papers for Konsojaya. In 1996, Hambali was invited to work on some minor construction projects with one of Sungkar's sons-in-law. In 1997, Hambali had helped Ba'asyir move into a small rented house opposite his own in Sungai Manggis.[84] And starting that same year, Hambali was occasionally asked to lecture to select students about jihad following Sungkar's regular sermons.[85]

Then came Hambali's big break. During a meeting of the markaz in the second half of 1997, he was selected by Sungkar to head Mantiqi 1.[86] He replaced Abu Bakar Ba'asyir, who was elevated to deputy amir. This propelled him into Jemaah Islamiyah's upper echelon, and with the promotion came opportunities for travel. Already in 1997, he had spent a month at Camp Abu Bakar. Then again in February 1998, he once more ventured to Mindanao, this time to escort three Malaysians to Camp Hudaibiyah for the short course.

Two additional trips were taken in early 1998. The first took him back to his West Java hometown of Cianjur. While there, he ventured to the town

---

For one week, the Arabs – one Kuwaiti and three Saudis – trained with firearms and practiced karate alongside the Indonesians. Among them was Umar Faruq, the al-Qaeda member rendered from Indonesia in June 2002.

[84] Hambali lived on Lot 564, Batu 18 ¼, Sungai Manggis; Abu Bakar Ba'asyir lived on Lot 872, Batu 18 ½, Sungai Manggis.

[85] Malaysian authorities believe Hambali conducted sixteen jihad training sessions between 1997 and October 2000. These sessions were attended by Malaysian radicals from the Malaysian Mujahideen Group (*Kumpulan Mujahidin Malaysia*, or KMM), a paramilitary group sympathetic to Jemaah Islamiyah that sought the overthrow of the Malaysian government. "Ambaran Pena – Riduan Isamuddin," p. 8.

[86] During Sungkar's tenure, the markaz met every six months.

limits to pay a short visit to ailing Darul Islam patriarch Ajengan Masduki, who had since reconciled with Sungkar after their falling out earlier in the decade. Though little of substance was discussed – Hambali mainly asked about Masduki's failing health – the fact that he made a courtesy call to such a senior figure in the Darul Islam movement reflected his added clout.

The second trip took Hambali to the Chittagong hill tracts of Bangladesh. Under orders of Sungkar, he had gone there to meet leaders of the Rohingyan Solidarity Organization (RSO) in order to discuss their possible inclusion under a Jemaah Islamiyah umbrella for an Islamic Southeast Asian super-state.

Before departing, Hambali had brushed up on the background of the RSO. The Rohingyas were Muslims from Burma who shared more in common – including language – with the peoples populating the Chittagong vicinity. During a 1978 crackdown by the Burmese government, hundreds of thousands of Rohingyas had fled to Bangladesh. Although most were eventually repatriated, a second round of persecution in 1991 displaced a quarter of a million people back into Bangladesh.

While these desperate masses were stewing in squalid refugee camps, liberation groups began to emerge. A patriotic liberation front was eventually formed; from this, a militant faction – the RSO – splintered from the more moderate mainstream. Although the RSO talked about returning to Burma to carve out an independent Muslim homeland – and took impressive publicity photographs at a paramilitary training camp ostensibly inside Burma – it was largely a fraud. In reality, its camp was in Chittagong; the RSO maintained no presence in Burma, and there is no evidence its members ever fired a shot in anger.[87]

Despite its reluctance to press home its fight, Hambali found the RSO to be a needy bunch. During a meeting with a representative named Salimullah, the latter could not stop talking of the need for help in procuring small arms. When Hambali could offer no easy answers, the discussion quickly fizzled to an anti-climax. Though not for want of trying, Hambali had come up short in bringing the RSO into the Jemaah Islamiyah fold.

---

[87] In 1989, the Indonesian cadre at Sadda trained a 40-man contingent ostensibly from Bangladesh. Nasir Abas, p. 61. Abas believes that the Bangladeshis were, in fact, Rohingyas. Interview with Nasir Abas, 24 July 2005.

For its part, al-Qaeda had been going through an equally eventful transition. Still unwelcome in Saudi Arabia (where the government froze his financial assets and revoked his citizenship in 1994), bin Laden had busied himself fleshing out his organization from the sanctuary of Sudan. But even among fellow radicals, he eventually wore out his welcome. In May 1996, after granting an interview to *Time* magazine, he was summarily expelled because the Sudanese authorities could no longer deny his presence.

One after another, Muslim nations across the Middle East rejected his appeals for asylum. Desperate, bin Laden called in a favor with the Afghans. Since 1992, a loose mujahideen alliance led by Burhanuddin Rabani had ruled Kabul. Sympathetically recalling his service during the Soviet war, Rabani granted him entry.

Once in Afghanistan, bin Laden was exposed to the chaos of Afghan politics. Outside of Kabul, a disparate patchwork of competing warlords ruled the land. Not attempting to play favorites, bin Laden initially settled in Jalalabad, probably because that vicinity's weak set of Islamic leaders afforded him a relatively free hand.

Four months after bin Laden's arrival, however, the situation changed dramatically. This came at the hands of the Taliban, a ragtag movement of poorly-educated religious students that had sprung up in the poverty-stricken refugee camps inside Pakistan during the Soviet occupation. Their conservative take on religion put even the Wahhabis to shame. All men, for example, had to grow fist-length beards; failure to do so drew mandatory beatings. Women were required to wear shapeless *burqa* gowns, their faces hidden behind mesh veils. No artistic depictions of living things were allowed. Even kite-flying was proscribed because, they decreed, only God was allowed to ply the skies.

What Taliban members lacked in intellect, however, they more than made up in fanaticism. Coalescing into a relatively effective military force from their powerbase in the city of Kandahar during 1994, they went on the offensive two years later and, on 11 September 1996, expelled the local mujahideen leaders controlling Jalalabad. A little over two weeks later, they pushed their way into Kabul and sent the ruling alliance into retreat. In short order, ninety percent of the country was under Taliban rule.

For bin Laden, the Taliban victories were a windfall. Not only did they offer him continued asylum in Jalalabad, but they allowed al-Qaeda to use some of the training camps seized from their defeated mujahideen competitors. In addition, Abu Zubaydah, the Palestinian militant who ran several camps in Taliban territory, formally declared himself an al-Qaeda member and placed his facilities under bin Laden's control.

Gaining momentum, bin Laden began to win over other key radicals. Several of the more extreme Egyptian jihadist groups, which had long been sympathetic to his theology, now formally merged themselves into al-Qaeda. This made Ayman al-Zawahiri, a 45-year-old former surgeon and leader of an Egyptian Islamic Jihad faction, the second most powerful man in al-Qaeda.

Arguably al-Qaeda's most important convert was terrorist freelancer Khalid Sheikh Mohammad (KSM). Ethnically from the border area between Iran and Pakistan, KSM had grown up in Kuwait. Hardly a radical as a youth, he had ventured to the U.S. to attend a Baptist college in North Carolina, graduating in 1986 with a degree in mechanical engineering.

Soon after, KSM had his first exposure to jihad. Within a couple of months after graduation, he flew to Pakistan to visit his brother, at the time serving at the MAK headquarters in Peshawar. Befriending the likes of MAK czar Azzam and mujahideen commander Sayyaf, he won approval to attend three months of training at Camp Sadda. Returning to Peshawar, he spent the next five years as an administrator for Azzam and Sayyaf.[88]

Over the following few years, KSM effectively led a double life. On the one hand, he took a legitimate job as an engineer with the Ministry of Electricity and Water in Qatar. This he maintained through 1996, traveling the globe on the behalf of Qatari technical projects.

On the other hand, he kept his hand firmly in the jihadist pot. Initially, he chose to contribute with his wallet. In 1992, he visited Bosnia to view the sectarian violence firsthand, but limited his involvement to monetary donations. The following year, after learning that his nephew, Ramzi Yousef, planned to bomb the World Trade Center in New York, he again gave cash.

But inspired by Yousef, KSM in the summer of 1994 ratcheted up his involvement to active planning of terrorist operations. Very quickly, he proved himself a master conceptualist of apocalyptic schemes, conjuring the idea as far back as 1994 of using asymmetrical weapons – fully-loaded airliners – in kamikaze attacks against strategic targets.

---

[88] Details of Khalid Sheikh Mohammad's background can be found in *The 9-11 Commission Report* (Washington, D.C.: Government Printing Office, 2004), pp. 145-149.

By early 1996, KSM's double life began to fray. With most of the Bojinka masterminds behind bars, and himself being pursued by U.S. authorities, he quit his job in Qatar, fled to Afghanistan, and renewed his relationship with his former mujahideen mentor, Sayyaf. Later that year, he won an audience with the recently-arrived bin Laden; during that encounter, KSM briefed the al-Qaeda boss on the kamikaze concept.

Listening to the plan, bin Laden liked what he heard. Although KSM never offered a formal pledge of allegiance to bin Laden, from that point forward he became one of his most influential planners. And given his fluency in English and extensive international travel, KSM served one other key role: reaching out to jihadi groups outside the Middle East.

Somewhere near the top of that list was Jemaah Islamiyah. While the synergy with al-Qaeda might have seemed obvious, there were key differences between the two organizations. In Jemaah Islamiyah, the vast majority of its members – and especially its leaders – were educated in conservative Islamic high schools and joined soon after graduating. The overwhelming majority of al-Qaeda members, by contrast, joined after their mid-twenties and did not have educational backgrounds in religion. Instead, they were from the natural sciences; the vast majority, too, were either professionals or semi-professionals.[89]

Such differences aside, Jemaah Islamiyah was predisposed toward being sympathetic to al-Qaeda. This became openly apparent in February 1997, when bin Laden issued another fatwa from Jalalabad, this one declaring war on the U.S. and Israel. Shortly thereafter, Sungkar traveled to Afghanistan and reportedly had a meeting with bin Laden. During their pleasantries, the pair discussed working together and perhaps joining forces.

While Sungkar stopped far short of confirming any formal merger, al-Qaeda had already found a greater ally in Southeast Asia: Hambali. Just as Sungkar had been won over by Hambali's perseverance, al-Qaeda had grown to see him as a dependable proxy. Perhaps his greatest advocate was KSM, who had first met Hambali in 1994 when the latter was approached to sign legal papers for Konsojaya.[90] Recalling that he was "very impressed" during that encounter,

---

[89] Statement by Marc Sageman to The National Commission on Terrorist Attacks upon the United States, 9 July 2003.

[90] Both Hambali and KSM overlapped at Camp Sadda during 1986, but did not meet each other during that

KSM made it a point to again rendezvous with the rotund Indonesian during a mid-1996 tour of Southeast Asia.[91]

⋙◆⋘

A little over one year later, in February 1998, bin Laden engineered a defining moment for his organization. Never one to shy away from publicity, he and al-Zawahiri that month arranged for an Arabic-language newspaper in London to publish yet another fatwa, this one in the name of the so-called Islamic Front for Jihad against Jews and Crusaders. Unlike his previous rants, however, this one intentionally blurred distinctions when it claimed that it was the duty of every Muslim to murder any American anywhere around the globe. Earlier, bin Laden had focused his wrath solely on U.S. servicemen in the Middle East, specifically those stationed in Saudi Arabia.

As if to drive home the point, the deputy head of al-Qaeda's military committee, Mohammad Atef, on 7 May faxed to London a new fatwa that restated the February threat. Another two weeks after that, bin Laden gave a videotaped interview in which he said he did not differentiate between American servicemen and civilians – they were all targets in his mind.

Predictably, the al-Qaeda pronouncements had ripple effects across the Muslim world. In Southeast Asia, the reaction from Sungkar was mixed. In a meeting of senior Jemaah Islamiyah officials in February, he told them of the need to join in the fatwa. But consumed by events inside Indonesia (where the Suharto regime was in its death throes) Sungkar offered no specifics as he stayed focused on domestic matters. He also disallowed Jemaah Islamiyah assets to be used against American targets.[92]

Hambali, by contrast, advocated far more aggressive engagement. Taking it upon himself to educate members of his Mantiqi 1 about the fatwa, he searched the Internet for the original Arabic text. After having it translated, he distributed it, as well as information about bin Laden, to all of his subordinates. Beginning in the first quarter of 1998, he also began preaching the need to start thinking of jihad against the U.S. and Israel.

---

period. Hambali, in fact, claims not to have made any significant or lasting acquaintances with Arabs or South Asians during his training in Pakistan.

His sermons proved prophetic. On 7 August, a car bomb outside the U.S. embassy in Kenya killed eleven Americans and 201 others; another 5,000 were injured. A simultaneous car bomb outside the U.S. embassy in Tanzania killed eleven as well, none of whom were American. Investigators soon pointed their fingers squarely at al-Qaeda.

The twin bombs were a watershed. Prior to the summer of 1998, al-Qaeda had largely provided funds and inspiration for terrorist attacks. The attacks on the embassies were different: both were planned, directed, and executed by al-Qaeda under direct orders of its leadership. Al-Qaeda had not only declared war on the U.S., but it had drawn first blood.

[91] KSM later claimed that Hambali served on the al-Qaeda media committee circa 1996. This claim is almost certainly in error. For one thing, Hambali was in Malaysia during 1996, making it hard to see how Hambali could have benefited the Afghanistan-based media committee. For another thing, given Hambali's poor English and limited computer skills, he could hardly have contributed to the workings of the media committee. In any event, Hambali has made no mention of alleged service in the al-Qaeda media committee during his extensive post-capture debriefings.

[92] In August 2001, a reliable informant provided the Indonesian State Intelligence Agency with a copy of a letter purportedly written by Sungkar and Ba'asyir in September 1998. In the letter, copies of which were allegedly carried to sympathizers inside Indonesia, the two clerics lauded bin Laden's 1998 fatwa. They further offered to assist any Indonesian religious leaders interested in traveling to Kandahar to meet bin Laden.

CHAPTER SEVEN

NEW MANAGEMENT

For Jemaah Islamiyah, 1998 looked set to be a year of opportunity. That May, Jakarta exploded in an orgy of violence as Suharto's 33-year iron grip corroded and crumbled with dizzying speed. Before stepping down, the cagey leader stage-managed the rise of his vice president and shameless cheerleader, B.J. Habibie. Physically short in stature and commanding none of his predecessor's unspoken Javanese presence, Habibie presided over what many saw as a lame duck administration marking time before a general election scheduled for the following year.

But despite the fact that, though sins of omission and commission, Habibie seemed to be steering the nation toward something approaching a true democracy, the Jemaah Islamiyah leadership refused to return from Malaysia. Fearful that memories were lasting, and that they might be arrested for fleeing the country back in 1985, both Sungkar and Ba'asyir chose not to end their self-imposed exile just yet.

Instead, the pair focused on expanding their own ranks. Key to this effort was Camp Hudaibiyah, the Jemaah Islamiyah facility running on the fringes of the MILF's Camp Abu Bakar. The 15,000-strong MILF was on a roll at the time, and had even started applying Islamic law within its territory during 1997.[93] That same year, the MILF's leaders had opened peace talks with the government; to win them over, the authorities had provided items like power generators and solar-powered water pumps for the MILF zone of control.

---

[93] In line with its implementation of Islamic law, the MILF executed two men – including one Christian – by firing squad during 1997. They had been charged with murder, robbery, and car theft.

Jemaah Islamiyah increased its financial support of its fellow Filipino jihad-ists. In June 1998, Hambali ordered the creation of a cover foundation spe-cifically to seek donations and channel these funds to the MILF. Known as *Pertubuhan al-Ehasan* (PAE), it was legally registered in Malaysia as a non-gov-ernmental organization and quartered in a Selangor shop-house.

In January 1999, however, the Philippine nexus suddenly came under fire – literally. The seven-month old administration of President Joseph Estrada, frustrated with the sputtering pace of negotiations, elected to press home its counter-insurgency campaign against the MILF. Not only did Camp Abu Bakar – and, by association, Camp Hudaibiyah – come under intense pressure, but transit between Mindanao and Indonesia became much more difficult.

By that time, the Jemaah Islamiyah leadership was contemplating an al-ternative. Already, word had already spread among the extremist community about the al-Qaeda training facilities in Afghanistan. During 1998, in fact, Mas Selamat Kastari, a 38-year-old bus mechanic who doubled as head of the waka-lah covering Singapore, had seen some of these camps when he ventured to Af-ghanistan to observe Taliban rule.[94] During that trip, he had even broached the subject of cooperation with al-Qaeda, including the establishment of a training program for Southeast Asians.

Jemaah Islamiyah's markaz was fully supportive of the concept. Initially, Zulkarnaen, the long-serving Sadda instructor, was tasked by fellow markaz members in late 1998 to negotiate training assistance from al-Qaeda. He was chosen because he had forged cordial ties to many top extremists since his Sadda days, including Zawahiri and KSM. But it was Mantiqi 1 chief Hambali, the outspoken proponent of al-Qaeda since bin Laden's February 1998 fatwa, who was dispatched by Sungkar in January 1999 to Karachi. There he rendezvoused with KSM and quickly won initial approval for formalized training assistance. Unlike the MAK-sponsored three-year military academy during the Soviet oc-cupation, which focused on paramilitary operations, this time somewhat fewer Jemaah Islamiyah candidates would participate, but they would partake in more specialized terrorist classes. This included such subjects as urban warfare, demo-

---

[94] Kastari had been among a group of Singaporeans that had received training in Afghanistan during 1993. Jemaah Islamiyah paid for Kastari and another Singaporean member, Jafar bin Mistooki, to make the 1998 trip to Afghanistan; they reportedly were "deeply impressed" by the Taliban administration. International Crisis Group, "Jamaah Islamiyah in Southeast Asia: Damaged but Still Dangerous," 26 August 2003, p. 11.

litions, surveillance, and forging documents.

Later that same quarter, Hambali headed back to Karachi for a second time. Joining him was fellow Mantiqi 1 member Faiz bin Abu Bakar Bafana. Born in Singapore in 1962, Bafana was a Malaysian citizen and Sungkar acolyte since 1987. He was also better educated and wealthier than the normal Jemaah Islamiyah adherent, managing his own construction company. Given his financial success, he was chosen to serve as the Mantiqi 1 treasurer. Both Hambali and Bafana were now escorting two other Malaysians – Zaini Zakaria and Zamzuri – who were the first two Jemaah Islamiyah members selected for the formalized training program under al-Qaeda.

From Karachi, the four made their way across Pakistan to the Afghan frontier. At the border, they took a halting four-wheel-drive ride on unimproved roads to the Taliban capital of Kandahar. Over a series of meetings with KSM and al-Qaeda's senior military commander, Mohammad Atef, both sides finalized details for a regular schedule of al-Qaeda training assistance.

Two weeks later, Hambali and Bafana returned to Malaysia. Although they had successfully escorted the two Jemaah Islamiyah trainees to Kandahar, Hambali noted a critical difference from the MAK days. In the eighties, would-be jihadists were ably assisted by MAK personnel during their transit from Karachi to Peshawar to Sadda. Host nation Pakistan not only tolerated this presence, but often assisted it.

Al-Qaeda, by contrast, had been labeled a terrorist organization after the Africa embassy bombings, and could count on none of the niceties inside Pakistan once accorded to the MAK. Moreover, the reclusive Taliban regime barely had any links with the outside world.[95] Jemaah Islamiyah members in Pakistan, as a result, had nobody to help them navigate to the frontier.

Hambali had a ready solution to overcome this transit dilemma. As in most countries with a sizable Indonesian student population, there was a large association comprising Indonesians studying in Pakistan, in this case appropriately known as Pakindo. As many of the Pakindo members were attending conservative Islamic schools, and might be predisposed toward sympathizing with a group like Jemaah Islamiyah, Hambali thought it possible to recruit select members of Pakindo to assist those transiting Pakistan to Afghanistan. Better yet,

---

[95] Beginning in July 1999, the Taliban regime was hit with U.S.-led sanctions for harboring al-Qaeda. The following month, the U.S. subjected Afghanistan's airline, Ariana, to Taliban sanctions.

Hambali felt that Jemaah Islamiyah should fashion its own Pakindo-style study group for the same purpose.

To flesh out this concept, Hambali reportedly turned to Abdul Rahim, the younger son of Abu Bakar Ba'asyir. Rahim had had a rather unusual upbringing. Before he had even become a teen, his father had sent him packing to the Afghanistan border during the Soviet jihad to spend time under Zulkarnaen's wing. From there he had enrolled in an Islamic high school in Faisalabad, Pakistan's third largest city and a textile center in Punjab province.

Rahim's performance at school was mixed. Of average intellect, some of his best marks were in computers and electronics. Seeking to give his son a more fundamentalist understanding of Islam, Ba'asyir allegedly directed him in the mid-nineties to Sana'a, Yemen, to study under Abdul Majid al-Zindani. Much like Abdullah Azzam, al-Zindani was a legend among the Arabs who fought in the Soviet jihad. He had been a key recruiter for the MAK, and was personally credited for steering thousands of Arab prospects to Camp Sadda. After the war, al-Zindani had established an Islamic university in Sana'a, reputed to be one of the more conservative in the region.[96]

By the opening of 1999, Rahim was back in Malaysia. With no employment prospects and unable to gain admittance in a local university, he spent several months doing little apart from studying for a driver's license. His future uncertain, Rahim ended up shadowing Hambali to relieve the boredom. Out of courtesy to Ba'asyir, Hambali tolerated his newfound protégé.

Rahim, it turned out, had something to contribute. When Hambali began brainstorming plans for a student study group in Karachi as cover for supporting Jemaah Islamiyah members heading to Afghanistan, Rahim lent his own international educational experiences and readily offered up ideas for a model.

Listening, Hambali realized the study group would need to have a strong leader to succeed. Isolated in Karachi, such a leader would need to be self-sufficient. He would also need to be of sufficient stature to defend Jemaah Islamiyah interests with al-Qaeda members. Contemplating possible candidates, he realized the position was perfect for Rahim. As the son of Ba'asyir, he would have instant recognition in both Jemaah Islamiyah and al-Qaeda. He was unmarried

---

[96] In March 2004, al-Zindani was accused by the U.S. of being a key recruiter for al-Qaeda. Late that year, al-Zindani earned international snickers when he announced his university had discovered a proven cure for HIV/AIDS: dedicated study of the Koran.

and could relocate quickly. He was fluent in Arabic, and already was familiar with Pakistan. Best of all, he already knew most of al-Qaeda's upper echelon from the MAK days.

When Hambali proposed the leadership slot to Rahim, his understudy immediately agreed. His father, too, offered his blessing. The decision made, Hambali passed along details of his Pakindo contacts who had earlier offered to provide some logistical support. Zulkarnaen, too, offered his own list of Pakindo acquaintances. Armed with this, Rahim packed his bags and headed west.

From the start, the Jemaah Islamiyah leadership was aware that al-Qaeda assistance came with strings attached. Back in 1998, Kastari had returned from Afghanistan with a message that al-Qaeda wanted help to conduct an operation in Singapore. During their early 1999 discussions with KSM and Mohammad Atef, Hambali and Bafana heard of al-Qaeda's desire to attack U.S. interests in Singapore. (Atef, it turned out, was preaching to the choir: Bafana was carrying with him an edited video that Jemaah Islamiyah's Singapore branch had made on its own. On it, they recorded the area around the Sembawang naval wharf and the Yishun Mass Rapid Transit station where U.S. military personnel congregated on the way to Sembawang. Jemaah Islamiyah proposed attacking U.S. nationals at that locale with al-Qaeda support. But aside from telling Bafana to short-list candidates and think about sourcing explosives, Atef remained noncommittal.[97])

In September, a new al-Qaeda request reached Southeast Asia. This one again came from Mohammad Atef; this time, he was asking Hambali if he could suggest a candidate to start a biological weapons program. Having forgotten most of his high school biology, Hambali himself was of little help. But he quickly thought of a Jemaah Islamiyah colleague who fit the bill: Yazid bin Sufaat. A 35-year-old Malaysian, Sufaat more closely resembled the profile of a typical al-Qaeda recruit (urban, middle-class professional with a science back-

---

[97] Jemaah Islamiyah's Singapore cell had first conjured the Sembawang attack back in 1997, but did not get around to making the video until 1999. Later in 1999, Singaporean Jemaah Islamiyah member Khalim Jaffar, while training in Afghanistan, gave an English-language briefing about the plot to Atef. Singapore Government White Paper, "The Jemaah Islamiyah Arrests and the Threat of Terrorism," 7 January 2003, pp. 11-12.

ground) than Jemaah Islamiyah (Islamic boarding school graduate). Sufaat's academic foundation was impressive: he had received degrees in both biology and biochemistry from California universities. After a stint in the Malaysian army, where he rose to the rank of captain and served as a technician in a medical brigade, he became a businessman and opened a lucrative testing laboratory in the Batu Caves suburb northeast of Kuala Lumpur.

Best of all, Hambali considered Sufaat a trusted friend. Not only had the two been attending Sungkar sermons for years, but Hambali and his wife had even frequented Sufaat's laboratory for fertility testing when they could not conceive a child.[98]

Taking Sufaat aside, Hambali quizzed him on his knowledge of biological weapons. He knew next to nothing, Sufaat admitted, but he was willing to do research. Thinking aloud, Hambali at that point recalled a family friend in Bogor, a city 60 kilometers south of Jakarta, who worked as a microbiologist at a government-run scientific research institute.

Wasting no time, both Hambali and Sufaat ventured to Bogor to sound out the biologist and assess his scientific abilities. For that initial meeting, they chatted about business opportunities and little else. Their initial impression of the candidate was not very favorable – he was a chain-smoking 40-year-old, Hambali later commented, who seemed fixated on the material things in life and probably had little stomach for conservative religious doctrine. But Sufaat saw reason for optimism, noting that the scientist, while no expert, would probably meet al-Qaeda's requirements. Too, the scientist desperately wanted to get an advanced degree overseas and was eager to earn extra cash to supplement his meager government income.

Before any further services could be rendered to al-Qaeda, Jemaah Islamiyah suffered a crisis on the home front. Its founder and ideological bedrock, Abdullah Sungkar, had developed severe heart trouble in June 1999 and checked himself into a Kuala Lumpur hospital for an operation.

By that time, the Indonesian government had offered amnesty to many of the religious dissidents persecuted under the New Order. Perhaps sensing that his own end was near, and yearning to return to Indonesia, Sungkar belatedly decided to test Jakarta's newfound tolerance by ending his self-imposed exile. Surprising, his homecoming proved extremely low-key. Though his anti-Suhar-

---

[98] Sufaat's company was named Green Laboratory Medicine, probably as an allusion to his religious affiliation.

to defiance over the years had resulted in sympathy in some corners, news of his return was thoroughly overshadowed by the media attention focused on the Indonesian presidential selection process set for early in the fourth quarter.

Sungkar's homecoming, too, proved extremely short. Within just a few weeks after his return, Sungkar died in Bogor on 23 October due to heart complications. His body was taken to Klaten, Central Java, the following day for burial.

Jemaah Islamiyah's leadership vacuum did not last long. Early the following month, Hambali and the other mantiqi leaders were beckoned to Solo to attend a ceremony in which Abu Bakar Ba'asyir was appointed as the new amir. While he had been Sungkar's understudy for decades, the cranky Ba'asyir came to the job surprisingly ill-prepared. After all, the soft-spoken cleric had largely toiled in the shadow of Sungkar, carrying none of his predecessor's commanding presence and few of his oratory skills.[99]

True to form, Ba'asyir first acts as amir were underwhelming. He reportedly opened the inauguration ceremony by asking if anybody had problems with his appointment. His audience offered no response. He then asked for persons to point out his flaws, promising to correct them. Again, his audience was silent. His subsequent speech, one in attendance later remembered, offered no clear vision for Jemaah Islamiyah or his views on jihad.

Despite this shaky start, it was early under Ba'asyir's watch that a series of significant changes affected the organization. First, the process for recruiting fresh blood into Jemaah Islamiyah was widened. Until that point, the organization had relied on word of mouth, and had focused heavily on those who had been attending Sungkar's sermons since his first years in exile.

But looking to draw in a new generation of adherents, senior members in each of the mantiqi now began acting as talent scouts. Under these new guidelines, they would observe a potential recruit for a year, then invite him to attend an intensive eighteen-month *tamrin* (Arabic for "training") course that covered all aspects of Jemaah Islamiyah's religious code. Each mantiqi was responsible

---

[99] Abu Bakar Ba'asyir vehemently denies his appointment as amir of Jemaah Islamiyah. However, countries such as Australia, Singapore, and the United States, as well as numerous journalists, all persuasively make this assertion. The Indonesian National Police also assert that Ba'asyir was named amir of Jemaah Islamiyah after Sungkar's death. See Indonesian National Police report, "The Investigation of the Series of Bombings Connect to Jama'ah Islamiyyah began with the Bali Bombings," 2003, p. 13.

for conducting a new tamrin cycle of up to twenty students every six months.[100] Of the 50 percent who passed, they would be eligible for pledging an oath of obedience to Ba'asyir. Then, and only then, would the recruit be exposed to Jemaah Islamiyah.[101]

Second, word quietly went out for an initial meeting of *Rabitatul Mujahidin*. Arab for "Mujahideen League," this forum was conceived by Jemaah Islamiyah as a discreet platform for Southeast Asian jihadists, all theoretically striving for Sungkar's vision of an Islamic super-state, to brainstorm ways to synergize. Arranged and hosted by Mantiqi 1, the league held its first meeting near year's end some 20 kilometers west of Kuala Lumpur in the home of Faiz Abu Bakar Bafana, the same Jemaah Islamiyah member who accompanied Hambali to Afghanistan. Attendees spanned the region: from the Philippines came the MILF's Abdul Hurairah; out of southern Thailand was Abdul Fatah; and from the Rohingyas in Burma came Salimullah, the same rebel leader who Hambali met the previous year.[102]

The biggest contingent at the meeting was from Indonesia. Representing Jemaah Islamiyah were Ba'asyir and Hambali. Out of Aceh came Abu Jihad, a shifty rebel who portended to lead a splinter of the Acehnese independence movement, but was widely suspected of being an Indonesian government informant.[103]

From South Sulawesi came businessman-*cum*-religious activist Agus Dwikarna. Easily the most complex character in attendance, Dwikarna was all things to all people. Charismatic, gregarious, and entrepreneurial, he was able to adapt to any social environment, comfortable mingling one day with senior politicians, the next with the poor and destitute. Dwikarna was also closely tied to religious extremists from his native South Sulawesi, including veteran Sadda instructor Syawal. Both he and Syawal had earlier arranged with Jemaah Islami-

---

[100] If a potential recruit was known to be pious and was already well acquainted with the Jemaah Islamiyah leadership, the tamrin course was not mandatory.

[101] In theory, bayat could only be offered to the amir of Jemaah Islamiyah. In practice, Sungkar had allowed proxies to occasionally fill in for him, especially for those offering oaths in Afghanistan and Pakistan. Ba'asyir reportedly was far more lenient in allowed various senior Jemaah Islamiyah members to accept bayat in his stead.

[102] Abdul Fatah had acted as the masul, or group leader, for Thai jihadists at Camp Sadda.

[103] Abu Jihad, who headed the *Front Mujahidin Islam Aceh* (Aceh Islamic Mujahideen Front), was coincidentally in Malaysia at the time in an unsuccessful attempt to purchase weapons from southern Thailand for his small Acehnese splinter group.

yah for select candidates from their province to venture to Camp Hudaibiyah for paramilitary training.

Over the course of a weekend, this diverse ensemble talked up jihad. Jemaah Islamiyah had hoped that its respective groups could cooperate and share resources for training, the procurement of weapons, and financial assistance. In reality, its accomplishments were limited to viewing some graphic pictures of Muslim casualties in the Malukus (where sectarian violence had broken out early that year) and examining some maps of the southern Philippines. No joint operations were discussed.[104]

A third change that came about early under Ba'asyir's tenure was a realignment of Jemaah Islamiyah against Western – especially American – interests. Previous manifestations of Islamic extremist organizations in the region – especially Indonesia-based entities like Darul Islam and its immediate progeny, Komando Jihad – had vented exclusively against domestic targets, especially government institutions. Now, largely owing to the influence of its Afghan alumni, the group had elected to participate in al-Qaeda's fight.

Part of this realignment was in a supportive role. Mantiqi 1, for example, hosted several al-Qaeda members passing through Malaysia. One of the more notable visits was by a 28-year-old operative named Issa al-Hindi. Born Dhiren Barot, he was an Indian Hindu (hence his kunya) until converting to Islam in 1992. Al-Hindi took his conversion to an extreme, serving as a paramilitary instructor in Afghanistan and fighting alongside fellow extremists in Kashmir. Fluent in English, he also authored a shrill tract entitled "The Army of Madinah in Kashmir." In it, he advocated a worldwide jihad by any means, including germ warfare.

In late 1999, al-Hindi showed up in Kuala Lumpur. The purpose of his trip to Malaysia remains something of a mystery. Staying at Hambali's Sungai Manggis house, he was ostensibly sent by KSM to learn about jihad in Southeast Asia under Hambali's tutelage. But as he was already a well-traveled and trusted al-Qaeda operator, this begs an ulterior motive. Before departing, he handed

---

[104] The exact number of attendees is in dispute. Hambali recalls about 15 persons were present. A report by the International Crisis Group put the number at over 20 ("Indonesia's Terrorist Network: How Jemaah Islamiyah Works," 11 December 2002, p. 12), though some of those alleged attendees – such as Aziz Muzakkar – vigorously denied the claim. Interview with Aziz Muzakkar, 2 May 2005. Complicating matters was the fact that a larger meeting was held on the campus of Universiti Islam Antarabangsa in Kuala Lumpur; from this, a smaller select group was invited to the tryst at Bafana's house.

Hambali a slip of paper bearing the names and addresses of contacts in South Africa and southern California. If Hambali were ever to land himself in those parts of the world, assured al-Hindi, those persons would provide assistance.[105]

As soon as al-Hindi departed, Hambali received a message from KSM to render assistance to an Arab jihadist named Tawfiq bin Attash, alias Khallad. Like bin Laden, he was a Yemeni who had grown up in Saudi Arabia, but he had been too young to participate in the anti-Soviet struggle in Afghanistan. But two years before the Taliban went on the blitz to seize control of that country, a teenaged Khallad ventured there to offer assistance. Three years later, in 1997, he lost his lower right leg in a battle with the Taliban's nemesis, a hodgepodge of guerrillas known as the Northern Alliance. Struggling on despite his handicap, he pledged loyalty to bin Laden and volunteered to be a suicide operative.

In 1999, Khallad moved one step closer to martyrdom. After persistent lobbying, KSM earlier that year had gained bin Laden's support for his earlier plan to simultaneously bring down numerous jetliners. Known within the group as the "planes operation," one phase of this was a resurrection of the Bojinka plot that involved downing airliners originating in East Asia. To gauge airport and aircraft security, Khallad, along with three other Arab suicide volunteers, intended to case flights in Southeast Asia near year's end. They would begin their reconnaissance from Kuala Lumpur, intentionally chosen because Malaysia did not require visas from Gulf state citizens. (This ease of access would later lead al-Qaeda to deem Malaysia a safe haven for its operatives in Southeast Asia; the group at no point contemplated attacks – even against Western targets – within Malaysia.)

In mid-December, Khallad and a fellow al-Qaeda member named Abu al-Bara al-Ta'izi landed in Kuala Lumpur and checked into a hotel near the city's international airport. As per KSM's orders, Hambali promptly rendezvoused with the pair and escorted them to his house in Sungai Manggis.

Khallad, it turned out, was in Malaysia for a second, more personal, reason. Although he theoretically wanted to give his own life in the near future, he apparently wanted to do it with a better artificial leg than that currently covering his stump. The Endolite clinic, located in the outskirts of the Malaysian capital, was known among the Afghanistan Arabs as a good source for fitting high-qual-

---

[105] This is almost certainly the same ethnic Indian named Issa al-Hindi who reportedly received two weeks of instruction at Camp Hudaibiyah in October 1999. See Nasir Abas, p. 164.

ity prosthetic limbs without asking too many questions. Hambali helped him contact the clinic, then drove both Arabs there the next day. After placing an order, and learning that parts for the prosthesis would not arrive from England for another two weeks, Khallad announced that he intended to wait in Malaysia.[106]

As his simple house could not handle two guests for a prolonged period, Hambali looked for an alternative. At that point, he recalled that Sufaat, who had recently accompanied him to interview the microbiologist in Bogor, had a three-bedroom condominium in a high rise on the outskirts of Kuala Lumpur. When asked, Sufaat immediately made it available as a safe house for these and future al-Qaeda guests.

Into the new year, Hambali and a pair of Malaysian Jemaah Islamiyah members attended to the two Arabs at the condominium. Two more al-Qaeda operatives – Saudis by the names of Nawaf al-Hamzi and Khalid al-Mihdhar – would soon arrive from the Middle East on 4 and 5 January, respectively. With Hambali helping to procure tickets, they fanned out from Kuala Lumpur early the next week to case regional airports. Three of them would also link up with more operatives in Bangkok, where they received large amounts of cash to fund future operations.

In the end, bin Laden judged the planes operation to be overly complex and ultimately cancelled the East Asia segment in the spring of 2000. But planning for the North American portion continued unabated. On 15 January, al-Hamzi and al-Mihdhar departed for Los Angeles; both would later be aboard American Airlines Flight 77 that crashed into the Pentagon. Five days later, on 20 January, Khallad left Bangkok for Karachi. He would later mastermind the October 2000 bombing of the USS *Cole* off the coast of Yemen, which killed 17 American sailors and crippled the warship.[107]

---

[106] The leg did not come cheap: U.S. investigators later found evidence that US$36,000 had been transferred to Malaysia to pay for the prosthesis.

[107] Among the other al-Qaeda members that stayed at Sufaat's condominium at various occasions in early 2000 were three Saudis: Yaqub al-Bahr, Hani Hanjour (who was later the pilot that crashed American Airlines Flight 77 into the Pentagon on 11 September 2001), and another known as Sokr. It is not known if Sokr is the same Saqr al-Madani that was nominated as a suicide operative for the planned attack in Pattaya.

While Hambali would later claim ignorance about the plotting in Sufaat's condominium – not implausible given compartmentalization of information by the Arabs – Jemaah Islamiyah was less innocent about other al-Qaeda plots. Perhaps the earliest example dates to late 1999 when, during a meeting between KSM and Zulkarnaen, the former asked the latter to begin surveillance against U.S. targets in Southeast Asia. Ideally, al-Qaeda wanted to hit the U.S. embassy in Bangkok. First, it was the second-largest U.S. diplomatic outpost in the world. Second, Thailand was a predominantly Buddhist nation; any collateral damage to Thai civilians, therefore, would not equate with Muslim casualties.

But the U.S. embassy in Bangkok was also an extremely difficult target. Not only was it split among several locales, but – unlike the East Africa embassies hit in 1998 – the main chancellery was far from roadside and appeared to be very secure. Al-Qaeda, as a result, resigned itself to finding alternate targets.

Hambali soon got wind of what those other targets might be. On 19 January 2000, he departed for Afghanistan on his third visit in two years. While there, he was told by KSM that Thai resorts were ripe for attack. Al-Qaeda operations chief Mohammad Atef, meanwhile, told him to case the U.S. embassy in Jakarta ahead of a possible suicide bombing. Thinking aloud, Atef even considered a kamikaze strike by a helicopter laden with explosives.

Returning to Malaysia, Hambali passed the request for Jakarta surveillance to Zulkarnaen. He, in turn, gave the task to Edi Setiono (alias Usman), a 39-year-old Jakarta resident, and 34-year-old Farihin Ibnu Ahmad (alias Yasir). Usman, the eighth of twelve children who eked out a living selling bottled water, had been in the Sadda class after Hambali. Yasir hailed from a family of religious conservatives: his father was among a group of Sundanese radicals implicated in a failed 1956 assassination attempt against President Sukarno, one of his brothers was a Ngruki graduate, and another brother was a member of Jemaah Islamiyah. Usman and Yasir had first befriended each other in Pakistan – Yasir had been studying religion in Karachi at the same time Usman was in Sadda – and both had later briefly worked at a Malaysian plantation.

Surveillance, the pair soon discovered, was easier said than done. Driving past the front of the U.S. embassy, they only managed a pair of blurred, off-center photographs of its entrance. So poor were the pictures, and so incomplete was Usman's final report, that Hambali was too embarrassed to forward it to Afghanistan.

Instead, Hambali himself ventured to Jakarta to do the job himself. Making multiple passes by the front of the embassy with Usman, Hambali was flustered by what he saw. Following the May 1998 riots in Jakarta, the embassy had significantly upgraded its outer defenses. Security was particularly heavy at the car entrance, Hambali noted, making a car bomb like those used in East Africa ineffective. Determining that further planning would require al-Qaeda experts, he prepared a report and sent it to Mohammad Atef via a Jemaah Islamiyah member heading to Afghanistan for training. He never received a response.

Somewhat better results were had while reconnoitering targets in Thailand. The impetus for this came after a visit to Afghanistan by a 43-year-old Malaysian member of Jemaah Islamiyah named Azhari bin Husin. Among his fellow extremists, Azhari was a rare breed. An engineering student at Australia's University of Adelaide in the early eighties, he had indulged in Western college life to such an extent that he returned home with no degree after four years. Suitably humbled over his poor academic showing, Azhari got serious and finished his undergraduate studies in Malaysia. More focused this time around, he departed for the United Kingdom and in 1990 earned a doctorate in statistical modeling at the University of Reading.

By now recognized as a gifted mathematician, Azhari returned to Malaysia and taught statistics for a time. He also began to specialize in property management and valuation theory; by 1993, he was a regional expert in the field. During that period, the ASEAN economies were going at full steam, and the property market was a boom industry. Azhari, in particular, was drawn toward job opportunities in Indonesia: not only was the Indonesian property sector particularly lucrative, but his wife's grandparents hailed from Bengkulu, Sumatra, and he had a sister working in Jakarta. Making the shift to the Indonesian capital in 1996, he landed the role as the director of research at a reputable property consultancy in the city's Central Business District.

Over the following year, Azhari struck co-workers as a timid and pleasant colleague with a nervous laugh. "He had the air of a bookworm, a goofy professor," said a British expatriate who worked in a neighboring cubicle. He also preferred a quiet, conservative life; despite constant prodding from his officemates he never partook in the Jakarta nightlife, instead claiming he needed to tend to an ailing wife.[108]

---

[108] Interview with Scott Butler, 18 March 2005.

Soon thereafter, Azhari's bubble burst. As the economic contagion rippled across Southeast Asia in mid-1997, the Indonesian economy began to implode. Its property sector was especially hard hit, and property consultancies quickly looked to shed themselves of pricey expatriates. Though his skills were no longer wanted in Jakarta, Azhari was reluctant to return home. Swallowing a salary cut, he headed for Gadjah Mada University in Jogjakarta to teach property management as a guest lecturer for six months.

Staying within the academic arena, Azhari and his wife by late 1998 were back in Malaysia and teaching at the Malaysian Technological University in Johor. It was to be a bittersweet homecoming. After years of faltering health, his wife was diagnosed with throat cancer soon after the birth of their second child. Though she survived, she lost her voice in the therapeutic process and was forced to forfeit her lecturing position.

It was at that point that Azhari had an epiphany. Rocked by his wife's illness, he turned to religion in a big way. For a person who had never outwardly shown much piety, his embrace of Islam quickly turned fanatical. In this, he found common cause with the puritan tenets espoused by Abdullah Sungkar's tight-knit community, which happened to be active in Johor administering the Luqmanul Haqiem pesantren.

For Jemaah Islamiyah, Azhari was a prize catch. With so few academics among its ranks, and apparently convinced of the sincerity of his relatively late religious conversion, its leaders fast-tracked his initiation into their organization. Leapfrogging over members with more seniority, in late 1999 he was chosen to receive al-Qaeda training in Afghanistan.

For Azhari, the Spartan amenities of Kandahar were a far cry from Johor or Jakarta. But throwing himself into his studies, he excelled; perhaps not surprising given his background in mathematics, he became particularly proficient in bomb-assembly and demolitions. He also made a favorable impression on senior al-Qaeda officers; before leaving in early 2000, KSM entrusted him with an envelope containing US$1,500. Noting the large number of Jewish tourists in Thailand, KSM said the money was earmarked for surveillance in the southern part of that kingdom.

Back in Malaysia, Azhari turned over the cash to Mantiqi 1. As the head of that mantiqi, Hambali looked for the right candidates to do the casing. His quick pick was Sufaat, whose manner and dress would let him easily pass for a tourist. But Hambali also wanted a Thai national to provide assistance. Contacting Abdul Fatah, who had attended the Rabitatul Mujahidin meeting late the previous year, he asked for a suitable assistant. Fatah led a sub-group of the Jemaah Salafi movement in southern Thailand; although it had no formal relationship with Jemaah Islamiyah, the group appeared sympathetic. Following Hambali's request, Fatah proposed Abu Hisham, an elderly, overweight Afghan alum who sported a wispy goatee.

Together, Sufaat and Hisham departed for Phuket in southern Thailand. With a camcorder in hand, they cruised its nightclubs, bars, and restaurants for a week. For another week after that, they frequented tourist destinations in Pattaya, the seaside resort town east of Bangkok.

Returning to Malaysia, Sufaat drafted a three-page surveillance report in English. Demonstrating his computer skills, he also edited a CD-ROM version of the video. Both were turned over to Hambali, who forwarded them to KSM with a trainee heading for Afghanistan.

This time, al-Qaeda responded. About a month later, KSM dispatched Abu Hazim al-Sha'ir to Malaysia. A 26-year-old Yemeni, Hazim was widely traveled and had served a stint as bin Laden's bodyguard. He came bearing bad news: KSM had viewed the CD-ROM and was annoyed that Sufaat had spent so much time videotaping girls in bathing suits. KSM was anxious for the Thailand operation to proceed, so Hazim headed to Phuket alone to conduct his own casing.

Huddling with Hambali once back in Malaysia, Hazim looked to fine-tune the plot. Pattaya would be their main target, and Hazim himself would be one of the suicide bombers; Atef nominated an al-Qaeda member named Saqr al-Madani as the second candidate for martyrdom. But as Hambali was convinced that they would need local Thai support to succeed, he once more contacted Abdul Fatah for assistance. Fatah would only need to provide minimal help, he assured; al-Qaeda had already nominated the operatives. But fearing blowback against his own Islamic network in southern Thailand, Fatah kept them at arm's length. Without Fatah's aid, Hambali told Hazim, Jemaah Islamiyah would be severely disadvantaged conducting operations in Thailand. This was relayed back to KSM, and the plan, reluctantly, was quietly shelved.

CHAPTER EIGHT

JIHAD: INDONESIA

I n June 2000, Mantiqi 1 organized and funded a second Rabitatul Mujahidin meeting in Malaysia. This time, the tryst was held in a rented apartment
in Kuala Lumpur. Apart from the new venue, however, much else was the
same. Aside from one new participant from a Malaysian opposition party, virtually all of the regional representatives from the first forum were there again. And
again, Indonesia fielded the largest contingent: Abu Jihad, Ba'asyir, Hambali,
and Dwikarna, among others, were all back. There, too, was Faiz Abu Bakar
Bafana, the Malaysian member of Mantiqi 1.[109]

Also like the first gathering of the talk shop, very little of substance was
discussed. Most of the extremist groups present were focused on their individual
struggles, and had little appetite for Jemaah Islamiyah's greater goal of pooling
resources to create an Islamic super-state.

But although Rabitatul Mujahidin had again come up short, Jemaah Islamiyah was hardly fazed. Indeed, the organization's problem during the first
half of 2000 was not that it did not have enough to do, but rather that it was
suddenly being whipsawed by too many activities at once. High on its crowded
agenda was participation in the various religious skirmishes flaring across the
Indonesian archipelago.

In general, these conflicts were rooted in local economics and population
shifts. On a handful of Indonesia's outer islands, populations had been traditionally tilted in favor of slim Christian majorities. As majorities, they had a

---

[109] In late 2000, Hambali sketched a crude Rabitatul Mujahidin logo and gave it to Bafana to re-design it on a
computer. The logo consisted of crossed Arabic swords framing a map of Southeast Asia with Arabic script
reading "Rabitatul Mujahidin" across the bottom.

lock on government power at the village, sub-district, and even district levels. They also dominated key sectors of the economy.

Such was the case in the southern Maluku island of Ambon. There, on what had once been a key Dutch bastion for control over the spice trade, Ambonese Christians had run the show for the vast majority of the years since Indonesia's independence. They had done so behind a veneer of stability, earning the island a reputation as a model of religious tolerance.

But during the country's robust economic growth in the early and mid-nineties, fundamental changes had occurred. Lured by better jobs on Java, and especially in Jakarta, the entrepreneurial Ambonese – many of them Christians – left their island in droves. To fill the less-desirable, less-lucrative jobs that had suddenly become vacant on Ambon, laborers from nearby South Sulawesi – mostly Muslims – filled the void.

Then in 1997 came Indonesia's economic crisis. Many of the wayward Ambonese, suddenly finding themselves out of work on Java, eventually headed back to their home island. To their dismay, they found changes had taken place in the interim. For one thing, non-Ambonese held scarce local jobs. For another thing, the delicate political balance in favor of Christians had shifted to the Muslims. With the status quo upset and tensions skyrocketing, all it took was a simple argument between a bus driver and a passenger from opposing religious blocs to set off the tinderbox.

During the New Order regime, such conflict would have been quickly and brutally stamped out. But during the impotent Habibie administration, communal violence, through sins of omission and commission, was allowed to thrive. Starting in January 1999, Ambon was fully aflame.

By the time of the first Rabitatul Mujahidin meeting, its attendees had already taken notice of the chaos in the southern Malukus. Although there was no denying that Muslims were dying in the struggle, it was also true that they were giving as good as they got. For that reason, there was debate among many Indonesian religious hardliners, especially within Darul Islam, as to whether the Ambon conflict could truly rate as jihad.

For Jemaah Islamiyah's Mantiqi 1, however, there was no debate: in their minds, the Muslim militiamen fighting on Ambon were jihadists worthy of support. Indeed, more so than the Jemaah Islamiyah elements based in Indonesia, Mantiqi 1 was predisposed to take a broader and more extreme version of jihad. This was because the majority of the Jemaah Islamiyah trainees receiving al-Qaeda training in Afghanistan had come from Mantiqi 1, and they were getting more religious indoctrination and vilification of infidels in addition to their traditional jihad training.

As head of that mantiqi, Hambali was fast to take action. In 1999, he arranged for Pertubuhan al-Ehasan, the non-governmental organization he set up in Selangor to help fund the MILF, to begin seeking donations at mosques around Malaysia for the Ambon "mujahideen." Over the next two years, an estimated US$18,000 was funneled to the Malukus.[110]

Others took an even more proactive approach. In mid-1999, a handful of hardcore Darul Islam members from around Jakarta and West Java excused themselves from that organization to form the grandiose-titled Abu Bakar Battalion. On paper it comprised six companies; in reality, it never amounted to more than sixty men. From this, a handful of members at year's end headed by sea toward Maluku.[111]

They were not alone. In January 2000, a paramilitary organization known as *Laskar Jihad* ("Holy War Army") was founded in Jogjakarta. The leader of the legion, Ja'far Umar Thalib, had studied in Pakistan for several years in the eighties (he also claimed, rather unconvincingly, to have engaged in major combat action against Soviet forces). Two months after its creation, a Laskar Jihad spokesman announced that the group intended to actively participate in Ambon. During April, after several weeks of high-profile paramilitary exercises at a private compound in Bogor – and repeated admonitions from the government – about 3,000 members recruited from across Java boldly departed for Maluku.

The dispatch of Laskar Jihad opened the floodgates for the arrival of other extremists. In what soon became a confusing amalgam of outside militants, among those arriving during 2000 were radicals from as far off as South Sulawesi, Java, and even Malaysia.[112] Some of these groups were secretive, barely

---

[110] Mantiqi 1 usually did not raise funds from mosques because of strict fundraising regulations in Malaysia. But according to Hambali, Ambon appeared to be an exception, with the authorities turning a blind eye.

[111] International Crisis Group, "Recycling Militants in Indonesia: Darul Islam and the Australian Embassy Bombing," 22 February 2005, p. 25.

[112] Nearly a dozen members of the Malaysian Mujahideen Group (*Kumpulan Mujahidin Malaysia*, or KMM) arrived in June 2000. The KMM was founded in October 1995 and had cordial ties with the exiled Jemaah Islamiyah leadership in Malaysia. A mention of a KMM member who fought in Ambon is found in *Asian Wall Street Journal*, 19 June 2002, p. A1.

tolerating their fellow Muslim jihadists. Further complicating matters, several generically referred to themselves as *Laskar Mujahidin* ("Mujahideen Army"). Too, aid workers complained that some of the militia, especially those from South Sulawesi, often dressed in Indonesian military camouflage and were difficult to differentiate from bona fide troops.[113]

The city of Ambon, not surprisingly, became a veritable war zone. Not unlike Beirut during the height of Lebanon's civil war, it became divided along religious quarters with a shaky green line separating the two. Marauding militiamen – Muslims and Christians – openly patrolled the streets with edged weapons and firearms. Others prowled the waters off the city on speedboats, laying siege to passenger ferries plying the bay. Homemade bombs exploded in markets and houses of worship on a weekly basis.

Throughout this period, Jemaah Islamiyah's contributions to the Ambon jihad were varied. Leading the effort was Zulkarnaen, the group's military czar. Over the preceding months, Zulkarnaen had been prowling eastern Indonesia in search of a worthy jihad. Initially, he had selected the conflict on the North Maluku island of Halmahera. To be sure, Halmahera was the scene of untold bloodshed. During the last couple of weeks of 1999 alone, an estimated 700 persons had been butchered.

But Halmahera's conflict had decidedly secular underpinnings linked to the profitable Gosowong gold mine which had opened earlier in 1999. Coincidentally, much of the adjacent sub-district had been settled by recent migrants – mostly Muslims – from the neighboring island of Ternate. Smelling an opportunity to squeeze the mine operators for land rights, these new arrivals began agitating to form their own district – which naturally did not sit well with the sitting district leaders, who were a mix of Christians and Muslims.

It was this tension that led to the bloody chaos that engulfed Halmahera beginning in late 1999. Looking to help what he pronounced as persecuted fellow Muslims, Zulkarnaen arrived on the island with a band of Javanese militants from Jemaah Islamiyah. His efforts quickly went nowhere. For one thing,

---

[113] Not helping matters was the fact that local police and military units took sides in the conflict, often assisting one side or the other of the warring factions. Perhaps the most egregious violator was the 733rd Airborne Battalion, which regularly intervened alongside Muslim jihadists. To help remedy the situation, the military in 2001 opted to send these paratroopers packing for a one-year assignment in Papua.

Muslims could be found on both sides of the conflict; during some of the largest skirmishes, longtime Christian and Muslim residents had banded together to repulse newcomers. For another thing, a particularly hardnosed Indonesian marine officer had been placed in charge of a military task force mandated with restoring order; with an even hand, he sent outside forces scurrying – Zulkarnaen included – as he brought about an enforced peace.

Down but not out, Zulkarnaen in early 2000 set his sights further north. By that time, a Philippine army offensive had razed Camp Abu Bakar (and Camp Hudaibiyah), leading Jemaah Islamiyah's military chief to begin weighing options for the creation of a new jihadist training camp closer to home. He eventually settled on Morotai, a small island located on the far northern tip of North Maluku. Morotai was a study in extremes. Its mountainous interior was so rugged that an Imperial Japanese army private was able to hide there undetected for twenty-eight years (he was finally coaxed out in 1973). Around its coast, meanwhile, was an imposing ring of mud and mangroves.

During World War II, General Douglas MacArthur had chosen Morotai for his launch point to retake the Philippines. His initial assault force to capture Morotai was compelled to blanket the coastal swamps with a web of raised catwalks. Some sixty-one thousand Allied personnel then poured onto the island, two-thirds of whom were engineers working feverishly to build docks and airstrips atop the soft seaside soil. Their efforts paid off. In short order, Morotai boasted a major military base with hard-surface runways and a comprehensive network of piers.

After only a few weeks, MacArthur forced his way into the Philippines, and Morotai was abandoned. Evidence of the island's brief service, however, abounded. Next to the harbor were hundreds of abandoned vehicles, from tractors to amphibious landing craft. Closer to the airfield, the rusting carcasses were those of planes.

For Zulkarnaen, Morotai's isolation was its biggest selling point. Staking out a remote corner of its interior, he began building a modest replica of Camp Hudaibiyah. Hambali, who visited the site soon after it opened, provided construction funds from Mantiqi 1's coffers. He also gave Zulkarnaen a speedboat to provide a ready link with other parts of the Malukus.

But despite a promising start, the Morotai camp floundered. Even before any students arrived for training, the local military outpost got wind of Zulkarnaen's construction activities. Opting not to risk a confrontation with the authorities, Jemaah Islamiyah abandoned the site.

Still unfazed, Zulkarnaen next looked for ways to stoke the ongoing Ambon jihad. In 2000, he began underwriting the dispatch of militia volunteers from Java, though never on the same scale as Laskar Jihad. Besides himself, other senior members of the group started visiting the island to assess the situation and meet their volunteers; Hambali, for one, would eventually make four visits to Ambon. They also extended material support. In the last quarter of 2000, for instance, the Jemaah Islamiyah markaz authorized the procurement of three tons of explosives for use on the island.[114]

To the west, another battlefield would hold the attention of Jemaah Islamiyah. Early in the second quarter of 2000, sputtering inter-religious clashes around Poso in Central Sulawesi erupted into full-blown fighting. Just as was the case on Ambon, the population around Poso was roughly divided between Muslims and Christians; many of the latter had migrated there in the fifties under pressure from Kahar Muzakkar's Darul Islam guerrillas. Also like on Ambon, the Indonesian government – first the Habibie administration, then Abdurrahman "Gus Dur" Wahid – was too hobbled by internal divisions to react forcefully to the carnage.[115]

For the first few months, Poso did not garner serious national attention. But on 3 June, media reports alleged that 200 Muslims had been massacred at Poso's Wali Songo pesantren. Reacting to this, the first jihadists from outside Central Sulawesi soon arrived on the scene. These militants were Muslim youths

---

[114] According to detained al-Qaeda member Umar Faruq, the explosives were to be used against a Christian gathering hall that would be holding a Christmas Eve mass. The plan was cancelled, however, when it was learned that some Muslim leaders had been invited to the service as part of a confidence-building measure between the warring communities.

[115] The undercurrent of religious tension around Poso dated back to the Kahar Muzakkar rebellion, during which time the government had sanctioned the formation of a so-called "Youth Movement of Central Sulawesi" to shield the younger generation from rebel recruitment. When the Darul Islam uprising began to run out of steam in the early sixties, this youth group splintered along religious lines into the "Christian Youth Movement of Central Sulawesi" and the Islamic "Tanjung Buluh Brigade." For nearly two decades, the presence of these religious youth militia was of little consequence. In 1992, however, violence broke out in Poso after insulting leaflets were found in that town. The perpetrator, a recent Christian convert, was later caught and sentenced to four years in prison. Three years later, violence again returned to Poso after several Christian youths were accused of throwing stones at a mosque and pesantren. Only the deployment of troops brought peace back to the community.

from South Sulawesi, who ventured across the border to support their religious brethren in July and August.

Others quickly followed. By the close of August, a small contingent of jihadists came from Jakarta and West Java; they hailed from the same group of hardcore Darul Islam members that had created the Abu Bakar Battalion the previous year.

Two months later, Islamic leaders held a congress in the South Sulawesi capital of Makassar. The purpose of the gathering was to discuss ways in which they could force the implementation of Islamic law in their province. By that time, Muslim paramilitary vigilante bands – usually armed with nothing more than sticks and machetes – were mushrooming around the country. Some of these vigilantes were used for securing the congress' venue – even to include the toilets and access to the *mushola* during noon prayers.

Although participants at the congress failed to make progress in implementing Islamic law, they did use the opportunity to create *Laskar Jundullah* ("Army of God") as an autonomous paramilitary wing. Heading Laskar Jundullah was Agus Dwikarna, the same savvy hardliner who had attended the Rabitatul Mujahidin meetings in Malaysia. In the interim he had also been named head of the "Crisis Handling Committee" (*Komisi Penaggulang Akibat Crisis*, or Kompak) for the eastern parts of Indonesia; in this role, he made videos of the violence taking place in Ambon and used them for fundraising and recruiting militia members.[116]

Very quickly, Laskar Jundullah was able to grow exponentially. As of September 2000, it was thought to number about 2,000 members spread among 22 districts across South Sulawesi. The overall commander was Agus Dwikarna; his chief-of-staff was Muchtar Daeng Lao (alias Ridha), an Afghan graduate who had been in charge of the Sulawesi students training at Camp Hudaibiyah.

Playing a key role, too, was Syawal, the longtime Sadda trainer who had also been instrumental in the Hudaibiyah program. Syawal had shaped up into

---

[116] During the same month that Dwikarna formed Laskar Jundullah in Makassar, an unaffiliated militant group with the same name was formed in Solo under the command of Mohammad Kalono. In October 2000, this group, armed mainly with bats and banners, spearheaded raids against several hotels across that city in an attempt to locate U.S. citizens and force them out of Indonesia. The reason for this "sweep" was because they were allegedly offended by criticism leveled at the government by U.S. Ambassador Robert Gelbard. Though the Solo militants were long on harsh rhetoric, they committed no damage nor inflicted any casualties.

an opportunistic freelancer, dividing his time between Laskar Jundullah, militants in Banten, and a host of other extremists around Jakarta. His relationship with Jemaah Islamiyah was particularly complex: though he had a familial link that carried significant weight – one of his two wives was the stepdaughter of the late Abdullah Sungkar – Syawal was known for his non-orthodox religious beliefs that, on face, ran counter to Jemaah Islamiyah's puritanism.[117]

In practice, Dwikarna's Laskar Jundullah proved to be an umbrella for hundreds, perhaps thousands, of young South Sulawesi males who answered the call to jihad. It began its paramilitary campaign that December, when dozens of its members destroyed a Makassar karaoke bar and café because it dared to operate during Ramadhan. The police offered no response to these acts of vandalism.

More serious, Dwikarna eventually deployed about 2,000 of his combatants to Central Sulawesi. Although their training was minimal and their weaponry (at least initially) largely limited to bats and machetes, they made a significant impact when they sided with the Muslim community in the simmering sectarian violence around Poso; just as was the case with Ambon, fighting – and the body count – sharply escalated.[118]

Just as with Ambon, too, still other extremists began to arrive. Although the bulk of its militia was on Ambon, Laskar Jihad diverted some of its men to the Sulawesi front. And when it saw that the central government was showing no backbone in Ambon, Jemaah Islamiyah, too, fielded a modest contingent from Mantiqi 3. "The jihad was just as bad in Poso [as Ambon]," Hambali would later recall. "But it was getting no attention from Gus Dur."[119]

---

[117] Syawal's other wife was the daughter of a controversial South Sulawesi cleric named Syamsuri, who unconvincingly claimed that he was the reincarnation of Kahar Muzakkar. According to Umar Faruq, Syawal wore around his neck an amulet with a vial of water into which Syamsuri had breathed – a mystical practice seen on Java that would have been seen as heretical by Jemaah Islamiyah adherents. Syawal later worked at a holistic center advocating New Age-style healing remedies that, again, was hardly in line with Jemaah Islamiyah tenets.

[118] During the Ambon conflict, Laskar Jundullah rotated a small stream of volunteers through that front. These militiamen often operated alongside Jemaah Islamiyah jihadists. The two groups maintained safe houses and weapons storerooms alongside each other in Ambon's Air Kuning district.

[119] There was a significant difference between Jemaah Islamiyah's intervention in Ambon and Poso. In Ambon, it sent money, material aid, and combatants. "In Poso, [its involvement] was 90 percent proselytizing and 10 percent combatants," said Mantiqi 3 leader Nasir Abas. "It proved to have a far more lasting effect." Nasir Abas interview.

The fighting in Ambon and Poso soon attracted the attention of foreign interests, including al-Qaeda. Playing a critical role in this effort was Umar Faruq, a lanky Arab born in Kuwait to Iraqi parents. Shortly before the 1991 Gulf War, a 20-year-old Faruq had been inspired by a fiery anti-Western sermon and abruptly decided to leave Kuwait for Afghanistan. There he gained admittance to Camp Khaldan – where he came into contact with Indonesians Syawal and Ridha – then had an uneventful spell alongside mujahideen in Tajikistan and another in Bosnia before returning for a second round of training in Afghanistan.

During his time in Afghanistan, Faruq made a couple of important contacts. The first was Abu Zubaydah, the Palestinian militant who was running the camps after the closure of the MAK. He also met several Filipinos from the MILF, who regaled him with tales of their tropical jihad. Faruq did end up going to the Philippines in late 1995, though not immediately to Mindanao. Along with another Arab from Khaldan, he was dispatched to Manila to seek entry into a flight school. In a forerunner to what became KSM's planes operation, their ultimate goal was to become proficient enough to commandeer a passenger plane on a suicide mission.

Failing to gain entry despite repeated applications, Faruq left Manila and headed south for a rendezvous with the MILF. Arriving at Camp Abu Bakar, he was the second member of what became a 35-man Arab contingent (he eventually became leader). There he trained for about a year, primarily in jungle warfare tactics. To his surprise, he met Syawal and Ridha, two acquaintances from Khaldan. He also befriended al-Ghozi, the Jemaah Islamiyah member who was instrumental in establishing Camp Hudaibiyah. It was al-Ghozi who allowed Faruq and three other Arabs to venture to Hudaibiyah to practice karate.

By 1998, Faruq was ready for a change. Indonesia held particular appeal for him for several reasons. First, the post-New Order chaos seemed to offer fertile ground for extremists. Second, Faruq already counted a stable of Indonesian contacts from his Khaldan and Hudaibiyah days.

With Syawal acting as guide, Faruq took a boat from Mindanao to Borneo in August 1998. Because his forged Kuwaiti passport had since expired, he illegally entered East Kalimantan by boat and then made his way down to Makassar. Once there, Syawal provided introductions to several religious hardliners in his hometown, including Dwikarna.

For the next few months, Faruq tried, unsuccessfully, to obtain an Indonesian passport using forged identity papers. Briefly detained by immigration officials in Makassar, he fled to Jakarta. There his Makassar contacts introduced him to a subculture of Islamic militants in the capital, many of whom were later affiliated with the Abu Bakar Battalion that dispatched volunteers to Ambon. One of these militants, Abu Zejid, would later give his daughter's hand in marriage to Faruq.

Over the ensuing year, Faruq sat in on meetings in which his father-in-law and fellow extremists vented against the authorities. For a time they talked up assassinating Megawati Sukarnoputri, who was a frontrunner in national assembly elections slated for June 1999. They also hatched plots to killed retired General Benny Moerdani – not coincidentally a Catholic – and assorted other dignitaries. Nothing became of any of these schemes.

Though short on action, Faruq was slowly becoming a valuable asset. His network of Indonesian sympathizers, in particular, was deemed valuable by al-Qaeda. By late 1999, he was receiving frequent telephone calls from the Middle East regarding the imminent arrival of Arab colleagues. Some of these referrals were being phoned in by Ibn al-Khattab, an Azerbaijan-based Chechen extremist with ties to al-Qaeda. Typically, Faruq would meet these short-term visitors – including Algerians, Egyptians, and Yemenis – and brief them on the Indonesian situation.

Another duty performed by Faruq was conducting a fact-finding trip to Aceh. This restive province was potentially of interest to al-Qaeda for several reasons. First, the Acehnese population was generally sympathetic to separatist rebels, many of whom ostensibly supported a strict interpretation of Islamic law. Second, Aceh was easily accessible from neighboring Malaysia. Third, the Acehnese rebels were perpetually in need of funds and army; al-Qaeda could theoretically help with both.

To further explore the possibility, Faruq and Syawal in mid-December 1999 took a boat to the east coast of Sumatra, then went to Aceh by bus. There they spent two days with Abu Jihad, the shifty Acehnese rebel who had attended the Rabitatul Mujahidin meetings.[120] The meeting was far from successful. In

---

[120] According to a participant at the meeting between Abu Jihad and Faruq, the former had arranged the trip because he wanted Faruq to help source firearms for his small, secular Aceh Islamic Mujahideen Front; however, no weapons or funds were ever turned over by Faruq to Abu Jihad. BIN memorandum from Staf Ahli Bidang Social Budaya, 25 November 2002.

particular, Faruq found the Acehnese woefully ignorant of Islam: just a week into the monthlong Ramadhan fast, they were openly eating during daylight hours. Worse, Syawal later whispered that Abu Jihad was suspected of being a government informant. Faruq duly reported these negative impressions back to Afghanistan.[121]

During this same time frame, Faruq made two important Arab contacts. The first was Achmad al-Moudi, a Saudi national who opened the Jakarta branch of the al-Haramain foundation in the summer of 2000. Al-Haramain traced its origins back to the eighties, when it was established by the Saudis to channel support to the jihad in Afghanistan. It was also widely seen as that kingdom's spearhead for spreading its Wahhabi precepts. Al-Moudi was especially well prepared for his Indonesian assignment, having previously served in Pakistan, Bangladesh, and Azerbaijan.

The second contact was a Saudi named Rashid. Posing as an al-Haramain representative, Rashid effectively became Faruq's handler and financier. Believed to have near-direct contact to bin Laden, Rashid used no fewer than eight aliases.

Over the course of 2000, Rashid and Faruq both focused on the violence flaring in the southern Malukus. To channel assistance to the Ambon jihadists, Rashid developed two paramilitary projects. The first, initiated during the second half of the year and funded via Al-Haramain, was known as the "Special Program." The aim of this was to provide paramilitary training to local (Ambonese) recruits, and to help procure weapons for them. Each cycle of instruction, which would last up to a month, would be provided to students free of charge.

To house the Special Program, Faruq and Rashid oversaw construction of a modest, isolated training camp (including a wooden schoolhouse) in the southern part of Ambon's Hitu peninsula. They then began assembling a Middle Eastern cadre to act as recruiters and instructors. Between late 2000 and mid-2001, the program was supported by twenty persons, including eight Saudis,

---

[121] On 9 July 2002, CNN reported that Faruq returned to Aceh in June 2000 along with top al-Qaeda officers Ayman al-Zawahiri and Mohammed Atef. For several reasons, it is almost certain that this alleged visit never took place. First, when Faruq was extensively questioned on this point on 18 July 2002 (and again on 2 January 2003), he readily admitted the earlier trip with Syawal, but adamantly denied ever meeting al-Zawahiri or Atef, much less traveling with them to Aceh. Second, neither KSM nor Hambali have indicated they knew of any 2000 trip to Southeast Asia by either al-Zawahiri or Atef. Had it taken place, they almost certainly would have contacted Hambali (especially since a Rabitatul Mujahidin meeting was taking place the same month.) Third, Abu Jihad, reportedly a government informant, never made any mention of the supposed visit to his government handlers.

four Yemenis, two Algerians, an Egyptian, and a Pakistani. Most of the foreign cadre remained in Indonesia for only a few months at a time.[122]

Rashid's second project was known as the "Cooperative Program," also known as "One Body." As the name implied, this was an effort to provide assistance for a range of Javanese and Sulawesi volunteers looking to fight in Ambon. For this, Rashid and Faruq maintained safe houses in Ambon and Sulawesi, financed the establishment of Jemaah Islamiyah jungle training camps on the Maluku islands of Seram and Buru, purchased firearms, and even procured a twenty-foot boat for gunrunning operations. Though unstated, the Cooperative Program was also an effort to provide some much-needed coordination among the various Islamic militias, who more often operated as autonomous bands rather than any integrated front.[123]

Helping bankroll these projects was Sheik Bandar (alias Abu Abdullah), the head of the al-Haramain branch in Damman, Saudi Arabia. Bandar was no stranger to Indonesia: one of his wives was an Indonesian from Surabaya, and the sheik had visited that city frequently since 1999. Bandar often carried bricks of cash to Indonesia during his visits, which were passed to either Rashid or Faruq for use in Ambon.

For personal reasons, Faruq – and, by association, his al-Haramain nexus – had tended to favor radicals from South Sulawesi. This was because the first Indonesians Faruq had met in Khaldan during 1991 were Syawal and Ridha, who were both from that province. Again in Mindanao, he forged the closest ties with Indonesians from South Sulawesi. And when he first came to Indonesia, his first acquaintances were in and around Makassar. Though he also had contact with a range of Jemaah Islamiyah personalities, they were far less intimate.[124]

---

[122] The Special Program eventually graduated four classes of about twenty students apiece. Seven graduates from the first class were sent to Pakistan in 2001 for further training at a school run by *Laskar-e-Tayyeba* ("Army of the Pious"), the militant Kashmiri group tied to al-Qaeda that was waging a separatist campaign against the Indian government in Jammu and Kashmir. The cost of sending the students to Pakistan was reportedly paid by al-Haramain.

[123] Far from cooperating, some of the jihadists nearly came to blows in Ambon and Poso; the relationship between Jemaah Islamiyah and Laskar Jihad was particularly frosty. Al-Haramain tried not to take sides, and is reported to have channeled funds to, among others, Laskar Jihad and Dwikarna's Kompak, which in turn was used to support Laskar Jundullah.

But among the highest levels of al-Qaeda, they continued to forge the closest regional links with Jemaah Islamiyah, especially Mantiqi 1. Reciprocally, Jemaah Islamiyah continued to support plots being championed by al-Qaeda. Some of these revolved around al-Qaeda's fixation with biological and chemical weapons. In the third quarter of 2000, while heading to tour the Ambon battlefield, Hambali and Sufaat again detoured to Bogor to meet with the microbiologist they had seen the previous year.

Not much had changed in the interim. Still looking to supplement his meager government income, the scientist handed his guests a box of Chinese ear mushrooms he had grown in his lab. Please look for markets in Malaysia, he implored the two Jemaah Islamiyah members. Most of their subsequent conversations were limited to mushroom cultivation and other business opportunities. But toward the end of their two-day stay, the tone changed. Probing gently, Hambali and Sufaat asked if the scientist could establish his own laboratory in Bogor. He answered in the affirmative.

Sufaat probed further. Five years earlier, Japanese doomsday cult members had produced sarin nerve gas and released it into the Tokyo subway system, killing a dozen and wounding 6,000. Sufaat asked the scientist whether he was familiar with sarin. He admitted he knew little about the nerve agent, but was willing to learn more.

Finally, Sufaat asked about anthrax. This spore was all too common to Indonesia, where a strain sometimes afflicted cattle herds. But a different, more deadly version was fatal to humans in even the smallest airborne quantities. Again, the scientist admitted knowing little about anthrax.

As the two Jemaah Islamiyah members departed Bogor for Ambon, they compared notes about the scientist. As during the first visit, Sufaat thought his abilities were sufficient for al-Qaeda's needs. Hambali, however, was less positive. The scientist was an innocent, he said, and they could not risk exposing him to their true intent. In the end, Hambali's pessimism won the day.

---

[124] Faruq eventually arranged for monthly al-Haramain stipends to be given to four Indonesians. Highest on the list was Syawal, who received 1 million rupiah a month. Ridha came in second with a 700,000-rupiah stipend, while Makassar-based extremist Nasir (alias Abu Jemiah) and al-Ghozi each got 400,000 rupiah. Of the four, only al-Ghozi was a Jemaah Islamiyah member; the other three were linked to Laskar Jundullah.

Another al-Qaeda fixation was targeting U.S. embassies in Southeast Asia. The latest round on this subject came in mid-2000, when senior Mantiqi 1 member Mukhlas ventured to Kandahar.[125] There he found Mohammad Atef to be in a particularly generous mood, agreeing to provide bomb-making experts, suicide bombers, and some operational material. Atef also turned over US$20,000 to cover the cost of surveillance and the purchase of fertilizer as the prime ingredient for a car bomb. In return, he wanted an attack on either the U.S. or Israeli embassies in Singapore.

Back in Malaysia, Mukhlas gathered a small circle of Jemaah Islamiyah colleagues to discuss al-Qaeda's requirements. Mas Selamat Kastari, head of Singapore operations, had already given thought to smuggling large amounts of fertilizer into the city-state. One method, he proposed, involved smuggling it in from Indonesia's Batam or Tanjung Pinang islands in small containers covered with food. Another option was to carry it aboard a boat from Malaysia, then transferring it to another boat while pretending to fish. Still another option was to bring it concealed in a car from Johor.

Before any decision was made, Kastari departed to conduct surveillance on both embassies. After a couple of weeks, he handed Hambali a typewritten report. The conclusion: both targets were extremely difficult. The U.S. embassy was ringed by walls topped by closed-circuit cameras; the Israeli embassy was tucked away in an upper floor of an office complex.

To conduct the actual attack, al-Qaeda had promised to send Jemaah Islamiyah bomb-making experts and suicide bombers. What they sent instead was Zacarias Moussaoui. Born in France of Moroccan parents, the 32-year-old Moussaoui had been schooled in the United Kingdom and had passport entries that spanned the globe. His extensive travels included a 1998 stint at Camp Khaldan, during which time he was formally inducted into al-Qaeda. He landed a fairly important role in the organization: KSM was leaning toward using him as a potential pilot for his planes operation. To become properly certified, KSM in September 2000 dispatched him to Malaysia to seek flight training.

Moussaoui, it seems, had other ideas besides the suicide route. Taking up residence at Sufaat's condominium, he made a half-hearted attempt to locate a

---

[125] Mukhlas was serving as both the wakalah commander in Johor and the head of the Luqmanul Haqiem pesantren.

flight school near Kuala Lumpur before giving up the search.[126] Striking out in a different direction, he instead offered to help Hambali pursue the scheme to build a car bomb to destroy the U.S. or Israeli embassies in Singapore.[127]

Over the ensuing month, some progress was registered. Using the money handed over by Atef to Mukhlas, Moussaoui and Sufaat purchased four tons of ammonium nitrate (using Sufaat's lab as a front) and stored it in a warehouse outside Kuala Lumpur. By way of comparison, four tons was twice what was used during the 1995 Oklahoma City bombing.

At that point, KSM learned of Moussaoui's extra-curricular activities and was not amused. Ordered to get serious about attending flight school, Moussaoui contacted a flight school in the U.S. state of Oklahoma via e-mail and got a positive response. Packing to leave, Moussaoui got last minute assistance from Sufaat in the form of a letter of recommendation from Infocus Tech, a computer company co-owned by his wife. It purported that Moussaoui was the company's marketing consultant for Europe and the United States; Sufaat falsely signed the document as the Infocus managing director. Letter in hand, Moussaoui in October headed for Oklahoma via London. The four tons of fertilizer, meanwhile, sat in the warehouse and the car bomb scheme went into remission.

---

[126] Moussaoui hardly made a good impression on his Jemaah Islamiyah colleagues; Hambali and Bafana saw him as skittish and prone to bizarre outbursts. Brief of Appellee, *United States of America v. Zacarias Moussaoui*, 4th U.S. Circuit Court of Appeals, pp. 25-26, 50.

[127] According to the 9/11 Commission Report, Moussaoui wanted the explosives to bomb planes destined for the United States. Hambali is adamant that the explosives were for the plot to bomb embassies in Singapore.

CHAPTER NINE

THE PROVOCATEURS

I t was Sunday, 28 May 2000, and sixty members of Medan's GKPI Protestant church were gathered for the morning's first mass. They had no reason
not to feel secure. Their church, after all, was situated in the midst of a
housing complex for army officers. Moreover, Medan, with significant percent-
ages of both Muslims and Christians, had long nurtured a reputation as a thriving cosmopolitan city where religious tolerance was deeply ingrained.

On at least that morning, however, their sense of security would prove fleeting. At 0830 hours, as the choir was singing a hymn, a blinding flash erupted
from below a rear pew. Most of the churchgoers instinctively ducked as wood
splinters sliced down the 50-meter length of the building's interior. Some 23
persons, mostly women, fell with various degrees of non-fatal shrapnel injuries.

As these casualties were rushed to area hospitals, word of the bombing filtered across the city's Christian community. Investigating their respective congregations, clergy found two more suspicious parcels later that morning: at the
HKBP Protestant church, an unclaimed package was discovered atop a table
before the day's second mass; at Christ the King Catholic church, another was
spotted below a chair. Inside both, police ordnance disposal experts found two-
kilogram time-bombs. Small nails had been mixed with the explosives to enhance their lethal nature.

In their subsequent investigation, the authorities made little progress. It
was not that there a shortage of possible suspects; rather, there were too many.
Almost since the day he took office, President Gus Dur had attracted legions of
detractors. This was partly due to his small legislative foothold in the national
assembly; a large bloc of assemblymen was already talking about legally voting

the president out of office during the upcoming August session. It was also due to Gus Dur's quirky, acerbic style which burned bridges instead of building them. In particular, he had alienated virtually all of the upper echelon of the military by his frequent rotating of the top brass.

But rather than narrowing down this list of suspects, the authorities performed a time honored waffle. During the relatively rare occasions when there had been disturbances to the peace in Indonesia prior to 1991, the New Order usually found it convenient to reflexively – and, often, unconvincingly – blame communist sympathizers. But after the Cold War was over, and especially after the social upheaval of May 1998, the Indonesian government found it convenient to remove politics from their generic boogeyman and start collectively referring to them as *provakators*. Without making any arrests, the North Sumatran police pinned blame for the Medan bombs on such provocateurs and let the case gather dust.[128]

Actually, the Medan events had been Jemaah Islamiyah's first tentative steps past the discussion phase and fully into the world of terrorism. Preparations dated back to Indonesia's social upheavals of mid-1998, when Hambali had taken it upon himself to violate territorial boundaries and deploy a cell of Mantiqi 1 members into his homeland (which actually fell under the purview of Mantiqi 2 and 3).

Chosen to lead the cell was Imam Samudra, a former honor student who had ventured to Sadda in 1991 for training. Brimming with defiance and rage, Samudra made for a fascinating character study. Part of this can be attributed to being a native of Banten, the westernmost portion of West Java where the local Islamic culture, though pervasive, is heavily colored by local traditions and is hardly conducive to Jemaah Islamiyah's jackboot conservatism. Samudra therefore was something of a misfit in his home environment; in the words of one anthropologist who has studied him at length, "He was the neurotic Brad Pitt character in *Twelve Monkeys*."[129]

---

[128] During the first week of June 2000, two sergeants working for the intelligence office in the North Sumatra military regional command were interrogated regarding the church bombs. They were briefly detained before being released by week's end. See "Dua Intel Kodim Medan Diperiksa," *Kompas*, 2 June 2000 and "Dua Intel Kodim Masih Ditahan Di Denpom Medan," *Suarya Karya*, 6 June 2000. The U.S. defense attaché visited Medan later that year and came away convinced that a senior army intelligence officer from the North Sumatra military region was responsible for the bombs.

[129] Interview with John MacDougall, 2 August 2005.

Samudra also seemed predisposed toward violence. "He was always incredibly intense," one colleague later lamented, "but he seemed to have no direction."[130] "He used to say, 'I know the perfect crime. Just wait and see,'" remembered another.[131]

But for all his intensity, for almost two years Samudra had done little besides talk tough. Prodded by Hambali, his cell finally, in the second quarter of 2000, mobilized itself to carry out a strike. It decided to target three houses of worship in Medan, no doubt because the roughly equally-divided religious community in that city was considered, like Ambon and Poso, to be fertile ground for instigating communal violence. (Indeed, a communiqué by the perpetrators would later explicitly state that they desired to turn Medan into a second front after Ambon.[132])

In the end, Jemaah Islamiyah's efforts did not have the desired effect. Far from sparking reprisals and inciting wider religious warfare, the bombs prompted the Medan populace to close ranks and swear off violence. Few made the connection with Ambon or religious extremists; rather, the most common assumption was that political opponents of Gus Dur were looking to make the executive branch appear unable to maintain stability. Jemaah Islamiyah, ironically, was the one looking impotent.[133]

If May 2000 had been a disappointing month for Jemaah Islamiyah, it was far worse for its Filipino compatriots in the MILF. The year had not started out that way. On 12 January, the administration of Philippine President Joseph Es-

---

130 Nasir Abas interview.

131 Interview with Al Chaidar, 26 July 2005.

132 By coincidence, just one day after the 30 May church bombing, a crude explosive device thrown from a passing car at Medan's upmarket Miramar restaurant shattered windows and wounded four pedestrians. It was never conclusively determined whether the target was the restaurant or the adjacent Catholic church. The culprits were never identified, though Jemaah Islamiyah was apparently not to blame.

133 A year earlier, another extremist group had tried to instigate a wave of religious violence. In April 1999, a small group of hoodlums-cum-Islamic extremists known as the Indonesian Islamic Mujahideen Army (*Angkatan Mujahidin Islam Nusantara*, or AMIN) planted a small bomb in the al-Istiqlal mosque in Jakarta. It apparently wanted to spark widespread communal violence just two months before scheduled national elections. The only appreciable reaction was in Makassar, where a mob of 1,000 set fire to a Catholic church in retaliation.

trada had agreed to a ceasefire on Mindanao. But liberally mixing the stick with the carrot, government planes continued bombarding MILF positions into the second quarter. Pouring in ground forces, Camp Abu Bakar by 19 May was effectively encircled. As month's end approached, pundits sensed Abu Bakar's days were numbered.

In nearby Camp Hudaibiyah, the Indonesian trainees and cadre knew better than to make a final stand. Marching down the mountain toward Camp Abu Bakar proper, they linked up with a rear guard column of Moro rebels and retreated along a jungle footpath for nine hours toward the city of Marawi.

Just short of Marawi, the Indonesian and Filipinos paused. They had come upon the MILF's second training locale, Camp Bushra. Named after the Syrian city along the pilgrimage route to Mecca, the outlook for the MILF looked bleak. With the sounds of battle ringing around Marawi, the retreat column had barely rested at Bushra before it decided to abandon that site as well.

Wading through the thick jungle for another seven hours, the Indonesians and some Moro escorts clawed their way up a nearby mountain. There, in a cramped clearing, they paused once more. While their remote perch was deemed sufficiently safe for the moment, the trail was too rugged to carry in any building materials. In those simple surroundings, they remained for a couple of days before they decided the situation was untenable. Leaving behind their MILF comrades, the Indonesians headed toward the coast and eventually found their way back to their homeland.

At the same time Camp Abu Bakar was smoldering, the second Rabitatul Mujahidin gathering was underway in Kuala Lumpur. In the margins of that June meeting, Hambali was fuming. The MILF had been generous in its support of Jemaah Islamiyah; in particular, its provision of training facilities had filled a critical void when the Afghanistan option had not been feasible. Now, given its reverses at the hands of the Filipino government – and a government dominated by Catholics at that – Hambali wanted revenge.

What he had in mind was taking a page out of the al-Qaeda playbook. A quantum jump from the amateurish devices in Medan, Hambali wanted to set off a massive car bomb in front of a Philippine embassy. Of all the Philippine embassies in the region, he settled on Manila's diplomatic outpost in Jakarta.

The Indonesian capital was chosen for good reason. First, Jemaah Islamiyah had a large and growing network across Java, including Jakarta. Second, for their jihadist efforts in Ambon, this network had already identified ready sources for precursor chemicals. Third, since the beginning of 1999, there had been a string of bombings in Jakarta – and the track record of the authorities in resolving these cases had been abysmal.[134] Unresolved, too, was the trio of bombs Jemaah Islamiyah had just tried to set off in Medan.

Emboldened by all this, Hambali was confident of success. When he told as much to Jemaah Islamiyah colleagues at the Rabitatul Mujahidin tryst, they listened in quiet approval. One later joked that the Indonesian authorities would instinctively accuse Filipino separatists, not domestic extremists.

Just as had been the case during the Medan bombing, Hambali would be turf raiding outside of his Mantiqi 1. This was partly a reflection of Hambali's proactive, aggressive interpretation of jihad, which ignored mantiqi boundaries in order to take the war to the infidels. But this was also a pragmatic reflection of finances. Of all Jemaah Islamiyah's area commands, Mantiqi 1 alone was able to keep its war chest full. In addition, Hambali largely controlled the spigot to Middle East cash through his al-Qaeda nexus. The markaz, he found, would not veto any operation if a mantiqi could source its own funds – and Mantiqi 1 readily had US$4,000 on hand for such a contingency.

Forging ahead, Hambali had already short-listed members in the Indonesian capital that would carry out the bombing. Heading the list was Usman, the Jakarta resident who had conducted the reconnaissance of the U.S. embassy the previous year. He would be assisted by Yasir, who had also participated in the embassy surveillance, and Yasir's younger brother, 33-year-old Abdul Jabar.

To provide logistical support for the Jakarta cell, Hambali turned to the group of Jemaah Islamiyah operatives living in East Java's Lamongan district. This included the pair of Amrozi, a 37-year-old high school dropout and motor-

---

[134] In January 1999, a business dispute led to the bombing of the Ramayana department store in Central Jakarta. The following month, a stick of dynamite went off at the Kelapa Gading mall in North Jakarta; this case remained unsolved. In April 1999, a small bomb went off at Plaza Hayam Wuruk. Four days later, a bomb was detonated on the ground floor of the al-Istiqlal mosque. A shadowy criminal gang masquerading as Muslim hardliners was later linked to both of the April 1999 blasts. And in June 2000, a bomb exploded in a ground floor bathroom at the Attorney General's office compound; this was believed to be connected to supporters of former President Suharto, who was facing corruption charges at the time.

cycle mechanic, and his slightly more cerebral younger brother, 30-year-old Ali Imron, a long-time Malaysian resident and Luqmanul Haqiem graduate. (The older brother of both, the intense Mukhlas, was a Luqmanul Haqiem teacher and Johor wakalah leader who at the time was in Afghanistan for meetings with al-Qaeda's upper echelon.)

Rounding out the conspirators would be two of Jemaah Islamiyah's top three bomb makers. The first was Dul Matin, a 35-year-old of mixed Arab parentage from Central Java who had attended a special MAK bomb circuitry course in Peshawar.[135] In 1999, Matin had gone to Mataram on the island of Lombok to work as a computer data processor. There he was remembered by co-workers for his uncompromising attitude; he reportedly insisted that taped religious sermons be played in lieu of the office radio, and browbeat female colleagues into wearing Islamic headscarves.

In January 2000, Matin had been in Mataram when the city unexpectedly erupted into an orgy of communal violence. After thousands of Islamic activists had gathered for a rally to show solidarity with their brothers in Ambon, they spilled onto the streets. By the time the authorities regained control two days later, casualties – primarily ethnic Chinese shop-owners – included 6 dead and 160 wounded. In addition, a dozen churches were razed. Dul Matin, reportedly, was among those running amok.

The second bomb maker was Fathur al-Ghozi, the Jemaah Islamiyah member most closely associated with the Philippines; revenge for the destruction of Camp Abu Bakar, therefore, would be deeply personal for him.

This group would follow a simple script. As taught by al-Qaeda, the car bombers would buy a vehicle – not rent one – far from the site of the intended bombing. All registration numbers would be filed off the chassis and engine. The bomb itself would be comprised of a simple recipe: three parts potassium chlorate for one part sulfur and one part aluminum powder. These components would be packed into six or seven containers and hidden beneath the seats in the back of the vehicle. Around these, jugs of kerosene would be placed to enhance the fireball effect.

All it took was a couple of cell phone calls from Hambali in early July to set the scheme into motion. The first went to Amrozi, who was told to purchase

---

[135] Nasir Abas interview.

the vehicle – preferably a van – for no more than 10 million rupiah. The second went to a MILF member named Solahudin hiding out in Cotabato, Mindanao. Solahudin, in turn, was told to contact al-Ghozi, a close acquaintance since the time both attended Afghan training. The instructions for al-Ghozi were simple: go to Jakarta, meet up with Usman, and monitor construction of a car bomb for use against the Philippine embassy.

That same day, Solahudin tracked down al-Ghozi in Cotabato and dutifully passed on the message. Using what little cash he had on hand, the latter immediately made his way to General Santos City, then boarded a ship bound for North Sulawesi. This province had become an underground highway of sorts for Jemaah Islamiyah members seeking to illegally transit to and from Mindanao; al-Ghozi himself had already entered the Philippines from the northern tip of Sulawesi on three occasions. Landing at Manado, he took another ship to the Jakarta waterfront, then made his way to an address provided by Hambali.

Arriving at that address – the same cramped residence in a lower-class East Jakarta district where Usman had lived since he was born – al-Ghozi introduced himself. Usman had already received his own call from Hambali and was expecting his colleague from the Philippines. Introductions were also made with Abdul Jabar, who showed up two days later.

As their first order of business, the three departed the following morning to rent a safe house to stage their operation. Finding a small but suitable residence with a garage in the nearby Duren Sawit sub-district, they paid the landlord 4.5 million rupiah in cash for the year and got a stern warning not to bring narcotics to the premises. With a tinge of irony, the three offered assurances they would not bring any illegal substances into the house.

Staging from there, al-Ghozi and Abdul Jabar set out to find their target. It did not take them long to locate the Philippine embassy in Jakarta's posh Menteng neighborhood next to the U.S. ambassador's residence. Sitting in a bus shelter across the street, they began to scrutinize the comings and goings from that address.

Striking up a conversation during their surveillance, Abdul Jabar asked why al-Ghozi had been chosen to help. "Do you know about Camp Abu Bakar?" asked the visitor from Mindanao.

Abdul Jabar admitted he had seen some television coverage of the Philippine army offensive. "It's totally gone," explained al-Ghozi. "We are getting our revenge for that."

As the pair continued their observations for the next few afternoons, they made a critical discovery. Each day between noon and 1230 hours, a black Mercedes would exit the embassy and drive a block west to a luxury residence situated next to the Bulgarian embassy. It would then pause momentarily as a security guard opened a heavy sliding gate at the foot the driveway. Judging from the suffix on the vehicle's diplomatic plate, this belonged to the Filipino ambassador; he apparently went home every day for lunch.

Al-Ghozi made another crucial observation. In the vicinity of the Philippine ambassador's residence, cars regularly parked on the sidewalk. While this was a bane for pedestrians, it was a boon for the terrorists. If they could put a car bomb next to the residence's driveway, he reasoned, this would be the optimal location to assassinate the embassy's highest official when he arrived for lunch.

Meanwhile in East Java, Amrozi had been busy procuring the vehicle to be used for carrying the bomb. As he ran his own motorcycle repair shop, this was not a particularly difficult task. In short order, he found a red Suzuki van in the price range stipulated by Hambali. Bringing it back to his repair shop – named Jilbab Motor Plus, after the headscarf used by Muslim women – he diligently filed off the serial numbers.

He soon received a second phone call. This time it was Dul Matin, who told Amrozi to buy the chemicals to be used in the bomb. Specifically, he wanted 200 kilos of potassium chlorate, 25 kilos of sulfur, and another 25 kilos of aluminum powder.

Amrozi was not the smartest member on the Jemaah Islamiyah roster, but he was arguably the most resourceful. Ever since Jemaah Islamiyah had started sending a trickle of jihadists to Ambon earlier that year, he had taken it upon himself to stockpile precursors for use in the Malukus. These he purchased at Tidar Kimia, a chemical supplier in Surabaya. As most of the components he sought had benign uses – potassium chlorate is a fertilizer, for example – he raised no eyebrows during his purchases. All were stored in an empty house he owned next to his own in Lamongan district. And as luck would have it, he already had on hand the quantities Dul Matin requested.

With the bomb ingredients and vehicle sitting in East Java, Yasir – Abdul Jabar's older brother – was brought into the picture. Now living in Cirebon in West Java, he was instructed by Usman to take a bus to Lamongan and bring back the Suzuki van with the chemicals inside.

Arriving in Lamongan one week before month's end, Yasir made his way to the al-Islam pesantren compound. Located in the tranquil hamlet of Tenggulun, 80 kilometers west of Surabaya, al-Islam had earned, like Ngruki, the reputation for pushing a hard-line curriculum. There was in fact significant synergy between the two, with many Ngruki alumni taking up positions at al-Islam.

Entering the boarding school during the pre-dawn hours, Yasir chanced upon Ali Imron. While working on the al-Islam staff, Ali was known as an inspiring orator. He was also prone to seething outbursts about the alleged threat from the United States and Jews.[136] Asked if his brother Amrozi had purchased the vehicle as instructed, Ali said it was parked 50 meters behind the pesantren.

Not wasting time, Yasir met up with Amrozi, inspected the vehicle, and declared that he would depart for Jakarta that night. He would go by way of Pemalang district, Central Java, in order to stop by the house of Dul Matin.

Although Yasir had the deadly serious mission of delivering a car bomb, the journey from Lamongan took on the air of a festive vacation. Ali Imron had elected to tag along for the ride, as had his brother Amrozi. Since they were passing through West Java, a female teacher at the boarding school named Infanah (who was also Ali Imron's niece) requested if she, too, could hitch a ride to Bandung. And since she did not know her way around Bandung, another member of al-Islam named Dadan was strap-hanging. Finally, a Jemaah Islamiyah member named Mubarok, who taught Arabic grammar at al-Islam, rounded out the group. Since there was not room for all six plus the bomb components in the Suzuki, Amrozi made available his own sedan to take three passengers and half the explosives.

Making their way to Central Java without incident, the two vehicles pulled into Dul Matin's house. There they found the skilled bomb maker along with another Jemaah Islamiyah member named Sarjiyo. A longtime friend of Ali Imron, Sarjiyo had trained in Afghanistan during the same timeframe; he had also spent two years in Mindanao.

It was under Dul Matin's supervision that the bomb began to take shape. Taking out the sacks of precursor chemicals, Sarjiyo mixed them by hand – nine kilos of potassium chlorate for every three kilos of sulfur and three kilos of aluminum powder. Combined in this fashion, the portions were loaded into plastic

---

[136] "The Hunt for the Terror Mastermind," *Tempo*, 25 November 2002, p. 16.

Darul Islam's original leader,
Sekarmadji Maridjan Kartosuwirjo.

Founders of the al-Mukmin pesantren in
Ngruki: Abdullah Sungkar (above) and
Abu Bakar Ba'asyir (left).

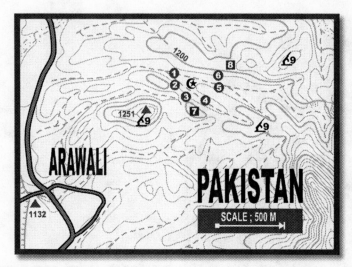

Abdul Rassul Sayyaf's Camp Sadda, located near the Pakistani cantonment at Arawali. Afghan members of Sayyaf's *Ittihad-e Islami*, who constituted the bulk of the students, trained at a string of faculties that specialized in communications (1), logistics (2), infantry tactics (3), engineering (4), artillery techniques (5), and cavalry/anti-tank courses (6). Arab students studied in a separate compound (7), as did Filipino students (8). Indonesian, Malaysian, and Thai trainees attended classes held in the mosque. Three anti-aircraft artillery emplacements (9) were on hilltops around the camp.

Two of the longest-serving Indonesian instructors at Camp Sadda: Zulkarnaen (left) and Ustad Syawal (right).

The remains of Philippine Ambassador Leonides Caday's Mercedes in front of his residence, 1 August 2000. (Courtesy *Kompas*)

Aftermath of the Atrium bombing,
1 August 2001. The injured Malaysian
terrorist Taufik Abdul Hakim, alias Dani,
would later lose his right leg.
(Courtesy *Tempo*)

Undated photo of Parlindungan Siregar,
the former Indonesian student who
brokered the visit of the al-Qaeda cell
from Spain to Poso.
(Courtesy Jason Tedjasukmana)

Members of the
al-Qaeda cell from
Spain visiting Poso,
July 2001. On the left
is Luis Jose Gallant
Gonzales, alias Yusuf
Galan.

Abdul Rahim Ayub, head of Jemaah
Islamiyah's Mantiqi 4 in Australia.

Undated photo of
Abu Bakar Ba'asyir and Ayub.

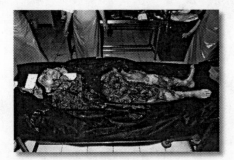

The body of Paddy's suicide bomber Fer
(alias Iqbal), October 2002. Aside from
his name, Fer remains an enigma: no
family member, colleague, or neighbor
ever stepped forward to provide more
information on his identity.

The most publicized photograph of Hambali (top). A computer altered version with goatee and minus glasses was circulated among regional security authorities in 2002 (left). In early 2003, Malaysian media sources published a photo purporting to show a clean-shaved Hambali (right).

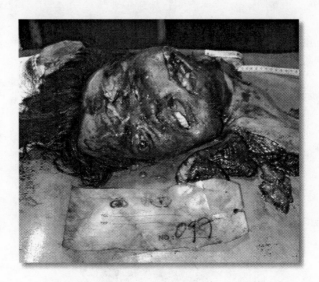

Severed head (above) recovered from the fifth floor of the J.W. Marriott hotel, August 2003. After limited reconstruction (below), family members and Jemaah Islamiyah colleagues linked it to Asmar Latin Sani (inset). DNA tests confirmed the identity.

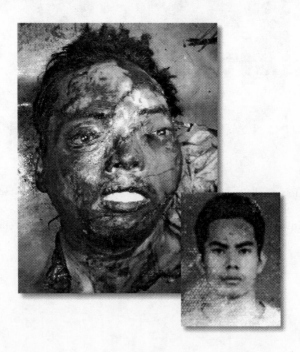

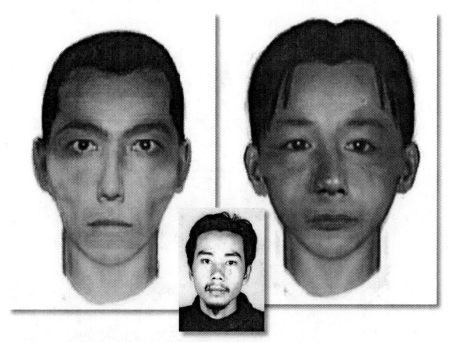

Police sketches of the two persons – later identified as Rois and suicide bomber Heri Gulon – who purchased the box truck used in the Australian embassy bombing. The sketch on the right bears a resemblance to Gulon (inset).

Masterminds of the Marriott and Australian embassy bombings: Azhari Husin (left) and Noordin M. Top (right)

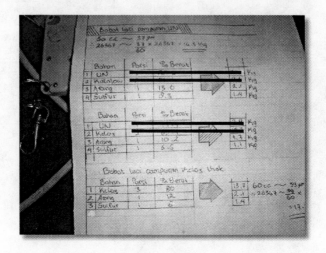

Azhari Husin's lecture notes on bomb construction, found in Cicurug, October 2004.

One of the Tupperware bombs discovered in Cicurug, October 2004.

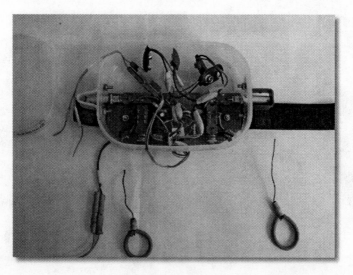

containers, each with a hole in the top for the insertion of a detonator. Dul Matin also loaded a briefcase into the vehicle; inside was a remote-detonation device he had jerry-rigged.

With Dul Matin and Sarjiyo joining for the remainder of the journey, the eight continued to Jakarta. Getting into the city at daybreak, they paused at a mosque on the eastern outskirts of the capital. Their road trip over, all but Yasir headed for the nearby bus station. Alone, Yasir continued in the Suzuki to the safe house in Duren Sawit. There he turned it over to Usman, al-Ghozi, and his brother for them to put the final touches on the bomb.

By that time, there was not much more that had to be done. Taking the plastic containers inside the house, blasting caps connected to detonation cord were inserted into the top of each. These, in turn, were connected to the remote detonation device rigged by Dul Matin. A second-hand walkie-talkie, also provided by Dul Matin, would set it off from a distance of up to 500 meters.[137]

Two days before the end of July, the three – Usman, al-Ghozi, and Abdul Jabar – piled into the Suzuki to do a reconnaissance of the ambassador's residence. Slowing down in front of their target, al-Ghozi noticed a large tree to the immediate right of the driveway entrance, and a public telephone to the right of that. He told the other two that the van should be parked between both.

In their own minds, they had set 1 August as the day to execute their deed. On the eve of that date, al-Ghozi had beckoned Abdul Jabar to assist in loading the bomb into the van. As a final touch, four plastic jugs of kerosene were placed around the ensemble. In addition, the license plates from East Java were changed with ones stolen from Cirebon. With an air of bravado, al-Ghozi took to lecturing his colleague. "You have never seen a real bomb go off," he said. "God willing, you will soon see one with your own eyes."

The next morning, al-Ghozi and Abdul Jabar awoke at the safe house. At 1000, Usman arrived and gave the bomb a final inspection. Usman then got into the van, while Abdul Jabar and al-Ghozi got aboard a motorcycle. Both vehicles peeled out of Duren Sawit.

---

[137] This was the first time that Jemaah Islamiyah would be experimenting with a remote-detonated bomb, but it was not the first time that such a device had been set off in Indonesia. In January 1999, a business dispute had led to a bomb being set off in the Ramayana department store on Jalan Sabang in Central Jakarta. The person who designed the device was a former officer in the navy's elite combat swimmer unit; he had rigged a pager to activate a blasting cap connected to dynamite.

Arriving in Menteng, the trio split. Abdul Jabar went to the Sunda Kelapa mosque and dropped off al-Ghozi, then headed to the nearby Keris Gallery shopping center and idled. Usman, meantime, drove straight to the Philippine ambassador's residence and parked the van, as planned, immediately to the right of the driveway. He then walked around the block to Keris Gallery and rendezvoused with Abdul Jabar.

Heading to Sunda Kelapa, the three briefly rejoined. After wishing his colleagues good luck, Usman alone departed aboard the motorcycle. Al-Ghozi and Abdul Jabar then walked the short distance to the bus stop in front of the Philippine embassy. The plan called for them to wait for the ambassador to depart, at which point Abdul Jabar would walk west and give the signal for al-Ghozi to activate the walkie-talkie.

Reality did not exactly follow this script. At 1230 hours, the Mercedes pulled out of the embassy. But due to light traffic, the chauffeur headed down the street faster than had been calculated. Unable to wait for Abdul Jabar to get into position, al-Ghozi raced down the sidewalk in order to get within 500 meters. Waiting until it appeared the Mercedes had slowed to pull into the driveway, he keyed the walkie-talkie. He instinctively turned away as the scene was engulfed in a fireball, followed a split second later by a deafening roar and concussion blast. Looking at his handiwork, al-Ghozi could only see a cloud of smoke and falling leaves.

⌘

Al-Ghozi had timed the detonation perfectly. As the targeted Mercedes was exactly abreast of the red Suzuki, the van disintegrated. The blast slammed into the side of the limousine, crushing its right flank and blowing its windows through the interior. Ambassador Leonides Caday, who habitually sat in the left rear seat, suffered four broken bones and was riddled with glass lacerations.

Others had it far worse. The 25-year-old security guard who was opening the sliding gate was dismembered. A female pedestrian was also instantly killed. The ambassador's driver barely clung to life with serious internal injuries. Nineteen others received shrapnel wounds. Buildings to either side and the front all lost their windows. Miraculous considering that the road was usually congested that time of day, just two other vehicles were damaged. One, a Daihatsu jeep, ran off the road and hit a tree. The second, a taxi, suffered a cracked window.

⤙❦⤚

Al-Ghozi and Abdul Jabar did not wait around to assess the carnage. Reversing direction, they got aboard a bus and took it a kilometer east, then switched to a *bajaj* – a motorized trishaw – for the rest of the way to East Jakarta.

Al-Ghozi soon left the city, taking a bus to his hometown of Madiun. Completely detached from the events he had just precipitated in Jakarta, he had a warm reunion with his parents and told them of his intent to get married in Malaysia. Keeping his word, he departed for Kuala Lumpur and soon had a wife in tow. He also used the opportunity to track down Hambali and present a detailed report on the bombing. Hambali's sole comment: "Excellent."

The Mantiqi 1 chief had reason for cheer. First, although the car bomb had failed in killing the Philippine ambassador, on a symbolic level the strike against Manila had been profound. Second, Jemaah Islamiyah had proven its ability to conduct a major terrorist operation in record time. Whereas al-Qaeda had taken years to plan and execute its car bombings – albeit on a larger scale – this one had been conceived and conducted in a little over a month.

Finally, Jemaah Islamiyah appeared to have gotten off scot-free. Some observers intuitively connected the blast with the offensive against Camp Abu Bakar, but they were clueless as to whether Moro separatists or Indonesian sympathizers were to blame. Others posited that the act might have been due to a personal grievance against the ambassador. Encouraged by all this, Jemaah Islamiyah began forging plans to take its struggle to the next level.

CHAPTER TEN

THE DOMINO THEORY

If there was any backslapping among the members of Jemaah Islamiyah after the bombing, it did not last. To the contrary, ever since the second quarter of 2000 there was a growing feeling of frustration among the group's leadership. The reason for this was due to events in Ambon and Poso. There, despite the best efforts by extremists from outside those regions, their Indonesian jihad was going nowhere. Indeed, the government by mid-year was showing progress in separating the warring factions in both the Malukus and Central Sulawesi.

Once again, Mantiqi 1 was in the forefront with a ready response. By mid-year, it had decided to continue with the campaign against churches that had started in Medan during May. Though that one-day blitz against three targets had come up short – only one bomb had detonated, and there were no fatalities – Mantiqi 1 was still intent on creating greater communal friction in that city, which in turn it hoped would start a domino effect and topple Indonesia's secular government. How it thought attacks against a small religious minority would cause that country's massive Muslim majority to rise up was not clear.

To head the renewed campaign, Hambali in June 2000 elevated his Malaysian lieutenant, Yazid Sufaat, to replace Imam Samudra. Two months later, Sufaat showed results. At 0600 hours on Sunday, 20 August, a two-kilogram bomb exploded outside a Protestant church on Jalan Bunga Kenanga. There were no casualties. Later that same morning, a second bomb went off in front of the house of Reverend J. Sitorus. Though the minister was unharmed, his son suffered ear injuries.

One month later came another pair of attacks. On 15 September, a bomb was found outside a Protestant church on Jalan Sudirman; the police bomb squad was able to remove it before detonation. Two days after that, assailants shot and wounded the chauffeur of the reverend from the church bombed the previous month.

This time, however, there was an arrest. On 17 September, the police detained 34-year-old Alawuddin Sitorus (alias Dani Sitorus, alias Abu Yasar) on suspicion of involvement in the Jalan Sudirman incident and the May attacks. Under interrogation, Alawuddin named three other members of his group.[138] He also mentioned the names Hambali and Imam Samudra – the first time either was publicly linked to terrorist acts – as the masterminds behind the bombings.[139]

Though one of their colleagues was in detention, the rest of Sufaat's cell barely took pause. On Sunday, 29 October, J.K. Surbakti, a minister with the Batak Karo Protestant church, was shot by two assailants. Though seriously wounded, he survived.

Two weeks later, on Sunday, 12 November, the cell struck again. This time, a time bomb encrusted with nails was placed in a plastic bag outside an auditorium where the Indonesian Communion of Churches was celebrating its fiftieth anniversary. Though all of the bombs thus far had been little more than glorified firecrackers – primarily breaking windows and eardrums but doing little other material damage – this time one of the nails found its mark, embedding in the skull of a passing 22-year-old woman. She died instantly.

Ironically, Jemaah Islamiyah's campaign was still not having its desired effect. Not only was the Medan populace staying cool in the face of such provocations, but few were making the connection to religious extremists or their ultimate cause. Following the fatal November blast, for example, a National Police spokesman pinned blame on Acehnese separatists. His boss, National Police Chief S. Bimantoro, claimed the attacks were likely tied to an economic or business dispute. And National Assembly speaker Amien Rais fingered "po-

---

[138] Under interrogation, Awaluddin Sitorus named three members of his cell: Indrawarman alias Toni Togar, Jabir, and Sueb. Of these three, Indrawarman, a Ngruki graduate and Sadda alum, was later apprehended after robbing a pair of banks in 2003. In 2003, the police stated that the Medan church bombings were the work of Awaluddin, Indrawarman, Nasrullah (alias Edi, alias Heru), Tono (alias Ramli, alias Regar), Ramli (alias Gugun, alias Agus), and additional unnamed accomplices. In July 2004, Awaluddin was released due to lack of evidence.

[139] A copy of "Polisi Tangkap Tersangka Pembunuh Tgk Nashiruddin," 29 September 2000, is posted on http://acehwatch.s5.com/beritautama/09/29b.htm.

litical thugs," a not unreasonable supposition given that some earlier bombings – most notably the 13 September blast at the Jakarta Stock Exchange building – were believed to be efforts to sow chaos during the trial of former President Suharto.[140]

⁓❧⁓

In October, while the Medan bombing campaign was still unfolding, Hambali convened a closed-door meeting of his top deputies. Their venue was the Kuala Lumpur office of MNZ Associates Management Services, an auditing firm owned by the Mantiqi 1 secretary, 32-year-old Malaysian accountant Zulkifli Marzuki (alias Ibrahim). Among the others in attendance were Faiz bin Abu Bakar Bafana, Mukhlas, Imam Samudra, Sufaat, Azhari, and Candra Nasrullah.[141]

For reasons not readily apparent, this cabal saw events in Medan as a winning formula. Building on the same theme, they now wanted to ratchet up the tempo by conducting simultaneous church attacks in up to ten cities spanning the Indonesian archipelago. For greater symbolic value, these attacks would be timed to coincide with Christmas Eve, 2000.

Such a major undertaking required detailed coordination and robust funding. Both of these topics were discussed during the MNZ tryst. As coordinators, Bafana, Azhari, and Imam Samudra would all participate in attacks on Batam island, Yazid would oversee Medan, and Hambali himself would oversee Java.

For funding, the group knew their Christmas blitz would not come cheap. Between transportation, safe houses, precursors, and inducements for accomplices, they estimated the price tag might reach as much as US$50,000. But even this amount was judged feasible, thanks in large part to the fact that a Malaysian Jemaah Islamiyah member named Masran bin Arshad had just couriered more than half that sum as part of an al-Qaeda donation brought back from Pakistan. And in a demonstration of his commitment to the cause, Sufaat of-

---

[140] "Detonator, Timer Found at Medan Bomb Blast Site," *Jakarta Post*, 14 November 2000; "Kasus Bom di Medan Persaingan Bisnis," *Media Indonesia*, 15 November 2000. In June 2000, a bomb exploded in a bathroom in the attorney general's compound in Jakarta; a suspect later said that one of former President Suharto's sons paid her to plant the explosive.

[141] Bafana, Surat Pernyataan (Lanjutan), pp. 4, 10. Nasrullah was a 30-year-old Indonesian member of Jemaah Islamiyah who worked in Sufaat's laboratory.

fered up US$10,000 of his own money.[142] For the rest, Mantiqi 1 normally had little trouble coming up with cash by soliciting its members for donations.

These key decisions made, the conspirators recessed. At that point, the professorial Azhari, who was rated as Jemaah Islamiyah's most skilled demolitions expert, went into action. In a basement apartment adjacent to the nearby International Islamic School, he conducted a bomb-making primer for Hambali, Sufaat, Bafana, and three other colleagues.[143] The plan was for them to pass on this knowledge to local cells when making bombs in each of the targeted cities.[144]

But before shifting its focus to Indonesia, Mantiqi 1 had one more event in Malaysia. During early November, Ibrahim rented a villa at a resort in Perak for the third convening of the Rabitatul Mujahidin forum. Virtually everybody from the first two gatherings was back and, again like the first two occasions, they talked up cooperation over a weekend.[145]

But after three tries, even the most enthusiastic proponent of jihad had to admit that Rabitatul Mujahidin was producing few tangible gains. And with Mantiqi 1 looking to conserve its funds ahead of the planned Christmas Eve operation, there was little appetite to sponsor a fourth meeting. After just a year, Rabitatul Mujahidin was no more.

By mid-November, Hambali and a small team of his closest Mantiqi 1 confidants left for Solo. This was actually Hambali's second trip to that city in three months. His earlier visit had come on the heels of a so-called Mujahideen Congress in Jogjakarta during early August.[146] That congress had given birth to the

---

[142] BIN document provided by a regional counterpart organization, "Pendedahan Yazid Sufaat Perkaitan Projek Keganasan di Indonesia dan Singapura."

[143] Bafana, Surat Pernyataan (Lanjutan), p. 9.

[144] During this same time frame, al-Ghozi also conducted a bomb-making session in Malaysia. Singapore Government White Paper, p. 37.

[145] Attending this session were two representatives from the Free Aceh Movement (Gerakan Aceh Merdeka, or GAM). During this tryst, Jemaah Islamiyah extended an invitation for GAM to send select members for a one-month paramilitary primer at joint Jemaah Islamiyah-MILF facilities in Mindanao. Taking up the one-time offer, forty GAM guerrillas made their way to the course in late 2000. Interview with Al Chaidar, 25 July 2005.

[146] The Jogjakarta congress concluded on 7 August 2000. This date was intentionally chosen because the Islamic State of Indonesia had been proclaimed by Kartosuwirjo on 7 August 1949.

Indonesian Mujahideen Council (*Majelis Mujahidin Indonesia*, or MMI), an overt umbrella organization intended as a discussion forum for the harder-line Islamic groups that were mushrooming across the country. Because Abu Bakar Ba'asyir had accepted the position of MMI's amir – in addition to his leadership of Jemaah Islamiyah – he had convened a one-hour informal markaz gathering in Solo shortly thereafter to discuss his decision with Jemaah Islamiyah's upper echelon.

This time, Hambali's trip to Solo was for the purpose of furthering the Christmas Eve operation. In line with Jemaah Islamiyah protocol, Mantiqi 1 needed formal approval before any attack could take place. But as was the case during the strike against the Philippine ambassador, Hambali expected the markaz would offer pro forma consent to any operation his mantiqi could fund from its own coffers.

He was not disappointed. Entering a hotel room near the Ngruki complex, he huddled with Bafana, Ibrahim, and Abu Bakar Ba'asyir. After he and Bafana reviewed their plans for Christmas Eve – and Ba'asyir was reportedly dismissive of the potential repercussions – he allegedly left with his needed authorization.

Later that same afternoon, Hambali and Ibrahim made their way to Jakarta. There they met with a select group of Jemaah Islamiyah members – including Philippine embassy veterans Usman and Abdul Jabar – at the same Duren Sawit safe house rented in July. Initially, Hambali was coy, highlighting alleged atrocities suffered by Muslims in Ambon and talking up the need to exact revenge.

Slowly, he shifted the topic of conversation. Revenge, said Hambali, would be best accomplished by killing priests. When someone in the group suggested that they assassinate clergy with firearms, Hambali disagreed. Rifles were too risky, he offered; explosives were a safer bet. He further suggested that it would be best to enter a church and place a bomb under the pulpit; if it was impossible to get inside, however, blowing it up near the church would suffice.

After planting these seeds, Hambali next went to the West Java provincial capital of Bandung. There, he held court in a budget hotel room with another select crowd of Jemaah Islamiyah members. Heading the group was Enjang Bastaman (alias Jabir), a Ngruki graduate and acquaintance of Hambali since the time they attended the same training cycle at Sadda.

Once again, Hambali started the conversation by denouncing Christian excesses against Muslims in the Malukus. He then steered them toward thinking of ways to strike back, and finally got around to suggesting that they attack churches.

At that point, he hit an unexpected snag. One of the group pointed out that Islamic law prohibited hitting a house of worship, Christian or otherwise. Scrambling for a Koranic verse to justify such an act, Hambali eventually argued that if such a locale was also used for non-religious activities, or to provoke others, it was fair game. Behind this fig leaf, plans proceeded.

Given that Mantiqi 1 envisioned the Christmas Eve attacks to take place in ten (later increased to eleven) cities, much depended on a multiplier effect. As overall coordinator for Java, for example, Hambali provided cash and selected a leader for each targeted province. Example: Jabir was charged with managing strikes in West Java. These leaders were then given considerable latitude in choosing subordinates to actually place the explosives in each targeted city. Considerable latitude, too, was given for what kind of bombs would be used: some eventually opted for rudimentary time bombs; others favored more sophisticated devices triggered by cell phones or pagers. The size of the bombs varied between 3 and 14 kilos.

The most ambitious attacks were set to take place in Jakarta. With Usman getting the nod as leader, he huddled in the safe house with several hand-picked confederates over the course of several days in early December. Among them were Abdul Jabar, Umar Arab (alias Umar Patek),[147] Husaib, bomb expert Dul Matin,[148] and a colleague from the bottled water business named Abdullah (alias Darwin, alias Asep).

Of this group, Abdul Jabar was dispatched on a buying mission. Scouring local markets, he purchased batteries, clocks, and some of the necessary precursor chemicals.[149] Taking these supplies back to the safe house, Dul Matin and Umar Arab took them upstairs and opened a production line for time bombs.

---

[147] As his name suggests, Umar Arab was of mixed Arab parentage. He was a close acquaintance of Dul Matin, who shared the same ethnic heritage; both, too, belonged to the same wakalah covering Central Java.

[148] Dul Matin was allegedly linked to a small explosion in October 2000 outside the Mataram office of the U.S. mining company PT Newmont. This is probably based on the fact that Matin had worked in Mataram until moving to Java shortly before the Christmas 2000 bombings. Security officers for Newmont, however, discount the idea that terrorists were behind the bomb and instead suggest that local authorities may have orchestrated the act in an attempt to milk the company for protection money.

[149] *Tempo*, 10 February 2003, p. 16.

Next, the bombers finalized their target list. In Jakarta, Usman's team had selected six churches – three Catholic, three Protestant – spread across the city. Of these, Abdul Jabar was to team up with Abdullah and hit an Anglican church in up-market Menteng, then another Protestant establishment in the southern suburbs near Halim airport. After surveying each building three times, the pair agreed that Abdul Jabar would drive past each locale, then wait as Abdullah walked back to the target and placed an explosive. The bombs would be set to go off around 2000 on 24 December, give or take an hour. With any luck, that time would coincide with a Christmas Eve mass.

With that minimal amount of planning, the Jakarta team readied themselves at sundown on 24 December. After breaking their fast in the safe house (it was the final days of Ramadhan), they divided in two: Abdul Jabar and Abdullah departed first in a motorcycle, the rest followed in a red Daihatsu Zebra van.

After taking circuitous routes from the safe house, at 1800 hours the two vehicles rendezvoused near a downtown bank. Abdullah walked over to the van, picked up a pair of green plastic bags, then returned to the idling motorcycle. Cradling the bags, he handed Abdul Jabar an envelope containing 300,000 rupiah; this sum was meant as a bonus to offset the risk of the operation and, on a more pragmatic level, presumably buy his silence if things went sour.

The motorcyclists then made their way to the Anglican church in Menteng. As planned, Abdul Jabar drove past and dropped off his accomplice. Abdullah, bomb in hand, walked back toward the target – and promptly got cold feet. Reluctant to get too close, he ditched one of the bombs under a fruit tree in the lot next to the church.

From there, the two went to the Oikumene church in the southern suburbs. Once again, Abdullah got a case of the nerves and ditched the bomb in the church parking lot. Without delay, Abdul Jabar then drove them back to the safe house.

A little over an hour later, at 2050, the first bomb rocked the Oikumene church. As was the case with the ones that had been going off in Medan since May, it was a relatively small device that packed a loud bang but a limited lethal radius. The front end of a single car was damaged in the resultant blast, but nobody was hurt.

Shortly thereafter, a string of loud explosions from the bombs planted by those in the Zebra van reverberated across the city. Alerted by the noises, a security guard outside the Anglican church patrolled the adjacent lot. Sighting the suspicious green bag, he alerted the police; the bomb squad subsequently defused the device before detonation.

The Jakarta bombers had not stayed around to view their handiwork. After rendezvousing at the safe house, they piled into the red Zebra van. With Usman at the wheel, they drove all night toward Dul Matin's house in Central Java. Arriving at 0600 on Christmas day, they caught word of the explosions on the morning's news.

Scenes like this were repeated in some thirty-eight locales in eleven cities across the country. A total of nineteen persons were killed and 120 wounded.[150] It could have been far worse: nearly half of the bombs in Sumatra were duds.

But it was in West Java where Murphy Law was in full effect. In Tasikmalaya, a three-man cell was supposed to target a local Catholic church. But because they had several Catholic acquaintances among the congregation, they opted to instead drive to nearby Ciamis district on the morning of 24 December. Assembling a pair of bombs in a beachside hotel, they made preparations to bomb an adjacent church – only to discover that there were no Christmas Eve services.

Making a frantic call to Jabir, the trio of bombers was told to instead target any "crowded place." To scout for options, two of the cell members took off in a Vespa, bomb in hand. Unfortunately for them, the jarring on the bumpy road set off the device. One of the bombers was killed instantly and the second, severely wounded, was captured by the police. The third bomber, hearing the explosion, threw the second device in a river and fled.[151]

---

[150] In Jakarta, eight bombs were placed at six locales, killing a total of six persons. In Bekasi, three bombs detonated by pagers were placed in the parking lot of a single church. In Bandung, a bomb went off during the afternoon of 24 December, killing four would-be bombers. In Sukabumi, two bombs were placed at two locations. In Ciamis, a bomb went off prematurely, killing one bomber. In Riau province (two locations in Pekanbaru and four locales in Pematang Siantur), six bombs killed seven persons. On Batam, four bombs were placed at four locations. In Medan, eleven bombs were targeted against eleven locations. In Mojokerto, four bombs were placed in four targets; one person was killed. And in Mataram, five bombs were placed at three targets; no casualties were reported.

[151] The third bomber, Holis, was ultimately captured in North Sulawesi in June 2004.

In Bandung, instead of more conventional time bombs, Jabir had ambitiously elected to outfit four devices with detonators triggered by GSM cell phones. Unfortunately for him, when he fitted his own phone in one of the devices, he forgot to change the SIM card; it went off in his face when somebody tried to call him. He and three members of the Bandung cell were killed. Two others – Iqbal, the head of the Bandung cell, and Aceng, the owner of the car repair shop where the explosion took place – fled the city but were eventually arrested on 16 January 2001 in Central Java.

⋘⋙

In all of its terrorist operations to date, Jemaah Islamiyah had never claimed responsibility. This had its advantages. After all, with the police making only glacial progress into their investigations of the Philippine embassy and Medan bombings, Jemaah Islamiyah saw no advantage in spoon feeding clues to the authorities and inviting a crackdown. This allowed them to conceive, plan, and execute operations in record time: the Philippine embassy attack took only about a month from start to finish, and the Christmas Eve strikes had a gestation period of a little more than two months. Al-Qaeda, by contrast, often took years to executive their plans.

On the other hand, the public was none the wiser to Jemaah Islamiyah's cause. This had been particularly frustrating for some of the more passionate members of the group, who welcomed the idea of drawing a spotlight to their ideals. Such was the case with Mas Selamat Kastari, head of the Singapore wakalah, who during the second half of 2000 actively lobbied for permission to strike at Singaporean government targets – and to claim credit for the attacks. His mantiqi boss, Hambali, had no problem with planning the strikes, but insisted that the wakalah claim responsibility in the name of a notional Singapore extremist organization in order to deflect true blame.[152]

During the Christmas Eve operation, Jemaah Islamiyah again chose the notional route. On Christmas day, fliers were left behind in Pekanbaru stating that

---

[152] Kastari was particularly incensed with the Singaporean government because he claimed their compulsory education program repressed Islamic culture and education. He suggested strikes against the ministries of education and Defense, but had not finalized any plans by the close of 2000.

the two bombs in that city were the work of an entity called the Badar Battalion of the Islamic Army (*Tentara Islam Batalyon Badar*, or TIBB).

This name held particular significance. The city of Badar, located between Mecca and Medina, was the site of the first major battle between Muslims and non-believers when the Prophet Mohammad and 300 of his followers had tried to lay siege to a caravan. The ambush failed and the caravan escaped – only to return with a thousand-man attack force. In their subsequent confrontation, the Prophet's men, though outnumbered, drove them from their defensive positions. Their victory was later attributed in part to divine intervention.

One day later, on 26 December, a message was e-mailed to several Indonesian media outlets. In it, the TIBB belatedly claimed credit for the three bombs that had detonated in Medan back on 28 May.[153] The TIBB further claimed that these bombs were preemptive strikes because a Christian army, acting on orders of the Vatican and in retaliation for what was taking place in Ambon, planned to launch an operation codenamed Richard I in Medan. (Richard I, better known as Richard the Lion-Hearted, was the great warrior king of England who led the Third Crusade in the twelfth century.) This alleged Christian army wanted to turn Medan into a second Ambon as of June. The e-mail, which warned of further attacks on churches, was signed by the TIBB commander, Abu Mutafajirat (Arabic for "Mr. Destroyer").

This e-mail was bizarre for any number of reasons. For one thing, it spoke of the 28 May bombs seven months after the fact but ignored all that had happened since. For another thing, even though Indonesian audiences were normally game for a good conspiracy, the charge of a Vatican plot sounded particularly sophomoric. And if the TIBB was claiming that it had gotten wind of an operation being dictated by the Vatican, they showed little understanding of Christianity by targeting two Protestant churches on 28 May for retribution.[154]

But while bizarre, the TIBB proclamations were a milestone for Jemaah Islamiyah. For the first time, it had made clear that religious extremists were responsible for at least some of the attacks, and that its motivation was tied to the perceived persecution of fellow Muslims in Ambon.

---

[153] The TIBB denied responsibility, however, for the bomb that went off the following day at Medan's Miramar restaurant.

[154] The contents of the TIBB e-mailed messages were also posted on the website www.tibb.cjb.net. According to Malaysian intelligence, TIBB was a name conjured in June 2000 by Sufaat's cell in Medan.

Trouble was, nobody believed it. Almost immediately, pundits cast suspicion on the Indonesian military. The most common media refrain: the simultaneous timing of the Christmas Eve bombings could only have been accomplished after meticulous planning, and the only organization with such a nationwide capability was the armed forces.[155] The military did this, argued the experts, in order to further embarrass the politically-besieged president. Though not for want of trying, Jemaah Islamiyah remained in the shadows.

❦

While all this had been unfolding in Indonesia, Hambali had not stayed in his homeland. Still infuriated with the Estrada government for its attack on Camp Abu Bakar, his Mantiqi 1 back in October had looked to strike at the Filipino authorities yet again. That month, al-Ghozi had returned to the Philippines with orders to contact the MILF and plan a joint operation. Doing as told, he had ventured to Marawi city and met up with a Sadda alum and MILF member named Muklis Yunos (alias Haji Onos, alias Saifullah Yunos). At 28 years-old, Yunos was in charge of the MILF's Special Operations Group, a unit that specialized in urban terrorist attacks. When al-Ghozi proposed a series of bombings to be funded by Jemaah Islamiyah, Yunos offered an enthusiastic response.

Much like the Christmas Eve campaign in Indonesia, Jemaah Islamiyah was prepared to offer only the barest amount of oversight. Besides providing inspiration, money, and minimal guidelines (the attacks were to be timed around New Year's Eve), it gave the MILF bombers complete latitude in conjuring and executing their plan.

For financial support, Mantiqi 1 treasurer Bafana during November began transferring increments of cash to a Philippine account opened by al-Ghozi. The latter then used this money to procure explosives in Cebu City.[156] After he and

---

[155] See, for example, "Year of Violence and Anarchy Ahead, Agency Warns Cabinet," *South China Morning Post*, 29 December 2000.

[156] Al-Ghozi had identified a legitimate shop in Cebu that would illegally sell him firearms and explosives. According to Hambali, if Jemaah Islamiyah military chief Zulkarnaen needed explosives in Indonesia, he would often order them through al-Ghozi's Cebu connection. Al-Ghozi would then charter a boat to smuggle the cargo from Mindanao to landing zones in Sulawesi. While not the safest method – given the heavy seas often encountered between the Philippines and Indonesia – this was considered secure because there was little patrolling by the Indonesian authorities in this region.

Yunos narrowed down their target list to five locales in Manila – the international airport, a shopping center across from the U.S. embassy, a bus terminal, a hotel, and a light rail transport (LRT) station – Yunos was charged with identifying MILF sympathizers that would place explosives.

To review the progress to date, Hambali and Bafana on 1 December flew from Kuala Lumpur to Manila. Met at the airport by al-Ghozi and Yunos, they were taken to a hotel in Quiapo, a district of the capital known for the large number of Muslim merchants in its bustling market. In addition to discussing the upcoming bombings, and handing over more cash, Hambali – recalling al-Qaeda's standing orders to attack the United States and its allies – requested a city map showing the locations of the U.S. and Israeli embassies. Before returning to Malaysia near week's end, Hambali personally cased the U.S. embassy, but later discounted it as a viable target because of its heavy defenses.[157]

On 30 December – Rizal Day, a Philippine national holiday that commemorates the execution of their national hero, Jose Rizal – Yunos and his accomplices mobilized. Shortly before noon, Yunos himself left behind a time bomb in the front car of an LRT elevated train. The subsequent blast at the Blumentritt LRT station left a dozen dead and 19 wounded. Three of the four remaining bombs detonated, killing another ten.

Much like the TIBB pronouncements after the Christmas Eve bombs, Jemaah Islamiyah chose to make a veiled admission of responsibility. A man calling himself "Freedom Fighter" – later identified as al-Ghozi – on 31 December called up a major Philippine newspaper and the Manila headquarters of the national police to claim credit. But though the Philippine authorities quickly assumed culpability by Moro separatists, they would remain ignorant of the Jemaah Islamiyah connection for more than a year.[158]

---

[157] Hambali later estimated that he turned over about US$4,000 for the December bombings in Manila.

[158] After looking more closely at the cell phone number used by Freedom Fighter, the Philippine National Police discovered that there were calls to and from Malaysia immediately before the bombings. One year later, it was learned that one of the calls was to a number used by Bafana. In 2002, nine persons were indicted for the bombings, including al-Ghozi, Bafana, Hambali, and six members of the MILF. Yunos was captured on 25 May 2003.

Though it had inflicted more fatalities against non-Muslims than during any of its previous operations, Jemaah Islamiyah was highly critical of its Christmas Eve blitz. On 26 December, Bafana and Ibrahim had ventured to the Kuala Lumpur international airport to meet Hambali. All three were somber: though details were sketchy, they knew there had been a premature explosion in Bandung and some of the bombers were dead.

On 2 January 2001, Hambali called all of his top lieutenants for a meeting at the MNZ office. Once more, they dwelled on the operation's shortcomings. By that time, they were also able to confirm the death of Jabir, which brought tears to the eyes of long-time friend Hambali.

Two weeks later, during a third meeting at Bafana's office in Selangor, their concern deepened. The media had just reported that Iqbal was captured, and Hambali knew that he would probably reveal that Hambali was a mastermind of the campaign.[159] Assuming that he would soon become a wanted man, Hambali panicked and made the snap decision to leave for safer climes in Pakistan. Turning to Mukhlas, the Johor wakalah commander who had overseen the bombings across Sumatra, he asked his colleague to be caretaker of Mantiqi 1.[160] He also told the gathering to consider a second round of church attacks in April, code-named Operation *Nanas* (Indonesian for "pineapple").

Hambali immediately returned to Sungai Manggis to inform his wife, Noralwizah. Their relationship was already strained, due in large part because she had been unable to conceive a child. They had sought fertility treatment to no avail, leading Hambali for a time to consider taking a second wife.

Now that he informed Noralwizah of their impending move, she was furious. Hambali had not confided to her about his involvement in the Christmas Eve bombings, but she had surmised as much given his recent travels and visible stress. But as angry as she was, she elected to join her husband in fleeing Southeast Asia.

Not wasting any time, Hambali visited his neighbor, Sarkom. The two had a lot in common: both were Indonesians from West Java, and both were mem-

---

[159] Another suspect, who had been captured on 2 December while carrying a bomb to Riau province, told police that he was paid by a person later identified as Imam Samudra.

[160] Besides being a member of Mantiqi 1, Mukhlas had served on Jemaah Islamiyah's shura council, a separate body which reported directly to the markaz. He was reportedly officially confirmed as Mantiqi 1 commander during a March 2001 meeting with Abu Bakar Ba'asyir in Solo.

bers of Jemaah Islamiyah (Sarkom was a member of the Selangkor wakalah). Leaving Sarkom with instructions to burn all documents left behind, Hambali and his wife said good-bye to Sungai Manggis.

Returning to Kuala Lumpur, Hambali spent a couple of days at Yazid Sufaat's condominium. Then, with US$5,000 in hand and a Malaysian travel document issued under his true name, he and Noralwizah crossed into southern Thailand.[161] The couple then took a flight from Phuket to Bangkok. From the Thai capital, Hambali sent an e-mail to Abu Haris in Karachi advising him of his imminent arrival. Like Hambali, Abu Haris was an Indonesian with permanent residency status in Malaysia; he spent time as a jihadist in Ambon before heading to Pakistan.

As planned, Hambali boarded a flight for South Asia. Stepping off the plane in Karachi, he and his wife were met by Abu Haris and hustled to the latter's residence. There they remained in seclusion for several weeks. He had good reason for caution: by the first week of February, his name had appeared in Indonesian newspapers, along with the fact that his wife was a Malaysian.[162] The Indonesian police had already taken their findings to the Malaysian police, only to be told that Kuala Lumpur would not yet issue an arrest warrant because Hambali was considered a religious figure deserving of protection.[163]

But realizing that his luck might not hold out, and that he might be subject to extradition from Pakistan, Hambali sought safer sanctuary. In early February, he and his wife crossed into Afghanistan and made their way to Kandahar. Though the setting was rustic, Hambali found himself among acquaintances. After all, he already knew most of the al-Qaeda upper echelon. And at month's end, with KSM providing introductions, he exchanged greetings with a lanky Yemeni surrounded by bodyguards.

Hambali had met Osama bin Laden.

---

[161] The Malaysian travel document, given to foreigners with permanent resident status, was virtually identical to a normal passport. However, it did not allow for visa-free travel anywhere in Southeast Asia except for Singapore. While using it, Hambali even needed a visa to travel to Indonesia.

[162] "Tiga Tersangka Peledakan Bom di Bandung Dicegah ke Luar Negeri," *Kompas*, 8 February 2001.

[163] "Dead End for Hambali," *Tempo*, 25 August 2003, p. 77.

CHAPTER ELEVEN

SCALES FROM THE EYES

Hambali's first meeting with Osama bin Laden proved somewhat anticlimactic. With almost no linguistic common ground, they shared little apart from the briefest of pleasantries. Four more incidental meetings took place in Kandahar over the next two weeks, including Hambali's attendance at a motivational speech in which bin Laden implored jihadists around the world to band together to defeat the United States. Delivered by bin Laden in Arabic, Hambali barely understood a word.

Language hurdles notwithstanding, the al-Qaeda leadership made early efforts to embrace the Southeast Asian fugitive. During the first days of March 2001, Hambali, along with other senior foreign jihadists residing in Afghanistan, was beckoned to Kabul. There, a giddy bin Laden announced that the Taliban government, ignoring world outrage, had decided to demolish the two massive Buddhas carved into the sandstone cliffs at Bamiyan. Construction of the colossal statues had started in the second century, and they still stood tall despite the ravages of Genghis Khan, centuries of intermittent warfare, and the harsh elements. For the Taliban, however, the Bamiyan Buddhas were un-Islamic graven images that needed to be destroyed.[164]

From Kabul, Hambali and his fellow jihadists were set to depart for Bamiyan to witness the event. At the eleventh hour, however, international conservationists begged the Taliban to construct a concrete wall in front of the cliff and spare the Buddhas. Frustrated by the ensuing delay, a dejected Hambali returned to Kandahar. He should have been more patient: almost as soon as he

---

[164] There was another reason for Taliban rage toward the Buddhas: the Bamiyan population was known to be sympathetic to the Northern Alliance, the main armed opposition to the Taliban. Destruction of Bamiyan's famed landmarks, therefore, was a form of revenge against the populace.

got back, he received word that the Taliban had rejected the compromise and, in a blaze of mortars, dynamite, tank fire, and rockets, had reduced the statues to sandstone and clay rubble.

Back in Kandahar, Hambali found a suitable house to rent with his wife. He subsequently dubbed his quarters "The Philippine House," intentionally selecting the name to conceal his own national origins; exactly who he was trying to confuse was not clear, as it soon became a bustling transit point for Indonesian and Malaysian students coming and going to al-Qaeda training camps.[165]

When not hosting these trainees, Hambali marked time at al-Qaeda's media committee house. The personnel assigned to that committee collected news from Arabic media outlets, especially al-Jazeera, then disseminated it in various languages to sympathizers around the world. They also produced propaganda videos, also for worldwide dissemination.

Very quickly, Hambali was tapped for a priority assignment. Picking up a theme from the previous year, al-Qaeda's senior military commander Mohammed Atef wanted to fast-track an anthrax program and asked Hambali if he had identified an expert that could establish and run a laboratory.

As it turned out, Hambali had the perfect candidate in mind. Yazid Sufaat, the Malaysian laboratory owner who had helped him brainstorm other candidates that could help al-Qaeda with a biological weapons program, had just arrived in Afghanistan to take a one-month terrorist primer at Camp al-Farouq near Khost.[166] As soon as Sufaat was finished, Hambali beckoned him to his Kandahar house, then, using his broken Arabic to the best of his ability, brokered an introduction to Atef.

Sufficiently impressed, Atef directed that the two meet with the al-Qaeda deputy commander, Ayman al-Zawahiri. Almost immediately, they were granted an audience with the Egyptian at the media committee house. Though it was the first time either had met al-Qaeda's deputy chief, it turned out they had

---

[165] "Gun Gun Rusman Gunawan," *Surat Tuntutan* (October 2004), p. 44.

[166] Select Jemaah Islamiyah members were being trained in a variety of advanced topics during this time frame. Azhari, for instance, had been given specialized instruction in the construction of car bombs and the use of mobile telephones as detonators; he later produced a 50-page manual and a CD-ROM for dissemination within Jemaah Islamiyah. During 2000, two other Malaysian operatives, Abdullah Daud and Wan Min bin Wan Mat, spent two months at a Taliban facility in Kabul learning surveillance techniques. A Singaporean member, meanwhile, was coached in forging passports.

common ground: after al-Qaeda's May 1996 expulsion from Sudan, al-Zawahiri had taken a four-month sabbatical in Malaysia on his way to Afghanistan.[167]

Al-Zawahiri wasted no time grilling Sufaat. Both were from the medical profession – al-Zawahiri the surgeon, Sufaat the medical technician – so the former was able to ask pointed questions about the Malaysian's schooling and lab experience. At no point did he talk about biological weapons or how al-Qaeda intended to use them.

Like Atef, al-Zawahiri concurred that Sufaat was the man to head their anthrax program. He immediately assigned a Yemeni and a Palestinian as understudies, then had Mohammad Atef allocate US$5,000 for Sufaat to purchase laboratory equipment.[168]

That May, Sufaat ventured to Karachi on the first of several purchasing trips over the ensuing quarter. After amassing what was described as a "roomful" of lab supplies, he sent word to KSM that he needed assistance transferring it to Kandahar. Two local al-Qaeda operatives soon arrived and helped load the crates into a truck belonging to a relief agency that regularly shuttled supplies to Afghanistan. While this cargo began the slow journey north from Karachi, Sufaat and his apprentices wasted no time returning to Afghanistan and taking over a room inside Kandahar's Omar Hospital. There, with a handful of microbiology journals and whatever rudimentary equipment was on hand, they began the tedious process of trying to isolate the anthrax strain.

Back in Southeast Asia, Jemaah Islamiyah had concluded that the Christmas Eve attacks had been a bust. Failing to incite greater communal friction, the group moved further away from being a regional jihadist organization and continued its transformation (which had actually started back in 1998) into a transnational terrorist organization. That did not mean it fully abandoned domestic targets in their respective nations. During the first quarter of 2001, for instance, Singaporean members of the organization conducted reconnaissance against the city-state's reservoirs, the causeway to Johor, and the ministry of defense.

---

[167] Al-Zawahiri and the al-Qaeda military chief, Mohammad Saleh, spent four months in Kuala Lumpur in 1996; curiously, there is no evidence that they met any members of Jemaah Islamiyah. Hambali, for one, convincingly denies meeting them during that period.

[168] Sufaat had actually proposed a budget of US$10,000, but al-Qaeda granted only about half that amount.

During the same period, other elements of the group developed a fixation with killing Indonesian priests. According to Mantiqi 1 treasurer Bafana, a series of meetings were conducted in Malaysia and Solo, during which time the assassination of priests was discussed by himself, Abu Bakar Ba'asyir, Mukhlas, Imam Samudra, and other top operatives. Specifically, plans were developed to attack a gathering of priests planned for Manado; they also broached the subject of killing then-Vice President Megawati Sukarnoputri. While the plotters assumed that Mantiqi 1 operatives would again spearhead these acts, Mukhlas, at least on this occasion, proved less aggressive than predecessor Hambali; he nixed these plans in July, stating that it would be more appropriate for an Indonesia-based mantiqi to play a lead role.

But more than emphasizing domestic targets, Jemaah Islamiyah was increasingly talking up attacks on Western interests. In early 2001, for example, members of Mantiqi 1 advanced plans to target U.S. warships docked in Singapore, possibly for a USS *Cole*-style attack. Others prepared a casing report on buses that ferried foreign students to one of the city-state's international schools; this report was passed back to Afghanistan, where two Arabs were designated as potential suicide operatives.

There were even early steps being taken for Jemaah Islamiyah to develop a cadre of indigenous suicide bombers. There is no overstating the cultural resistance that this effort was sure to face. Unlike other parts of the world where suicide was all too common, like among the Palestinians and Tamils, suicide was usually only seen in affairs of the heart in Southeast Asia – and very rarely then. And of those few previous suicides by Southeast Asian insurgents, they were committed on ideological grounds (communist guerrillas giving their lives during the Vietnam War) rather than theological ones.[169]

---

[169] There are numerous examples of combatants during the Vietnam conflicts –on all sides – sacrificing themselves in the heat of battle. However, there are extremely few documented examples of coldly, precisely-planned suicide missions. One of the exceptions: on 27 September 1950, a female Vietnamese agent, masquerading as an ailing passenger, carried a time bomb aboard a French naval vessel and stayed with the device until it detonated, sinking the ship. Nguyen The Bao, *Cong An Thu Do: Nhung Chang Duong Lich Su* [Capital Public Security: Historic Events] *1945-1954* (Hanoi: People's Public Security Publishing House, 1990), pp. 186-88. (The author is indebted to Merle Pribbenow for pointing out this incident.) It has been alleged that religious extremists conducted a suicide attack in Mindanao during October 1997, but the two operatives were from Egypt and Saudi Arabia rather than homegrown militants. In fact, the October 1997 incident appears to have been a more conventional guerrilla raid with assault rifles and grenades – not a deliberate suicide assault – against the civil relations officer attached to the 61st Infantry Division; he was targeted because his public affairs campaign vilified the MILF.

Jemaah Islamiyah, taking a page from al-Qaeda, was determined to change all that. According to Malaysian intelligence sources, during the first quarter of 2001, Yazid Sufaat, who had just arrived in Afghanistan for training, was asked to help identify four Indonesian commercial pilots who might be enticed into giving their lives on a mission.[170] And during the same time frame, Zaini Zakaria, the 34-year-old Malaysian who had received al-Qaeda training back in 1999, was contacted by KSM and urged to enroll in a pilot school. Hard at work on the planes operation at the time, KSM envisioned Zaini for potential follow-up kamikaze hijackings.

Despite this transformation, word did not reach all of Jemaah Islamiyah's rank and file. When a handful of operatives struck again in the third quarter of 2001, they fell back on the tired formula of attacking churches. Spearheading this round was the group's brooding, intense pit bull, Imam Samudra.

Samudra had already found ample opportunity to turn his outspoken militancy into deeds. As head of the original Jemaah Islamiyah cell dispatched to Medan, he had been pivotal in the church bombings that rocked that city since May 2000. He had also attempted to set off a large device in a Pekanbaru church during early December (the courier was arrested before detonation), then had coordinated several strikes against Batam houses of worship as part of the Christmas Eve 2000 campaign. Witnesses later claimed that he had person-ally conducted reconnaissance in at least one of the Batam churches.[171]

Samudra's turn as a terrorist, it seemed, took a heavy physical toll. Plump and balding, by mid-2001 he looked older than his 32 years. But appearances notwithstanding, he was game for another round of church bombings that July. Not playing favorites, he had his eye set on one Protestant and one Catholic congregation in the Indonesian capital.[172]

---

[170] Although a Southeast Asian intelligence service identified four Indonesian pilots by name, and further claimed that they had traveled to Karachi to meet al-Qaeda members, an investigation by the Indonesian authorities could find no pilots by those names or any other evidence to corroborate those allegations.

[171] "Police Unveil Bali Attack Suspect's Computer Files," *Taipei Times*, 8 July 2003.

[172] There is no evidence that the July 2001 church bombings, or the abortive 1 August Atrium bombing, were operations that underwent the formal Jemaah Islamiyah approval process. Rather, Imam Samudra appears to have used his own initiative to conceive, organize, and execute the operations. He also apparently used his own personal funds, reportedly turning over 10 million rupiah to Usman from donations given for the Ambon jihad and money he earned selling cloth in Malaysia.

To help carry out the attacks, Samudra turned to Usman, the same Jakarta-based operator who had been involved in the Philippine ambassador car bomb and the Christmas Eve blitz. Another Jakarta native, Agung al-Faisal (alias Solahudin, alias Dedi Maulana), was also brought into the operation.

A fourth conspirator, Taufik Abdul Hakim (alias Dani), added an international dimension to the affair. A Malaysian national and university graduate, Taufik had the right pedigree by marriage: his brother-in-law was 35-year-old engineer Zulkifli Hir, a leader of the Malaysian Mujahideen Group (*Kumpulan Mujahidin Malaysia*, or KMM), a shadowy militant ensemble that sought to overthrow the elected Malaysian government and replace it with an Islamic one.

Taufik had pronounced radical leanings of his own. In 1993, he had ventured to Afghanistan and trained for two years at a string of terrorist camps. In search of a jihad to implement his newfound skills, in June 2000 Taufik and eight other Malaysians opted for the Malukus. After being rebuffed in Halmahera (where the conflict was already winding down), they eventually found better prospects on Ambon. They remained there through the following April but, growing bored after a de facto stalemate largely segregated the two warring communities, he and a fellow jihadist headed toward Java and eventually made their way to the western end of the island.

From contacts made in Ambon, it was not hard for Taufik to seek out like-minded souls. The new province of Banten (previously part of West Java), in particular, proved especially fertile. Though the Islam generally practiced in Banten was tinged with the region's rich history of mysticism and local traditions – something that would make a Wahhabist cringe – a radical fringe had grown more aggressive of late. This fit well with Banten's martial culture; in the words of one senior intelligence official, the Bantenese are "Indonesia's Gurkha wannabes."[173]

Living up to this reputation was a fiery Islamic activist named Cecep Bustomi, who in 1998 had established a radical paramilitary organization known as Hizbullah in the district of Pandeglang. This group began staging raids against nightclubs, bars, and outdoor festivals (especially those that featured music and dancing) across the province; many of these establishments decided to close as a result, putting a damper on Banten's once substantial tourist industry.

---

[173] Interview with MB (State Intelligence Agency), 30 August 2005.

In August 2000, Hizbullah overstepped in a big way. While attempting to break up an outdoor cultural event near the city of Serang, its members confronted one party-goer and beat him to death. Unfortunately for them, the victim was a member of the army special forces group based in Serang.

Realizing he needed to conduct damage control, Bustomi ventured to the special forces encampment the following morning to offer an explanation. Apparently, his apology was not accepted; when he was returning to his residence, his vehicle was flanked by pairs of masked men on motorcycles. Volleys of automatic weapons fire were directed into the vehicle, killing Bustomi instantly. Hizbullah subsequently went into remission.

Though Hizbullah was no more, there was a second group of extremists mobilizing around Pandeglang. This group was led by Kang Jaja, an ambitious, independent-minded Darul Islam chieftain who headed Banten's youth militia wing. A strong proponent of jihad, in 1999 he had sent a small contingent of followers to train at Camp Hudaibiyah, then a steady stream of volunteers to fight in such battlefields as Ambon and Poso. Closer to home, by mid-2001 he had set up an Islamic commune, with an associated paramilitary camp, in Saketi sub-district, Pandeglang. It was here that Taufik stayed for a time, along with nine other Malaysian radicals who were on the run from authorities in their own country.

Taufik eventually gravitated toward Jakarta. There, he befriended Banten native Samudra, who was keeping a low profile in the capital in the wake of the Christmas Eve bombings. Enlisted into Samudra's latest plan, Taufik, along with Usman and Agung, moved on 22 July to simultaneously hit the Santa Anna Catholic church and an HKBP congregation during Sunday morning services. The bombings were a near-repeat of the Medan formula and, like in Medan, achieved the goal of inflicting Christian casualties: a combined total of 56 persons were injured, though none died.

In a city numbed by the frequency of such attacks, the blasts garnered little attention in the Jakarta press. Unfazed, Samudra wasted no time seeking his next target of opportunity. Reportedly, it resulted from a chance encounter. During an evening at the Atrium mall – a downscale shopping center in a crowded working-class district of Jakarta – a cohort caught sight of some well-dressed church-goers boarding a bus at the mall entrance. Discreet inquiries revealed that charismatic Christian services were held in an upper floor of the mall each Wednesday night.

Hearing of this, Samudra saw opportunity. Given that the church service finished at 2100 hours, and the worshippers normally filed into the bus fifteen minutes after that, he planned on detonating a bomb next to the vehicle at precisely 2115 hours. Participating in the strike would be nearly the same team – Agung, Taufik, and Usman were all back. They were joined by two others: Abdullah, the veteran of the Christmas Eve bombings, and a radical named Ibrahim, who was an acquaintance of Taufik.[174]

With explosives and a detonator obtained by Samudra, the cell assembled a bomb and placed it inside a Dunkin Donuts box. Then on the afternoon of Wednesday, 1 August, they visited the Atrium on a reconnaissance mission. That evening at 2000 hours, Usman drove Taufik and Agung back to the mall. Lingering briefly near the bus stop, Agung set down the box and briskly walked away.

Seconds later – whether because the timer was set wrong or the box had been jarred – the bomb went off prematurely. Unfortunately for Taufik, he had lingered behind a moment too long and absorbed much of the blast; he later lost his lower right leg. Four other passersby fell with non-lethal injuries.[175]

The Atrium bombing would prove a watershed event for regional law enforcement. The injured Taufik was immediately taken into custody and upon interrogation fingered the rest of his cell. Within two weeks, Usman was in custody and started connecting dots between the Atrium, the Christmas Eve bombings, and the attempted assassination of the Philippine ambassador.

At the same time, the police searched the memory chip in Taufik's cell phone and found a frequently dialed number in Saketi, Pandeglang. When the corresponding address was raided on 13 September, thirteen persons were arrested, including one Malaysian instructor; numerous weapons and explosives were confiscated.[176]

---

[174] The choice of the Atrium has caused some speculation. Faruq, citing hearsay, incorrectly claimed that the bomb was part of an assassination attempt against Megawati Sukarnoputri, who had succeeded Abdurrahman Wahid as president in July.

[175] This was not the only bomb to detonate at the Atrium. On 11 December 1998, an explosive device went off near an automatic teller machine in the mall; this was a criminal rather than terrorist act. On 23 September 2001, a bomb went off in the mall's indoor parking lot; this was believed tied to a business dispute.

[176] *Buku Putih Bom Bali* (Jakarta: PTIK Press, 2004), p. 202.

As the scales began to fall from the eyes of the Indonesian police, headway was also being made in Malaysia. This was set against a backdrop of an increasingly aggressive KMM, whose members in 2000 and early 2001 were responsible for a series of political crimes, including an attack on a police station, the bombing of several churches and Hindu temples, and the November 2000 assassination of Christian assemblyman Joe Fernandez.

The KMM's undoing came in May 2001, when five of its members attempted to rob a Southern Bank branch in a Kuala Lumpur suburb. A security guard fought back, killing two of the militants and capturing a third. One of the two who managed to escape was Taufik's brother-in-law, Afghan alum, and U.S. university graduate Zulkifli Hir; he was thought to have sought sanctuary in Indonesia.

After interrogating the detained militant, only then did the Malaysian authorities belatedly realize the existence of a fundamentalist group in their midst. As it turned out, many KMM members were also supporters of the main opposition political party, the highly orthodox *Partai Islam SeMalaysia* (PAS). This caused a sea change in the thinking of Kuala Lumpur authorities: whereas before they had been more than tolerant of radicals on their soil (and had refused earlier Indonesian entreaties to move against Hambali), they were now more than happy to crack down on the KMM. Of the ten KMM militants in detention as of early August, seven were PAS members. This included KMM leader Nik Adli Nik Abdul Aziz, who also happened to be son of the PAS spiritual advisor.[177] And in an abrupt about-face – if not a bit of a stretch – a senior Malaysian police official now said that Abu Bakar Ba'asyir and Hambali, as well as three KMM members, were now wanted in connection with the murder of assemblyman Joe Fernandez.[178]

These KMM arrests, and the fact that religious militants were now being fingered for terrorism in Indonesia, was not exactly news to that country's State Intelligence Agency (*Badan Intelijen Negara*, or BIN). By the end of the first quarter of 2001, multiple tips from that agency's intelligence network confirmed the involvement of religious extremists in the Christmas Eve 2000 blasts. Most of its sources were informants of varying degrees of reliability. One of them,

---

[177] Nik Adli Nik Abdul Aziz had attended the second meeting of the Rabitatul Mujahidin.

[178] Singapore White Paper, p. 8. The link to Ba'asyir and Hambali must be considered extremely unlikely; Hambali would later comment that he was in Indonesia during the murder of Fernandez but assumed the involvement of the KMM.

who had run a business in Saudi Arabia, was recruited when his investment went sour and, needing emergency help to flee the kingdom, became indebted to the intelligence representative at the Indonesian embassy. Another was a cash-strapped Sundanese who had sought out the BIN deputy chief at a mosque in search of monetary handouts. Still another was a sometimes Acehnese separatist who had been recruited by the BIN chief when the latter was the military commander for northern Sumatra.

One of BIN's best sources was not an informant but a full-fledged penetration agent known as Dadang. As Islamic activist since his university days, he had approached Indonesian intelligence in March 1985 and volunteered his services to the state. Embracing him, BIN operatives encouraged his subsequent two-year educational stint in Saudi Arabia. By 1992, he had successfully ingratiated himself among aging Darul Islam veterans. The following year, he ventured to Malaysia for two months to meet fugitive clerics Sungkar and Ba'asyir. And in mid-2000, he attended the founding congress of the MMI.

Throughout this time, Dadang passed regular reports back to Indonesian intelligence. For just as long, however, his information received scant attention. This changed during the second quarter of 2001, when the agent attended an MMI gathering in Jogjakarta. Mingling among the attendees – many with Jemaah Islamiyah links – he heard fellow radicals commiserating that the Christmas Eve bombings had been ineffective. This information, which seemed to corroborate the involvement of extremists in the attacks, was duly relayed to Indonesian intelligence. "After that," recalled Dadang, "my reports were given more credence."

While Jemaah Islamiyah seemed complicit, BIN's scanty knowledge about that organization indicated it was an extremely large target to investigate. During mid-year, the BIN chief tasked his deputy chief with narrowing down the list of likely suspects. Intuitively, the deputy knew where to look: the half a dozen contingents of would-be Indonesian jihadists who had ventured to Afghanistan since 1985 were surprisingly cohesive – they had even organized an alumni gathering in Solo in 1999 – and, given their exposure to demolitions and other martial skills, were exceedingly dangerous.[179]

---

[179] In mid-2001, the Indonesian government, belatedly concerned with the large and growing number of Indonesian nationals training in Afghanistan, had decided to discuss the issue with the Taliban government. Through the offices of their Pakistani military intelligence counterparts, BIN had tentative plans to dispatch two senior officers to Kabul that July. This trip was initially postponed and, after 11 September, cancelled. Interview with Muaman Ali, 22 July 2004.

By late June, information from BIN's informants was starting to paint a more complete picture of Indonesia's Afghan ensemble. While the total number of veterans was unknown, the deputy chief narrowed this down to a list of twelve top alumni. Of these, one of the most respected was Abu Rusdan (alias Abu Hamzah, alias Thoriqudin), a native of Kudus, Central Java, who had gone to Afghanistan in 1986. Though unknown to BIN at the time, Rusdan was secretary in the Jemaah Islamiyah markaz, the third-highest position in the organization that placed him in charge of day-to-day operations.

Initially, BIN wanted to place all twelve under surveillance. But after years of negligence and shrinking budgets, its surveillance teams were woefully short of equipment and funds. Focusing solely on Abu Rusdan, the head of the surveillance directorate scrounged some operable telephone taps, loaded three fellow members into a Kijang van, and on 5 July departed Jakarta for the two-day drive to Kudus. A little over two weeks later, on 21 July, they were making transcripts of Rusdan's conversations. Their operation was codenamed *Jarum*, a reference to the famed Djarum brand of clove cigarettes manufactured in that city.

Their deployment proved timely. On 6 August – five days after the Atrium bombing – the Jarum team in Kudus recorded some intriguing phone chatter. That morning, an unidentified Indonesian male called the Rusdan household with bad news. A cell phone had been found on Taufik, said the caller, and its directory contained the names of mutual friends and affiliated organizations. Pausing to absorb the news, Rusdan turned professorial. Inform those persons on the cell phone directory to be exceedingly careful, he said in an even tone. Every time they forge a contact, he added, it entails risks – even if the risks are not immediately apparent. While short of a smoking gun, the gist of this conversation (as well as those of additional calls recorded over the next two days) strongly indicated that Abu Rusdan's network was linked to the blast.

The government soon faced other evidence of international terrorism close to home. During August, a raid at an al-Qaeda safe house in the Middle East yielded a startling discovery. Among papers reportedly found in the house was a detailed sketch of the U.S. embassy in Jakarta. At the time, it was not known who had made the sketch or if an attack was imminent. There was some speculation that a Yemeni hit team might have entered Indonesia for that purpose, but no further details were known.[180]

As news of the sketch was passed to the Jakarta embassy, the U.S. state department issued a strongly worded travel advisory for Indonesia during that same month. This caused considerable angst among Indonesian government officials, who demanded to know the reason for the alert. The new BIN chief, A.M. Hendropriyono, who had just assumed his post on 10 August, was given a confidential briefing by U.S. counterparts within days after taking office. The gist of these briefings was then passed to relevant Indonesian officials and the protest died down.

A few days later, al-Qaeda again became an item of discussion at BIN. This came about after a longtime government informant, meeting Hendropriyono for the first time, looked to burnish his credentials by presenting a two-page photocopy of a letter purportedly written by the late Abdullah Sungkar and Ba'asyir. Dated 10 September 1998, the letter relayed a message from "Shaikh Usamah bin Ladin" to unnamed Islamic clerics in Indonesia. Besides urging them to pursue bin Laden's 1998 fatwa to liberate the Arab peninsula from "American infidels" and to prepare for a world jihad against the United States, the missive offered assistance to any cleric who wished to visit bin Laden in Kandahar.[181]

Later that same month, President Megawati confirmed plans to travel to the U.S. to meet President George W. Bush on 19 September. It was to be her first overseas trip as head of state. Joining her would be the BIN chief; counter-terrorism was to be on his planned discussion agenda. As part of a briefing paper, Hendropriyono intended to take to Washington, he requested that his

---

[180] Said then-U.S. Ambassador Robert Gelbard: "…we knew from external sources, multiple sources, that an al-Qaeda team was coming into Jakarta to try and blow up the embassy." See "Moving Targets in a Strike Zone," *Sydney Morning Herald*, 23 November 2002. Despite the countless interrogations of al-Qaeda members since 11 September 2001, no further details have ever emerged to corroborate the dispatch of a Yemeni hit team to Indonesia in mid-2001.

[181] Although Ba'asyir refutes the authenticity of the letter, there is reason to believe otherwise. For one thing, it surfaced before al-Qaeda shot to worldwide prominence on 11 September 2001; therefore, it is less than likely that a forger would have tried to smear Sungkar and Ba'asyir by linking them to a relatively obscure Yemeni militant. Second, the letter specifically mentions that bin Laden at the time was in Kandahar under the protection of the Taliban, but was trying to mediate with other Afghan factions opposed to the Taliban. This detail, which would have been significant for a short time in 1998, was largely forgotten by the time the letter surfaced four years later.

agency prepare a preliminary list of religious extremists involved in anti-government and paramilitary activities. This list was largely completed by the end of August.

Eight days before their trip, on 11 September, events in New York and Washington placed counter-terrorism on the top of everyone's agenda. In reaction, the chief of intelligence ordered his subordinates to refine the August list of extremists into a more complete report that would be brought to the U.S.

By the third week of September, this English-language report, totaling 24 pages, laid out BIN's findings to date. Many details were lacking. Still, it contained numerous items of interest. For example, it noted that foreign militants were suspected of operating on Indonesian soil. This included a Saudi "mujahidin instructor" named "Syeh Hussein," and a Kuwaiti national named "Umar Faruq." Indeed, Faruq was mentioned three times in the report, including a reference to his visits to Aceh, Ambon, and Sulawesi. Syeh Hussein, meanwhile, was said to have entered Indonesia in June 2000 and was allegedly living in Jakarta.[182]

The report also included the names of 36 Indonesian militants. Among them were four persons said to be based in southern Thailand, six in Kuala Lumpur, one in Mindanao, and three in Sabah. In addition, it gave thumbnail sketches of several paramilitary groups, including Laskar Jihad, MMI, and, in the briefest of mention, Jemaah Islamiyah.

Apart from the scant details in the report, BIN had little other information about the persons listed. In hindsight, much of it was inaccurate or woefully outdated. Some of the militants, for example, were already dead or in custody. And while Hambali does rate a mention, the report claims he had moved to Saudi Arabia. For all its shortcomings, however, the report was a milestone in that it belatedly recognized a network of religious radicals – foreign and local – was actively taking up arms across Southeast Asia.

---

[182] Syeh Hussein was an alias used by Rashid, the Saudi from al-Haramain.

CHAPTER TWELVE

THE SECOND FRONT

It was late on the afternoon of 11 September when word of the terrorist attacks in New York and Washington, D.C. flashed through Kandahar. Those al-Qaeda members in the know quickly brought their brethren into confidence, and for a short time the mood was festive and celebratory.

But for Hambali, the giddiness almost immediately gave way to the dark realization of the profound detrimental effect the attacks were likely to have on Jemaah Islamiyah. This was true for several reasons. First, by Hambali's own estimate, Jemaah Islamiyah was still four or five years away from having an adequate cadre in terms of quality and quantity. Mantiqi 1 was the only one that was properly developed; Mantiqi 2 and 3, by contrast, suffered major personnel shortfalls. And Mantiqi 4, which had been recently created to theoretically cover Papua and Australia, consisted of less than two dozen Indonesians residing in Australia.

Second, Jemaah Islamiyah did not yet have a proper paramilitary training program in place. Although the MILF had recreated some of its Mindanao camps, Jemaah Islamiyah was not sending a regular flow of students to the Philippines.[183] Moreover, future training in Afghanistan was now probably out of the question given the almost certain reprisals that would forthcoming from the United States.

---

[183] After Gloria Macapagal-Arroyo became president of the Philippines in January 2001, she reversed the policy of her predecessor and pulled the military back from MILF strongholds in Mindanao. As a result, the MILF was able to reestablish Camp Bushra and a series of other sites, the most significant of which was Jabal Qubah (the name of the mountain north of Mecca) in Maguindanao. As of mid-2001, a handful of Jemaah Islamiyah members had arrived for training at Camp Jabal Qubah.

Third, there was not even full agreement within the organization on its direction. Hambali and his Mantiqi 1 comrades welcomed the idea of targeting the West and were prone to fuse the goals of Jemaah Islamiyah and al-Qaeda. But others, especially in the markaz, sought little or no outside help. Several, too, were cautious of targeting Western interests because they did not yet see local political conditions conducive for wider attacks.

Fourth, and perhaps most importantly, it soon became apparent to Hambali that the al-Qaeda leadership had not fully considered the next steps for itself, not to mention its allied jihadist movements, after carrying out KSM's planes operation. Through the end of September, in fact, many of the top al-Qaeda personalities were preoccupied with setting up their own avenues of escape before the U.S. military launched its expected counterattack.

Virtually alone, KSM was belatedly trying to firm up a follow-on wave of terrorist operations around the world. During the first week of October, he ventured to Hambali's Kandahar house to brainstorm schemes for opening a second front in Southeast Asia. Hambali used the opportunity to remind the al-Qaeda operations chief of the long-standing plan to strike at an international high school in Singapore. KSM, however, preferred that this operation be temporarily shelved – not because of the age of the student victims, but because he foresaw difficulties in smuggling explosives into the city-state now that its authorities were on high alert.

Instead, KSM saw greater potential in hitting targets in the Philippines. Already, he had dispatched one al-Qaeda member – Mohammed Mansur Jabarah – to scope out potential operations in that country and, if need be, act as a suicide operative. KSM also had received assurances that Jemaah Islamiyah member al-Ghozi could readily source explosives in the Philippines.

Thinking aloud, KSM ran down a litany of other potential operations. Oil tankers plying the Straits of Malacca, he said, were vulnerable to explosives placed on their hulls. Vulnerable, too, were U.S. oil interests in the Philippines. The two also spoke of striking at U.S. servicemen during annual U.S.-Thai military exercises.

Hambali left the meeting without agreeing on any single plan of action. Shortly thereafter, he was dramatically reminded that time was of the essence. During the pre-dawn hours of 7 October, fifty Tomahawk cruise missiles and fifteen U.S. and British bombers combined for the opening volley in Operation

Enduring Freedom. In four waves coming every ninety minutes, Kandahar and Kabul shook from the aerial bombardment. The airfields in both cities were rendered inoperable and power grids destroyed. Worse for al-Qaeda, the Taliban, and their Jemaah Islamiyah guests, U.S. President George W. Bush promised this would be only the first salvo in a "sustained and relentless campaign."

With Kandahar still smoldering, Hambali made his way to the al-Qaeda media committee house. There he chanced upon Ayman al-Zawahiri and Mohammed Atef; apart from a brief request from Atef for assistance in attacking the U.S., British, and Australian embassies in Jakarta, both were too busy planning their escapes to discuss details with the Indonesian.

KSM, by contrast, was still determined to set into play an eleventh-hour round of operations. The next week, he returned to Hambali's house for what would be their last face-to-face meeting. First, realizing that it was futile to remain in Afghanistan, he ordered Hambali to carry on the fight from Southeast Asia. And because the Indonesian and Malaysian authorities would be actively looking for him, Hambali was urged to instead head for a less obvious destination like Thailand.

Hambali concurred, though there was a problem. His Malaysian travel document was almost full of visa chops. Worse for him, it was issued in his true name – and this was almost certainly on the watch-lists of regional immigration officials. As it was therefore of limited value, he opted to leave this behind. Instead, KSM had a visiting member of Jemaah Islamiyah, Miqdad Syed Hassan, offer Hambali his genuine Indonesian passport; Hambali needed only to substitute his own photograph.[184]

Next, KSM and Hambali agreed on a method of communication. To provide an extra level of protection, they planned to use intermediaries to pass e-mailed messages back and forth. They also agreed on some simple code words; "rice," for example, would mean "money."

As almost an afterthought, the conversation turned operational. KSM asked Hambali if he could find a Malaysian or Indonesian pilot to participate in a second wave of kamikaze attacks in the United States. As al-Qaeda realized that U.S. officials would be scrutinizing Middle Eastern nationals, KSM

---

[184] Hambali's Malaysian travel document was retrieved by KSM and later used by al-Qaeda terrorist Ahmed Khalfan Ghailani, alias Ahmed the Tanzanian. A Tanzanian citizen linked to the 1998 embassy bombings in Africa, Ghailani was captured in late July 2004 after a 10-hour shootout in Pakistan.

knew that the next crop of suicide pilots would need to carry passports from other countries, like Canada, France, or Southeast Asian states. He hinted that their targets would be tall buildings or nuclear facilities in the Midwest or California.

KSM's fixation with Southeast Asian pilots was not exactly new. Al-Qaeda, in fact, had been trying to source Indonesian commercial pilots since the first quarter of 2001. It had come up short finding one with airline experience, though a single Mantiqi 1 member, Zaini Zakaria, had already graduated from a pilot school at KSM's behest. Hambali had no ready ideas for a second candidate, though he promised to keep looking.

In actuality, KSM envisioned Jemaah Islamiyah members for a range of suicide operations. Over the previous few months, he had pieced together an elite cell of Southeast Asians who had pledged to martyr themselves on al-Qaeda missions against the United States. Probably to overcome language barriers, all of them were English-speaking Malaysian nationals and all were longtime members of Mantiqi 1. Heading the cell was Masran bin Arshad, a trusted operative who had couriered money from Pakistan on previous occasions and most recently had been assisting Sufaat set up his rudimentary anthrax lab in Kandahar. The rest of the cell included Nik Abdul Rahman Mustafa (alias Afifi), Mohammad Farik bin Amin (alias Zaid, alias Zubair), and Bashir bin Lap (alias Lillie, alias Nazri). KSM had chosen well, as all four of these would-be martyrs now saw themselves as more al-Qaeda than Jemaah Islamiyah.

For his part, Hambali by mid-October was ready to flee Kandahar for the safer climes of Pakistan. He would be joined by his wife, as well as the wife of Masran bin Arshad; Masran himself planned to stay behind for a few more days to fine-tune plans with KSM for the Malaysian suicide cell.

Their exodus proved surprisingly uneventful. Together with a driver and an Afghan guide provided by KSM, Hambali and the two women were taken to Spin Bolak, the border town controlled by a sizable Taliban contingent. There, Hambali paid a fistful of Pakistani rupees to cross the border and then, using a combination of buses and taxis over the next day, reached Karachi. From that city's bus station, Hambali placed a call to an al-Qaeda acquaintance named

Abu Ahmad al-Kuwaiti. They were promptly picked up and whisked away to Abu Ahmad's house in a quiet residential neighborhood.

Over the next three weeks, Hambali led a surreal existence. The city, he found, was teeming with displaced al-Qaeda members, many of them marking time in an exceedingly conventional manner. While shopping at the bazaar, for example, he ran into Abu Hazim al-Sha'ir, the Yemeni who had twice gone to Malaysia to oversee joint operations with Jemaah Islamiyah.[185]

Other encounters were with members of the Malaysian suicide cell, who had taken up temporary residence in a Karachi apartment. For a time they were joined by Richard Reid, a British drifter and Muslim convert who was carrying a pair of shoe bombs fashioned in Kandahar.

Hambali also chanced upon Sufaat, the Malaysian helming the al-Qaeda anthrax program under Ayman al-Zawahiri. Sufaat had made little progress in isolating the anthrax strain prior to 11 September, in large part because the bulk of his equipment had yet to arrive from Pakistan. During the interim, he had been giving biology lessons to two al-Qaeda apprentices, a Sudanese and a Palestinian who previously worked as a technician at a medical lab in Karachi. As both apprentices had graduated from a Pakistani university in Hyderabad, they suggested that Sufaat enroll as a student at that university's biology department; using his student status as cover, he could discreetly continue their anthrax testing in Pakistan.

But Sufaat yearned to return to Southeast Asia. Thinking aloud with Hambali, he suggested the possibility of shifting the anthrax program to Indonesia. He also mentioned a media report that the aircraft carrier *Kitty Hawk* – which was the centerpiece of the U.S. naval battle group launching strikes against Afghanistan from the Arabian Sea – would be passing by Singapore in the coming months en route to its home port in Japan; resurrecting KSM's earlier plan to recruit Indonesian commercial pilots, Sufaat talked up using a suicide operative to crash an airliner into the U.S. warship.[186]

Hambali promised to give further thought to these ideas when he himself returned to Southeast Asia. Before parting, he warned Sufaat not to go directly

---

[185] Abu Hazim al-Sha'ir, who real name was Khalid Ali bin Ali al-Hajj, was thought to be a top al-Qaeda operations officer as of 2003. He was killed in a firefight in Saudi Arabia on 15 March 2004.

[186] Undated report from a regional intelligence agency, "Pendedahan Yazid Sufaat Berkaitan Projek Keganasan di Indonesia dan Singapura."

back to Malaysia because immigration officials were no doubt alerted to his name.

Toward the end of November, Hambali was ready to make the trip to Thailand. To lessen any scrutiny he might face, he booked tickets for himself and his wife via Colombo, Sri Lanka. Before leaving, he had a final meeting with Abu Ahmad al-Kuwaiti. His al-Qaeda host used the opportunity to hand him a bundle containing US$20,000. The money, he was told, was authorized by KSM to use "any way he saw fit."

The plane flight to Bangkok via Colombo was without incident. Hambali's doctored Indonesian passport – under the name Syed Hassan – passed the inspection of Thai immigration officials. His wife's passport, issued under her true name, also raised no red flags.

From Bangkok, the pair headed south. Arriving at the Thai city of Narathiwat, Hambali made an unannounced visit to the house of Abdul Fatah. A member of Jemaah Salafi – the Thai group sympathetic to Jemaah Islamiyah – Fatah was the fellow Sadda veteran who had attended the earlier Rabitatul Mujahidin trysts. Despite these commonalities, Fatah's support for aggressive jihad was qualified: fearful of a backlash against their proselytizing by Thailand's Buddhist majority, he had rebuffed Hambali's earlier requests to participate in joint al-Qaeda strikes.

This time around, Hambali merely asked Abdul Fatah that he give shelter to his wife while he attended to business elsewhere in Southeast Asia. He also asked that Fatah place a call to a Jemaah Islamiyah member to meet him on the Malaysian side of the Thai border. After a single night in Narathiwat, Hambali on 4 December continued south and, avoiding border checkpoints, illegally slipped into Malaysia.

Hambali soon learned that a great deal had happened in Malaysia over the previous months. Much of it centered around Mohammed Mansur Jabarah, an al-Qaeda member he had briefly met four months earlier in Karachi.[187] A Kuwaiti by birth, Jabarah was an interesting case study. At the age of twelve, he had immigrated with his family to Canada and enjoyed a seemingly normal adolescence. Under the surface, however, his religious views during his late teens

---

[187] Hambali had briefly gone to Karachi with Sufaat in August during one of their purchasing trips for laboratory equipment.

had hardened following media coverage of the violence in Chechnya. During a vacation to Kuwait following high school graduation, he and his brother came into contact with al-Qaeda sympathizers and were hooked. To the chagrin of his father, Jabarah postponed his university education and in the summer of 2000 ventured to Pakistan, ostensibly for religious study.

In fact, Jabarah was ushered across the border into Afghanistan. There he underwent a series of courses in terrorist tactics, broken by a short spell fighting the Northern Alliance alongside the Taliban.

One year on, Jabarah had received instruction in everything from urban guerrilla tactics to mountain warfare. He was also granted three separate audiences with Osama bin Laden, during which time he had been invited to join al-Qaeda; not until a fourth meeting, in July 2001, did he agree. After pledging loyalty, he was bundled off to Karachi for additional tutoring under the auspices of KSM. With an eye on the calendar, KSM wrapped up the tutorial after two weeks and ordered Jabarah out of Pakistan by no later than 11 September. Specifically, the al-Qaeda operations chief wanted his student to head for Southeast Asia, telephone some Jemaah Islamiyah contacts provided via Hambali, and carry out some ambitious terrorist attacks against U.S. targets in the Philippines. Jabarah was provided with US$10,000 to finance the scheme.

Normally, a potential recruit like Jabarah probably would not have merited such personalized attention by bin Laden. But as al-Qaeda members with non-Arab passports were at a premium, the Canadian Jabarah became an instant, if not unlikely, linchpin. And because KSM had an inkling of the international pressure they were likely to feel after 11 September, he needed his protégé out of South Asia before that date.

Doing as he was told, Jabarah was in Hong Kong watching television when news broadcasts reported the events of 11 September. By the following day, he reached Kuala Lumpur and over the next few days made contact with Mantiqi 1 secretary Zulkifli Marzuki and treasurer Faiz bin Abu Bakar Bafana. He also rendezvoused with Ahmed Sahagi, a Saudi member of al-Qaeda who had once served as a bin Laden bodyguard and had attended some of KSM's training in Karachi alongside Jabarah; he was now designated as a suicide bomber.[188]

---

[188] Hambali was told that another al-Qaeda member named Abu Musab al-Hashiri was designated as a suicide volunteer for Southeast Asia.

As the group huddled, Jabarah conveyed KSM's desire to conduct a strike in the Philippines. To realize this, he and Sahagi intended to travel to Manila and needed help getting in touch with al-Ghozi, who they were told was with MILF colleagues in the southern part of that country.[189]

As planned, Jabarah and Sahagi shifted to Manila in early October. After waiting for just under a week, they were able to link up with al-Ghozi at their hotel. Touring the city, they filed past the U.S. and Israeli embassies. Both were daunting targets. Just as Hambali had determined the previous year, the U.S. embassy was heavily fortified and set too far back from the road to be within effective range of a truck bomb. Too, the Israeli embassy was in a high rise ringed by heavy security. Worse for them, al-Ghozi said he needed time and money to procure at least four tons of explosives.

Souring toward targets in Manila, the trio headed to Kuala Lumpur for further discussions. Showing good tradecraft, meetings with Ibrahim and Bafana were held in a car circling the capital. They quickly agreed that the Philippines was a poor venue for strikes. As an alternative, Bafana suggested that they consider Singapore; the previous month he had already alerted local Jemaah Islamiyah members about a possible operation by Jabarah and al-Ghozi.[190]

On 16 October, Jabarah took a bus to Singapore. With introductions provided by al-Ghozi, he and Sahagi accompanied the Jemaah Islamiyah cell in a tour of the city-state, camcorder in hand. A range of potential targets was observed – the docks, commercial buildings with major U.S. firms, the British and Australian high commissions – but topping the list were the U.S. and Israeli embassies.

Returning to Kuala Lumpur for another tryst, they began to fine-tune their plan. Jabarah agreed to seven targets, starting with the two embassies. Truck bombs driven by al-Qaeda suicide operatives would be used, each filled with about three tons of ammonium nitrate. As Jemaah Islamiyah in Malaysia was still storing four tons (purchased through Sufaat's lab) since late the previous year, they needed an additional seventeen tons.[191] Al-Ghozi also wanted to get a large amount of dynamite to set off the fertilizer.

---

[189] During this period, Jabarah used the alias Sammy, while al-Ghozi went by the name Mike.

[190] Singapore White Paper, p. 27.

[191] *Ibid*. In March 2003, Malaysian authorities recovered the four tons of fertilizer buried near the border of Singapore at the home of a cousin of Taufik Abdul Hakim, the hard-luck Atrium bomber. Ressa, *Seeds of Terror*, p. 212.

Over the next month, Jabarah and his Jemaah Islamiyah colleagues sought to procure the necessary explosives. This was easier said than done. Money was not an issue, as Jabarah had requested, and received, an additional US$30,000 in early November from an al-Qaeda courier in Kuala Lumpur. But as Jemaah Islamiyah had already discovered during earlier scheming, purchasing such large quantities of fertilizer and smuggling it into Singapore was difficult during the best of times; it was doubly difficult during the period of heightened vigilance after 11 September. The same was true for bringing in the dynamite, which al-Ghozi sought from distant sources in the Philippines.

This was the state of affairs when Hambali entered Malaysia in early December and booked himself into a Kuala Lumpur hotel. Over a series of individual meetings with Ibrahim, Bafana, Jabarah, and his Mantiqi 1 successor, Mukhlas, he was hardly pleased with their progress. For one thing, al-Ghozi was experiencing delays in finding an adequate amount of explosives. For another thing, he knew al-Qaeda wanted Southeast Asian attacks done at the earliest possible opportunity – probably to divert attention from Afghanistan – but a strike in Singapore required extra time associated with smuggling in the explosives. Overriding the decision of his colleagues, he ordered them to set aside plans for Singapore and refocus attention on Philippine targets.

Unfortunately for Jemaah Islamiyah, regional authorities – for once – were one step ahead. During the days immediately after 11 September, an informant had alerted the Singaporean authorities to the fact that a citizen of Pakistani extraction, Mohammad Aslam bin Yar Ali Khan, had bragged of his ties to Osama bin Laden and claimed he had participated in the Afghan jihad. Aslam was placed under surveillance, but on 4 October had abruptly left the country for Pakistan; he subsequently crossed into Afghanistan to fight on behalf of the Taliban.

Though their primary target had slipped their dragnet, the Singaporeans shifted focus to Aslam's known associates. During mid-October, they were seen meeting with several foreigners, one of whom was later identified as Jabarah. They were also seen exchanging several thousand dollars into local currency, and trying to obtain large quantities of ammonium nitrate.

By this time, the Singaporean government knew something was afoot but had yet to connect the dots. On 3 December, however, its hand was forced. On that date, the media reported that Aslam had been captured by the Northern Alliance and was turned over to the U.S. military. Fearing his associates might go underground, Singaporean police on 9 December arrested an initial group of six Jemaah Islamiyah members. Coincidentally, Sufaat was arrested on the same day while trying to enter Malaysia.

As word of the arrests reached Hambali, he knew that Jemaah Islamiyah was losing the initiative. Leaving Kuala Lumpur, he ventured to Johor Baru and on 13 December grouped with several top Mantiqi 1 members. While they could not plan and execute a large-scale attack under the current circumstances, he urged them to conduct smaller bombings to retaliate for the Singapore detentions.

While Hambali was still in Johor Baru, Bafana arrived in town. He was on his way to Singapore, he said, to meet his brother. Hambali adamantly warned him not to go, but to no avail. Perhaps predictable, he was arrested during a subsequent round of seventeen arrests during the third week of December.[192]

With the loss of Bafana, Hambali feared his days were numbered. Not only did Bafana have current information on impending operations, but he knew of his most recent movements in Malaysia. Hambali realized that he had to leave fast; moreover, because his doctored Indonesian passport was in the name of a fellow Jemaah Islamiyah member, he wanted alternate travel documents.

Obtaining a false passport was not a simple proposition. A Singaporean member of Jemaah Islamiyah had received specialized al-Qaeda training in this field, but he was merely able to substitute photographs in documents that would not stand up to close scrutiny; his skills did not extend to digitalized photographs or cases where complicated seals covered part of the photograph. In any event, the Singaporean crackdown made it prohibitive for Hambali to enter that country to seek out his assistance.

But from his years working in Malaysia, he knew of a viable alternative. Many Indonesians looking for blue-collar work outside their country exited

---

[192] Of the 23 persons detained in December 2001, thirteen were convicted as members of Jemaah Islamiyah, two were MILF sympathizers who were released but not allowed to leave the country, and eight were set free.

via boats illegally plying the Malacca Strait from the Riau island chain. Before departing, the workers often obtained passports from the Indonesian immigration office on Tanjung Pinang island. The immigration officers at that post were known for expediting documents without asking too many questions.

Taking this route in reverse, Hambali waited on the beach for two days until, for the sum of US$150, he found a maritime smuggler to illegally take him from Johor Baru to Batam. A short ferry ride from there had him at Tanjung Pinang. True to their reputation, the immigration officers were sufficiently pliable. For a modest fee, Hambali applied for a new Indonesian passport under the assumed name of Hendrawan. A week later on 24 December, he had the document in hand. While the passport was genuine and the photograph was his, all the biographic details were false. Significantly, he was now clean-shaven in an attempt to alter his trademark full-bearded image.

While in Tanjung Pinang, Hambali had been doing more than simply waiting for the issuance of his passport. Placing a call to Amrozi, the resourceful Jemaah Islamiyah member in East Java, he asked that he send word for Zulkarnaen – Jemaah Islamiyah's military chieftain – to make his way to Medan for a meeting.

Boarding another ferry near year's end, Hambali arrived in Medan and took up residence in a safe house arranged by a local Jemaah Islamiyah operative. After a short wait, Zulkarnaen arrived on 4 January 2002. Acquaintances since the Sadda days, the pair wasted no time brainstorming a course of action. Recalling a request conveyed by Mohammad Atef (who had since been killed during a U.S. airstrike in Afghanistan) for attacks on Western embassies in Jakarta, Hambali suggested that this would be a preferred option. Dipping into the wad of cash allocated by KSM, he turned over US$11,000 to Zulkarnaen.

While accepting the funds, Zulkarnaen did not appear particularly enthusiastic. Promising he would use the money to buy explosives in East Java, he did specify which embassy, if any, he intended to target. On that noncommittal note, the two parted ways.

The next day, 5 January, Hambali looked to test his new passport. Boarding a flight from Medan to Phuket via Singapore, he received no undue scrutiny. Unfortunately for him, his comrades in Jemaah Salafi were less forgiving. When he headed for Narathiwat to pick up his wife, he found Abdul Fatah's nerves were frayed to the breaking point. Over the previous days, a steady stream of top

Jemaah Islamiyah members – Mukhlas, Azhari, Noordin M. Top, Wan Min bin Wan Mat, Ibrahim – had entered southern Thailand to evade the dragnets in Malaysia and Singapore. Without complaint, Fatah had helped them find sanctuary in Yala.

Fatah was also more than willing to accept Jemaah Islamiyah cash. Fearful that the Malaysians would freeze their bank accounts or confiscate their savings, Mukhlas had brought with him US$14,000 of Mantiqi 1 money. Drawing on suggestions from Fatah, he invested this in a Yala rice company headed by Jemaah Salafi members.

But there were limits to Fatah's hospitality. Pushing him over the edge were the photographs of Hambali that were starting to appear in regional newspapers. In as courteous a tone he could muster, he told Hambali that he was not welcome to spend the night.

Rebuffed, Hambali and his wife looked to lose themselves in the urban confusion of Bangkok. With the assistance of a Jemaah Salafi operative seconded by Fatah, they arrived in the Thai capital and began looking for suitable accommodations.

Back in Hambali's native Indonesia, the reaction toward religious extremists was markedly different than in Malaysia or Singapore. Prior to 11 September 2001, that country's civilian intelligence agency, BIN, had already placed telephone taps on Abu Rusdan as part of Operation Jarum. The head of BIN had also prepared a report on religious extremists ahead of his 25 September visit to CIA headquarters.

But during the second half of September and much of October, even these minimal measures seemed to be running counter to the shrill outcry by elements of Indonesian society against the U.S.-led war on terrorism.[193] For example, groups like the MMI and Islamic Youth Movement (*Gerakan Pemuda Islam*) announced plans to send volunteers to fight against U.S. forces in Afghanistan. Despite travel restrictions placed by the Indonesian government, several hun-

---

[193] On 23 September 2001, hard-line Islamic groups in Solo conducted a sweep of area hotels, ostensibly to force U.S. citizens out of the country. On 28 September, several thousand persons held an anti-American rally outside the U.S. embassy. Several thousand protesters again massed outside the embassy on 8 October.

dred volunteers allegedly departed for South Asia, though they ultimately found themselves unable to progress beyond Pakistan.[194]

At the same time, several paramilitary groups in Solo and Jakarta threatened to "sweep" American and other Western citizens from Indonesia. A sweep was conducted in a number of Solo hotels, though no foreigners were actually harmed.

Against such activity, the Indonesian government initially offered little response. Not until 18 November was its hand forced – and this due to events taking place in Spain. On that date, flamboyant Spanish judge Balthasar Real Garzon issued a statement concerning evidence of an extensive al-Qaeda presence in Spain. According to Garzon, an al-Qaeda cell had been operating in that country since 1994. Moreover, he revealed that a captured member of that cell, Yusuf Galan, was in close touch with Indonesian radicals and had trained in Sulawesi. Hundreds of al-Qaeda members, he claimed, had gone to Sulawesi from Europe for such paramilitary instruction.

While there was reason to take Garzon's claims with a grain of salt – he was a showman known to relish the limelight and could well be prone to hyperbole – BIN knew there was proof of radical activity in Sulawesi, especially around the beleaguered town of Poso.[195] In this, there had been participation from a myriad of extremist groups, including Laskar Jundullah, Laskar Jihad, and Jemaah Islamiyah.

On a parallel, but separate, track, an al-Qaeda cell had in fact taken note of Poso from half a world away. This was largely the result of Parlindungan Siregar, an Indonesian national who had ventured to Spain's *Universidad Complutense de Madrid* in 1987. Remaining in Spain after his scholarship money ran out, Siregar supported himself by offering his services as a translator and martial arts instructor for children.

Siregar also happened to befriend Imad Eddris Bakarat Yarkas (alias Abu Dahdah), the head of an al-Qaeda cell operating in Spain. In October 2000, Siregar returned to Indonesia but remained in contact with Yarkas. By now enamored with radical Islam, he ventured to Poso and met Omar Bandon, a Sadda

---

[194] There was considerable doubt that any would-be Indonesian jihadists even reached Pakistan, with cynics claiming that the Jakarta-based recruiters were merely collecting donations for their own personal gain. Still, such boasts persisted for several months: in December 2001, Laskar Jundullah leader Agus Dwikarna falsely claimed that a dozen of his South Sulawesi militants had reached Afghanistan. Undated BIN information report, "Kegiatan Agus Dwi Karna," p. 1.

[195] Garzon was the same judge who had secured former Chilean leader Pinochet's arrest in London in 1998, and he had later issued arrest warrants for all 48 members of Argentina's 1976-1983 junta.

alumni. Growing close, the two cemented ties when Siregar married Bandon's sixteen-year-old daughter.

With Bandon soon taking up arms against Christians around Poso, Siregar sent word to Yarkas about the unique opportunities available in Central Sulawesi. Not only was there an active jihad taking place, but the area around Poso was sufficiently isolated to allow for discreet paramilitary training.

In May 2001, Yarkas came to Indonesia to make his own assessment. Traveling on a false passport via Bangkok and Jakarta, he arrived at the town of Palu, linked up with Siregar, and then drove down to Poso. From there, they took a boat ten kilometers east along the coast.

For Yarkas, the locale was perfect. Situated near a jungle camp run by Bandon, he found an abandoned Christian settlement consisting of ten hut clusters. Already present were a mix of Filipinos, Malaysians, and even an Australian. It was estimated that the settlement could potentially house up to six hundred trainees. Siregar himself was tapped to act as a martial arts instructor.

Returning to Spain, Yarkas made arrangements to channel al-Qaeda money to Poso. In July, he dispatched a fellow cell member, Yusuf Galan, to bring cash to Siregar in order to properly bankroll what was now dubbed Camp Mujahidin. Plans called for a facility to train thirty Filipinos, fifteen Malaysians, two dozen Europeans, and four Australians. Implementation of the plan was to take place before year's end.

None of this was yet known to BIN when Judge Garzon made his comments in November. To investigate the claims, a BIN officer was rushed on 7 December to Central Sulawesi to search for Siregar (whose name appeared in Garzon's deposition). It was quickly determined, however, that the target had already fled to Java.

While the manhunt for Siregar was a bust, some compelling evidence came from eyes in the sky. Courtesy of a counterpart organization, satellite imagery of Poso's vicinity was shared with BIN; this showed what appeared to be an abandoned camp consistent with a training facility. Following from this, on 13 December, Hendropriyono announced the likely presence of an al-Qaeda training camp near Poso. The following day, he publicly stated that there had been foreigners in the vicinity.[196]

---

[196] See "Puluhan WNA Dimasukkan ke Poso," *Media Indonesia*, 14 December 2001.

While his statements were met by derision by numerous prominent Islamic figures, more proof followed.[197] On 23 December, BIN's deputy for foreign affairs rushed to Spain for meetings with police and defense officials. There, he was given the interrogation results from Galan, as well as significant items found in Galan's possession: airline ticket stubs to Indonesia, a passport with immigration stamps from Indonesia, and two photographs of himself and other al-Qaeda members in the Poso jungle.[198] BIN subsequently determined that the Poso camp was probably abandoned shortly after the 11 September attacks, and certainly by the time the al-Qaeda cell was smashed in Spain.

In December, two events elsewhere in the world focused attention on Indonesia. The first took place in Kabul, which Taliban and their al-Qaeda allies had vacated in a rush. A check of the bombed-out house of Mohammed Atef revealed the videotape of Jemaah Islamiyah's Singaporean cell members performing surveillance of American targets. Meanwhile, another house contained a detailed sketch of the U.S. embassy in Jakarta. This was the second such sketch found among al-Qaeda documents.

The second event was the 22 December attempted bombing of an American Airlines flight from Paris to Miami. Richard Reid, a British drifter and Muslim convert, had tried – and failed – to detonate a bomb hidden in his shoe; had he been successful, the damage to the aircraft's skin would have caused sufficiently rapid depressurization to tear apart the plane in flight. This was the same British national who had been living in a Karachi apartment with several Malaysians.

After Reid was taken into custody in the U.S., investigators in several nations quickly began to piece together his links to al-Qaeda cells across Europe and the Middle East. In particular, he was connected to a Pakistani national named Muhammad Saad Iqbal Madni, who in turn had been in touch with al-Qaeda operatives in the Kandahar area. Further investigation indicated Madni went on the run shortly before Reid was apprehended, and was believed to have gone to Indonesia.

---

[197] Din Syamsuddin, the general secretary of the Indonesian Council of Islamic Clerics, was among the more outspoken when he said on 14 December, "It is not useful to state that there is a group at Poso that is part of the al-Qaeda network." *Media Indonesia*, 14 December 2001.

[198] BIN report, "Al Qaeda di Poso (Menerut Laporan CSD/Badan Intelijen Tertinggi Negara Spanyol)," undated.

During the final week of December 2001, BIN was alerted to the likely presence of Madni on Indonesian soil. He was thought to be using his real name, and had possibly sought refuge in East Jakarta. His passport details, obtained in Afghanistan, were eventually forwarded to Indonesia.

Based on this limited briefing, BIN operatives initiated a search for Madni shortly before year's end. Limiting the search to East Jakarta, information was eventually gleaned about a Middle Eastern or South Asian national who had recently rented a room in the vicinity. He was said to spend his time sequestered in his quarters, and did not host visitors.

On 5 January 2002, intensive surveillance of the suspect's apartment was initiated. After five days of continuous surveillance – during which time no one was seen entering or exiting the apartment – special forces personnel assigned to BIN moved in during the evening hours. As they entered his room, however, they found no one home. A check with the landlord revealed that Madni had taken a trip to Solo (he claimed he was visiting his stepmother).

Uncertain when Madni would return from Solo, the special forces personnel maintained a vigil at the suspect's apartment. At 0600 hours the following morning, an unidentified person of possible Arab ethnic origin was observed approaching the building and entering the suspect's room. When confronted by Indonesian personnel, he did not resist. On his person was found a doctored Pakistani passport in Madni's name.

Over the next 48 hours, Madni was kept in Indonesian custody. During that period, he repeatedly attempted to bribe his way to freedom (his initial offer was one million rupiah, but this figure escalated sharply over the course of his confinement). Although he did not reveal much during questioning, he did admit that his father had taught at the Saudi embassy-sponsored Arab Language Institute in Jakarta for a decade and that he had visited the country several times in the past. Because of this connection, he had opted to flee to Indonesia.[199]

After two days, Madni was prepared for extradition to a third country.[200] On his way to the airport, he made one final attempt to bribe Indonesian authorities. This time, his offer stood at 100 million rupiah. The amount was not

---

[199] "U.S. Behind Secret Transfer of Terror Suspects," *Washington Post*, 11 March 2002.

[200] Because he also carried an Egyptian passport, Madni was rendered to the Egyptian General Intelligence Service. Media reports claim he was flown out of Indonesia on a Gulfstream V jet chartered by Premier Executive Transport Services. "Terror Suspects' Torture Claims Have Massachusetts Link," *Boston Globe*, 29 November 2004.

accepted, and Madni was summarily expelled from Indonesian soil. Though there were unanswered questions about whom he may have contacted while in Indonesia, no beneficial feedback was offered to BIN regarding the questioning of Madni – perhaps not surprising given the stretched resources at the time among intelligence organizations in the Middle East and elsewhere.

On the same day Madni was whisked out of Indonesia, Hambali arrived in Bangkok. Still unsatisfied that his new Indonesian passport offered him sufficient cover, one of his first orders of business was to obtain an alternate identity. Bangkok, he knew, had a thriving black market in stolen tourist passports; many were sought out by Chinese nationals looking to illegally enter the U.S. or Europe. Finding a Pakistani national who dealt in such items, he had his photograph inserted in a Spanish passport under the name Alejandro Gonzales Davidson.

Over the course of the month, Hambali also began holding court with a growing roster of displaced colleagues. One of the first to arrive was al-Qaeda's Jabarah, who had been laying low in a Bangkok hotel since the close of the previous year. Jabarah was not the most welcome comrade under the circumstances: after the December arrest of the Jemaah Islamiyah network in Singapore, he had been identified from his immigration form and was now the subject of an international manhunt. Much like Hambali had been rebuffed by Fatah, it was now Hambali's turn to break contact and urge Jabarah to leave the kingdom.[201]

Hambali was far more forthcoming with his fellow Jemaah Islamiyah members. During January, both Ibrahim and Azhari arrived in Bangkok from Yala. The next month, they were joined by Mukhlas, Noordin Top, and Wan Min bin Wan Mat.[202] With this quorum, they held their first post-11 September strategy session to brainstorm future operations in Indonesia.[203]

---

[201] From Bangkok, Jabarah unsuccessfully attempted to get a visa for Myanmar. He then flew to Dubai, and finally shifted to Oman. He was arrested there on 9 March and rendered to the United States. Ahmed Sahagi was reportedly detained at the same time and deported to Yemen. See U.S. Department of Justice report, "Information derived from Mohammed Mansour Jabarah," 21 August 2002.

[202] When Mukhlas was promoted to Mantiqi 1 commander, Noordin Top became head of the Luqmanul Haqiem pesantren and Wan Min bin Wan Mat took over as head of the Johor wakalah.

[203] Jemaah Islamiyah operational planning in Indonesia between September 2001 and January 2002 had been haphazard. Imam Samudra, venturing from Indonesia to Malaysia in December 2001, had requested funds from treasurer Bafana for the purchase of dynamite for an unspecified operation; as this was not approved by Hambali, the funds were denied. In the same month, Mantiqi 3 ordered its wakalah in Mindanao to send five M-16 rifles, three pistols, and thirty kilos of dynamite to Indonesia for an unspecified operation. Bafana report, "Surat Pernyataan," p. 7; Deni Afresio interrogation report, pp. 45-52.

Much like the discussions between Hambali and KSM the previous year, their talks covered a wide range of potential targets. Mention was made of the U.S., British, and Australian embassies – as per the late Mohammed Atef's request – but there was general agreement that those targets were too heavily fortified to achieve success.

They saw more promise, by contrast, by looking toward the seas. To achieve surprise, all of those present thought it was a good idea to shift to maritime targets rather than those on land. Linked to this, they talked up the concept of sending members to a Malaysian resort for diving classes; six persons were even short-listed as good candidates.

Hambali, it turned out, had a perfect scenario for a maritime strike. When he had been aboard the ferry from Tanjung Pinang to Medan late the previous year, he had seen oil tankers docked near a fueling station at Dumai. He thought these would be ripe for a *Cole*-style suicide attack. As an alternative, Mukhlas suggested the use of Jemaah Islamiyah frogmen to place explosives on their hulls while moored.

Other ideas soon came to the fore. Mukhlas favored an attack on the ExxonMobil facility in Aceh. And both Mukhlas and Hambali thought there was promise in a strike against the U.S.-operated gold mine on the island of Sumbawa. They also broached the merits of hitting nightspots on Bali, though no specific clubs were mentioned. In the end, Hambali rated the Dumai operation as the most promising, followed by the ExxonMobil facility and the Sumbawa gold mine. Hambali, however, gave his "local brothers" leeway in selecting the best target from among those discussed.

On that note, the meeting adjourned. For the time being, Hambali and Ibrahim planned to hide out in Bangkok. The rest looked to make their way south, where they would begin the execution phase of opening a second front in Indonesia.

CHAPTER THIRTEEN

BALI

By the beginning of 2002, the war against terrorism in Southeast Asia was progressing in fits and starts. Some of the most important gains were scored in the Philippines. Acting on a tip from Singaporean intelligence officials, for example, Filipino authorities arrested al-Ghozi on 15 January as he was preparing to leave on a commercial flight for Malaysia via Bangkok.[204] He then divulged information that led Filipino police officers to storm his General Santos City safe house. Not only did they find over a ton of explosives he had earlier procured for use in Singapore, but they also found seventeen M-16 rifles destined for militants in Indonesia. Four Filipino accomplices were arrested, though one managed to flee to MILF-controlled territory.[205]

Two months later, on 15 March, the Philippine authorities scored another coup when they arrested Laskar Jundullah leader Agus Dwikarna. His arrest had been a complicated affair. In early March, Dwikarna had gotten word (via South Sulawesi business colleague Abdul Jamal Balfas) that Thai mining investor Prasan Sirinond, active in East Kalimantan, was planning to dispatch a Thai

---

[204] After "Freedom Fighter" called the Philippine National Police to claim credit after the December 2000 Manila bombings, the police identified the cell phone number. Monitoring of this number revealed calls made to and from Malaysia before the bombings; one of these calls was traced in 2001 to Faiz bin Abu Bakar Bafana. Late that same year, explosives suppliers in Cebu City informed the authorities that a person was trying to purchase an usually large amount of explosives. This information, plus details emerging from interrogations of Jemaah Islamiyah suspects in Singapore, led Philippine authorities to pinpoint al-Ghozi.

[205] Al-Ghozi was sentenced to seventeen years in prison and interned at Camp Crame in downtown Manila. On 15 July 2003, he and two fellow prisoners pried open faulty door hinges and made their escape past sleeping guards. During the course of an ensuing nationwide manhunt, he was shot dead while resisting capture.

coal exploration team to look at a new vein exposed by an earthquake in the mountains of Mindanao.

Seeing an opportunity to strap-hang on the Thai delegation for his own purposes, Dwikarna told Sirinond (via Balfas) that he had excellent local knowledge of Mindanao. What's more, there had been a spate of kidnappings in Mindanao, and Dwikarna broadly hinted that he had Filipino contacts who could shield the Thai during their travels into the countryside. Pushed, Sirinond agreed to bring along Balfas, Dwikarna, and a third Indonesian from Kompak.

By that time, Dwikarna had been under scrutiny by Indonesian intelligence officers for months. During a 5 March telephone conversation tapped by BIN, Dwikarna was heard talking about a contemplated venture between Laskar Jundullah and the Abu Sayyaf Group in the Philippines.[206] That same week, Dwikarna called his wife to say he was going to General Santos City in the southern Philippines to meet with "Islamic brothers."

BIN had dutifully informed its Philippine counterparts, the National Intelligence Coordination Agency, of Dwikarna's imminent arrival. Tracking him, however, was easier said than done. The three Indonesians had routed their trip through Bangkok, ostensibly to view a Thai mine on their return. But when BIN's Thai counterparts were belatedly alerted on 11 March, they could not mobilize in time and the Indonesians disappeared into Bangkok for the night.

Murphy's Law, it turned out, was playing no favorites. When the Indonesians returned to Bangkok's international airport on the morning of 12 March to continue their journey to the Philippines, they missed their flight. This meant they would not be able to continue their next leg to Manila until the following morning. This also meant that they would not be able to join the Thai engineering team venturing into the Mindanao heartland, which had gone ahead and was scheduled to depart from General Santos City the next morning.

Despite the snafu, the Indonesians transited through Manila, spent the night, and arrived in General Santos City on Tuesday morning, 14 March.

---

[206] There was already a history of contact, albeit limited, between Indonesian extremists and the Abu Sayyaf Group (ASG). During 2000, the commander of Mantiqi 3, Nasir Abas, had instructed the ranking Jemaah Islamiyah member at Camp Hudaibiyah, Zulkifli (alias Deni Afresio), to expand his contacts with Filipino militants beyond the MILF. Afresio subsequently ventured to Jolo to meet with leaders of the ASG. From this meeting, a short-lived exchange program ensued, with a handful of Jemaah Islamiyah members going to Jolo and a trickle of ASG militants receiving training at Camp Hudaibiyah. On his own initiative, Afresio later participated in fourteen bombings across the southern Philippines, some with the MILF and some with the ASG. Deni Afresio interrogation report; Nasir Abas interview.

Though Dwikarna had been busy on his cell phone, a promised reception party at the airport never materialized. At their downtown hotel, a Filipino Muslim, identifiable by his Islamic goatee, met him in the hotel driveway and conferred briefly.[207]

On that anti-climactic note, the Indonesians pushed to return home. On Wednesday, 15 March, they boarded an early morning flight to Manila. When they returned to the airport later that evening for an ongoing flight via Bangkok, the authorities were – literally – waiting at the door. Descending on the three Indonesians, law enforcement officials placed them in custody because explosives residue and detonation cord were allegedly found in their luggage.

Shortly after the arrests, regional politics intervened. Because the Indonesian from Kompak had political pull in Jakarta, the Filipino government was enticed into releasing him and Balfas. Dwikarna, however, did not have it so good. By that time, the captured al-Ghozi had revealed his ties with Dwikarna to the Filipino police. Confirming this, al-Ghozi's home phone number in Madiun was found in the memory of Dwikarna's cell phone. What's more, the Filipinos noted that General Santos City was a hotbed of MILF activity; they were convinced that the Indonesians had come to meet MILF representatives and assess the damage done by al-Ghozi's arrest.[208] Collectively damned by this evidence, Dwikarna was sentenced to 17 years in prison by a Filipino court. In his absence, Laskar Jundullah quickly began to atrophy.

Malaysia was proving equally aggressive in its counter-terrorism campaign. Between December 2001 and July 2002, a total of 23 persons were arrested in that country, including four Indonesians and three Singaporeans. Added to the earlier arrests in Singapore, Jemaah Islamiyah's Mantiqi 1 – save for a handful of operatives who fled to Indonesia – was effectively crushed.

Within Indonesia, by contrast, the counter-terrorism record was still decidedly mixed. In the face of shrill comments from top politicians unequivocally

---

[207] Interview with Prasan Sirinond, 16 July 2005.

[208] The Filipino authorities were also concerned that Dwikarna was planning an attack against the largest company in General Santos City, Century Tuna. This was because when Dwikarna's airport reception failed to materialize at General Santos City, they had accepted a cheap Century Tuna corporate hotel rate suggested by a tour guide at the airport. When they took a city tour later that same day to mark time, it had included the Century Tuna facilities at the port. Sirinond interview.

denying the presence of foreign radicals in Indonesia, BIN – fresh off the Madni rendition – was proactively trying to stave off of the possibility.[209]

In some cases, BIN's chase turned up nothing. On 18 January 2002, for example, they were briefed by Australian counterparts about 28-year-old Melbourne resident Jack Terrence Thomas (alias Jihad Thomas, alias Abu Khair Ismail), who was possibly the Australian said to have trained at the al-Qaeda-sponsored Poso camp. Married to the daughter of a retired Indonesian police officer in Makassar, Thomas was also thought to have ventured to Kandahar for paramilitary instruction in mid-2001. Assuming that his wife was still in Makassar – and that she would still be in touch with her husband – Australian intelligence officials asked their Indonesian counterparts to place her under surveillance.

After several weeks of telephone tapping, the operation was bearing little fruit. Though several calls were placed to Australia, the wife's conversations did not touch on the location of her spouse. Then, after a little more than one month into the surveillance, she and her child abruptly left Makassar via Jakarta, then departed overseas. Their final destination was not known.[210]

Another dry hole was the case of Sheikh Ahmed Salim Swedan (alias Sheikh Ahmad Salem Suweidan, alias Sheikh Swedan, alias Sheikh Bahamadi, alias Ahmed Ally, alias Bahamad, alias Ahmed the Tall). Born in Kenya in either 1969 or 1970, the six-foot Swedan had managed a trucking business before being drawn into the al-Qaeda cell established in that East African nation. He was implicated in the August 1998 bombing of the U.S. embassy in Kenya; the U.S. government had posted a multimillion-dollar reward for information leading to his apprehension or conviction.

---

[209] Vice President Hamzah Haz repeatedly cast doubt on the possibility of foreign terrorists within the country; as late as 19 March 2002 he publicly stated, "I promise there are no terrorists in Indonesia." *Kompas Cyber Media*, 19 March 2002.

[210] The Australian authorities were especially eager to track down Jihad Thomas because John Walker Lindh, the so-called American Taliban, revealed in December 2001 that he trained alongside a Melbourne resident near Kabul. Not until 4 January 2003 did Jihad Thomas surface in Pakistan, where he was promptly arrested. His lawyer, however, insisted he was not the same person fingered by Lindh. In May 2003, another Melbourne native and terrorist suspect, who went by the name Abu Jihad, slipped the authorities and headed to Egypt, where he was detained on a visa violation. Jihad Thomas was subsequently repatriated to Australia, and it remains uncertain whether he or Abu Jihad was Lindh's colleague in Afghanistan, or which of the two – if either – was the Australian at Poso.

On 7 March 2002, BIN was alerted to the fact that Swedan had sought refuge in Indonesia. Specifically, he was reportedly hiding in Malang, East Java. Special forces members assigned to BIN were immediately mobilized to track down this al-Qaeda target. When a raid was conducted that same week, however, it was discovered that Swedan had boarded a flight out of Indonesia the previous day. He whereabouts remain unknown.[211]

One more false start took place in May, when a foreign counterpart organization notified BIN that a suspected Yemeni terrorist named Bekkayee had entered Jakarta. The target was tailed for several days, then detained and questioned while attempting to board a flight for Europe. As it turned out, he had the same name as a top al-Qaeda operative but was actually a shoe salesman looking to expand into the Indonesian market; he lamented that he was repeatedly a victim of mistaken identity at airports around the world.

BIN finally hit pay dirt with the case of Umar Faruq. During January 2002, an informant reported a Kuwaiti named Faruq had been seen in the vicinity of Bogor. This set off warning bells, since a Kuwaiti with that same name had been included in the September 2001 report prepared prior to the BIN chief's visit to the United States.

Focusing on this individual, by early February BIN sources had been able to determine that Faruq was in Bogor near the border with Sukabumi. By mid-month, an informant claimed to have actually seen the elusive Kuwaiti.

Though BIN did not yet know it, Faruq had been extremely busy over the previous months. At the close of November 2001, he had ventured to Central Sulawesi to participate in an operation designed to reignite communal tension in that vicinity. During the evening of 1 December, he joined a gathering of fifty Laskar Jundullah guerrillas. Confiscated video later showed him joining in prayer and then being presented with an M-16 rifle. Further video clips, taken between 2232 hours on 1 December and 0015 on 2 December, show an assault in Poso; this time frame coincides with an attack on the village of Sepe, where almost 200 Christian huts were set ablaze.

---

[211] During that same month, BIN dispatched personnel to the island of Lombok. This came after an embassy in Jakarta relayed information from a longtime expatriate resident in Bali about an alleged suspicious residence in Lombok that was host to sixty Arab males. When BIN personnel arrived at the location to investigate, they found nothing.

Although Laskar Jundullah rated this operation a success, it did not maintain the momentum. Faruq subsequently returned to Jakarta after a major disagreement with Dwikarna.[212] For the time being, he retreated to Bogor to live in a remote hamlet with his wife's extended family. He did not remain long. During January 2002, at the urging of al-Haramain's Rashid, he dispatched an Indonesian colleague named Nasir (alias Nafar) to survey of possible religious and military training sites on the island of Kalimantan. Rashid reasoned that Kalimantan was a good locale because it was large and did not have a heavy concentration of security forces.

Nasir was a good pick to make the survey. Hailing from Kalimantan, he had trained in both Afghanistan and Pakistan during the early nineties. With houses in both Makassar and East Jakarta, Nasir had met Faruq soon after the latter arrived in the country.

After a brief trip to the East Kalimantan city of Balikpapan, Nasir returned to Jakarta with a video of his survey. But before this could be shown to Rashid, plans were forwarded in late January for Faruq and Nasir to lead a small group back to Balikpapan in order to conduct a month-long "Call to Jihad" course at the Hidayatullah pesantren.[213] Joining them would be Syawal, the senior Laskar Jundullah operative who had fought alongside Faruq at Poso in December, as well as Aris Munandar, the head of the MMI's Department of Inter-Mujahideen Relations.

By late February, word of the militant proselytizing at Hidayatullah had reached Jakarta. A 25 February report from a counterpart intelligence agency correctly listed the names of three persons dispatched to Kalimantan, including Nasir, Syawal, and Abdul Hadi (an alias used by Faruq).[214] Nothing further apparently resulted from this "Call to Jihad" session, though not for want of trying.

Upon returning to Jakarta, Faruq remained in frequent telephonic contact with Abu Zubaydah, the senior al-Qaeda operations officer he had known since his time in Afghanistan, and Ibn al-Shaykh al-Libi, a Libyan who had been head

---

[212] The disagreement stemmed from an argument between the Arabs and Indonesians. Dwikarna was allegedly irate over the fact that the Arabs insisted on videotaping their actions, which he deemed a security risk. He was also irate that al-Qaeda, through al-Haramain, was not turning over what he felt were enough funds.

[213] Faruq's father-in-law was affiliated with Hidayatullah.

[214] Officials from the Hidayatullah pesantren admit that Aris Munandar and Ustad Syawal conducted self-defense instruction there in January, but deny Faruq was present. See *Tempo*, 2 December 2002, p. 22.

of an al-Qaeda training camp. Faruq by this time was contemplating a return to Kuwait on an authentic Indonesian passport. His previous attempt to get a passport – in Makassar during 1999 – had resulted in a brief detention. This time around, he had managed to get fake identity papers from sympathetic government employees in Ambon that listed his name as Mahmud bin Ahmad Assegaf, allegedly born in Ambon in 1971. With these papers, he had been able to get an Indonesian passport on 27 February 2002.[215]

There were problems, however. Faruq wanted to depart with his wife and two daughters, but the immigration office was dragging its feet on issuing the additional passports. In the meantime, Zubaydah (al-Libi was captured in Pakistan in January 2002) urged Faruq to make preliminary plans for large-scale car and truck bomb attacks against U.S. embassies in the region on or near the 11 September anniversary in 2002.

By that time, Faruq could turn to few assets. Rashid's Cooperative Program in Ambon and Sulawesi had already fallen apart due to infighting among the Indonesian counterparts from Laskar Jundullah and Jemaah Islamiyah. Likewise, Rashid's Special Program – the unilateral effort to train paramilitary cadres in Ambon – had also hit hard times. This was in part because several of the Arabs that had ventured to Ambon as trainers (especially the Egyptians and Yemenis) had started bickering among one another, and several had returned to the Middle East after 11 September. Moreover, Indonesian security authorities in Ambon had belatedly started cracking down on foreign nationals arriving on that island; Faruq learned that at least one al-Qaeda instructor – an Algerian who went by the kunya Huzaifa – was detained by Indonesian authorities during early 2002 and deported via Jakarta.[216]

To further his plans, Faruq turned to his remaining allies in Jakarta. Among foreigners, there was Rashid and Abu Daud (alias Seyam Reda), an Egyptian-born cameraman who had accompanied Faruq to Poso in December 2001. There was also Ahmed al-Moudi, the Saudi national who headed the al-Haramain branch in Jakarta. Faruq's relationship with al-Haramain was a two-way street.

---

[215] Faruq's father-in-law helped him get false documentation (including a forged birth certificate, identification card, family card, and marriage book) in Ambon during 2000, shortly before the father-in-law was killed during skirmishes on that island. Faruq took the fake documents to Bogor and paid a middleman three million rupiah to expedite the processing of his passport.

[216] This deportation almost certainly corresponds to Shahni Farid, a 32-year-old Algerian who was deported from Ambon on 27 March along with Hussein al-Zahrani, a 27-year-old Saudi national.

Al-Moudi had given Faruq US$3,500 of al-Haramain money for his planned return to Kuwait. But in April, Faruq had ventured to Surabaya to take delivery of US$99,000 from Sheikh Bandar, the al-Haramain branch chief from Saudi Arabia; Faruq subsequently turned over this money to al-Moudi.

Present in Jakarta, too, was Gharib (spelling variant Ghareeb), a Somali who held a Bosnian passport.[217] In his early thirties, Gharib was director of Yayasan Aman, a front foundation located near Hotel Sentral in East Jakarta. Aman had been started with 30 million rupiah in al-Haramain funds delivered by Faruq. Far from running a humanitarian charity, however, Gharib was fully responsive to Rashid and had been instrumental in sending Ambonese students from Rashid's Special Program for paramilitary training in Pakistan.

Finally, there was Zein al-Din (variant Zein al-Deen), an Egyptian who for the past year had been an instructor in Ambon for Rashid's Special Program.

From this cast, Faruq helped delegate tasks for coordinated attacks to take place on or around 11 September. Zein al-Din, for one, was assigned with planning attacks against U.S. targets in East Timor; funds for this were provided through al-Haramain. Faruq himself made plans to conduct an 11-day reconnaissance trip that would take him through Singapore, Malaysia, Thailand, Cambodia, Vietnam, Brunei, and Borneo (Malaysia) to scout out U.S. diplomatic outposts before returning to Jakarta.

Before he could leave on this trip, Faruq wanted to settle the issue of his wife's passport. To expedite the process, he resorted to paying US$2,500 to a middleman who claimed close connections to immigration officials. Faruq obtained this money from Gharib, the Somali who headed Yayasan Aman.

Faruq's attempts to get a passport opened up an opportunity for BIN. By mid-April, a longtime BIN informant had been able to make fleeting contact with Faruq during the latter's attempts to deal with immigration officials. When the informant offered to help, Faruq offered his cell phone number.

Immediately, BIN passed Faruq's number to regional and international counterparts. This led to several astonishing discoveries. First, Filipino intelligence sources informed BIN that Faruq's number was in the memory of Dwikarna's cell phone. And on 27 April, it was learned from Pakistani officials that Faruq's number was also in the memory of a phone used by Abu Zubaydah,

---

[217] Gharib had fought in Bosnia with the "Afghan" contingent organized under the 3 Corps; in appreciation, he was awarded a Bosnian passport.

the al-Qaeda operations officer who had been arrested in Pakistan back on 28 March.

Faruq, meanwhile, was proving to be a moving target. In late April, he had taken leave of Bogor to implement his latest terrorist scheme. Every year since 1995, the U.S. Navy's Pacific Fleet had sponsored a series of bilateral Cooperation Afloat Readiness and Training (abbreviated as "Carat") exercises in Southeast Asia. These exercises, designed to enhance regional cooperation, focused on humanitarian and disaster relief projects. During each year since 1996, a portion of the exercises were held in Indonesia. The 2002 Carat series was set to begin on 17 May in Surabaya with some 1,400 U.S. sailors, marines, and coastguardsmen arriving on four ships.

As the Carat exercises were given significant publicity, Faruq had learned details from the press. Deciding that this was a target ripe for a suicide attack like that conducted against the U.S.S. *Cole* in Yemen, he looked for extremists willing to partake in martyrdom. Realizing that suicide was a bit extreme for local tastes, he asked Gharib, the Somali heading Yayasan Aman, to find Middle Eastern volunteers. Gharib, however, was preparing to go back to Bosnia to renew his passport and could not spare time to assist. Unable to recruit on his own, Faruq quietly shelved the idea.[218]

Meantime, the incriminating evidence against Faruq continued to mount. During May, American sources found a cell phone link between him and Ibn al-Khattab, the late Chechen commander with ties to al-Qaeda. That same month, a photo of Faruq was shown to Abu Zubaydah, who was proving somewhat cooperative with interrogators; Zubaydah positively identified the photograph as that of his Kuwaiti colleague trained in Afghanistan.[219]

Unaware that the dragnet was closing, Faruq was engrossed in terrorist planning during late May. Listing his wife's name on the license for a notional agricultural business, he purchased a ton of urea fertilizer in Bogor. This was to be used in the explosives package targeted against the U.S. embassy in Jakarta. Over the course of several shuttles, at least half a ton of the urea was picked up

---

[218] Media sources later reported that six Middle Eastern terrorists were thought to have slipped into Indonesia in May as part of the plan to attack Carat vessels. The alleged presence of these six terrorists was never corroborated.

[219] On 17 May, it was learned that Faruq's old cell phone number (he changed numbers frequently) was found among the possessions of an al-Qaeda prisoner taken to U.S. detention facilities in Cuba.

by a driver employed by Imam Hanafie, a Jemaah Islamiyah member, and stored at the latter's house in Jakarta.

By that time, BIN became aware that Faruq had succeeded in getting a false passport and was a flight risk. To prevent this, the head of BIN authorized his arrest. On the night of 4 June, a special forces team seconded to BIN ventured to Bogor. Approaching the suspect's house, the team entered at 0200 hours the next morning.

What followed next was a case of déjà vu. Just as during the initial attempted arrest of Madni, Faruq was not at home. Instead, the team found eight members of his wife's extended family.

The BIN team knew it was in trouble. In particular, it feared that word would soon leak of their presence, especially since neighbors in the hamlet had undoubtedly seen it approach. Remaining huddled inside the house, its members took pains to ensure that no members of the family attempted to alert Faruq or his wife via telephone.

Thinking fast, BIN operatives placed a call to the informant that had earlier established contact with Faruq. They dictated to him a message for Faruq, which the informant relayed via cell phone shortly after sunrise. The wife's passport was ready, the informant told the Kuwaiti, and he could pick it up at a mosque in Bogor later that morning. Faruq said that he was seeing a friend off at the airport, but that he would rendezvous in the early afternoon.

As promised, Faruq arrived at the mosque. When he was surrounded by special forces personnel seconded to BIN, he resisted slightly before being taken to the Bogor immigration office. Over the next two days, immigration and police intelligence officers attempted to interrogate him. Though he spoke some Indonesian, the detainee was not proving cooperative. Found in possession of a fraudulent passport, Faruq was flown on 8 June to the U.S. detention facility at Bagram airbase, Afghanistan.

While Faruq had been hustled out of the country, word had not leaked to the press.[220] Taking advantage of this, BIN had looked to move swiftly against his foreign colleagues. Most, however, appeared to have departed the country.

---

[220] For several days, Faruq's wife had no clue her husband had left the country. On 6 June, she telephoned the wife of Agus Dwikarna in Makassar to enquire whether she had heard of his whereabouts from Laskar Jundullah operative Mochtar Daeng Lao, or if she knew the telephone number of Gharib, the Somali who headed Yayasan Aman.

The one exception was Abu Daud, the cameraman who had been in Poso, who apparently returned to his East Jakarta home after a short absence.

Daud was something of an enigma. Born in Egypt, he had ventured to Germany in the early eighties to study math. There he married a German national and became a naturalized citizen. Remembered for his brooding personality, he ventured to Bosnia-Herzegovina in 1995, ostensibly to manage a car rental business.

His Bosnian tenure was not all business, however. Daud's company was linked to Middle Eastern extremists, many of them Afghan veterans who were looking to participate in the Balkan jihad. According to his wife, he was in touch with al-Qaeda members and took part in a firing squad that killed a Serb.[221] Daud also helped produce propaganda videos to solicit donations for the jihadists from the Middle East. He reportedly received two awards from the Bosnian leadership for these efforts.

In 1998, Daud took leave of the Balkans. Making his way to Saudi Arabia, he sought employment with a media company the following year. Later shifting to Qatar in early 2001, he attempted to land a job as a photographer for the al-Jazeera television network. Unsuccessful in this endeavor, he moved to Indonesia in the third quarter of that year. Linking up with Rashid, he obtained funding through the al-Haramain foundation and was able to secure a two-year lease on a Jakarta house without any visible means of support.

For the next year, Daud applied his photographic expertise while filming scenes of communal violence for fundraising videos. When his house was raided on 17 September 2002, the authorities found eighteen explicit videotapes, including Laskar Jundullah students navigating a jungle obstacle course and footage of Faruq and Syawal during the Poso attack. Daud was subsequently jailed for ten months on visa violations, then deported back to Germany.

By comparison, the Indonesian authorities were far less decisive against homegrown extremists. To be fair, there had been some arrests. The largest crackdown

---

[221] "Two Firms Linked to al-Qaeda, Saudi Intelligence Agency," *Chicago Tribune*, 31 March 2004. Daud's estranged wife later detailed her recollections of his Bosnian tenure in her memoirs. See Doris Gluck, *Mundtot* (Berlin: List, 2004).

had taken place back in September 2001, when police raided the paramilitary training camp in Pandeglang, Banten.

But efforts against Jemaah Islamiyah were all but absent. When Abu Bakar Ba'asyir was summoned by the police on 24 January 2002, for example, the cleric was released after a single morning of light questioning; emboldened, he continued (if not escalated) his verbal support for extremism.

So confident was Jemaah Islamiyah that most of its upper echelon – down to the wakalah leaders – converged in April 2002 for an administrative meeting at Puncak, the mountain resort area just two hours outside Jakarta. There, the leaders selected Abu Rusdan, the Sadda veteran who had been the focus of the BIN wiretap since July 2001, to act as their caretaker amir because of Ba'asyir's preoccupation with his MMI role.

On an operational level, most of Jemaah Islamiyah's leadership did not appear to be in any particular rush to conduct its next major operation. In May, several of its top members had gotten around to meeting at a Solo house rented by bomb maker Dul Matin. Thinking aloud, Mukhlas said he wanted to stage a strike against the Australian international school in Jakarta, but rhetorically noted that the defenses around that site were prohibitive.

Running down the list of targets discussed with Hambali back in February, they recalled the U.S.-operated gold mine on the island of Sumbawa. That same company, they noted, maintained an office in Mataram on the island of Lombok – and Dul Matin was intimately familiar with Mataram from his earlier employment as a data processor.[222] Since he was currently marking time as a used car salesman, Matin quickly agreed to return to Lombok on a month long reconnaissance mission.

Meanwhile, the impatient Imam Samudra was agitating for faster action. Since mid-2000, he had been quietly preening a small cadre of youthful understudies from villages in his native Banten. In doing so, Samudra was turf raiding to an extent: these recruits actually saw themselves as Darul Islam devotees, not Jemaah Islamiyah; at least one had even received basic paramilitary training at a Darul Islam camp set up in the neighboring Sukabumi district. But Samudra

---

[222] Indonesian National Police officials claim that Dul Matin was linked to a small bomb that detonated outside PT Newmont's Mataram office in October 2000. *Buku Putih Bom Bali*, p. 236. Officials from PT Newmont, however, downplay this speculation, suggesting instead that local authorities may have perpetrated the act to milk the company of protection money.

was on good terms with the local Darul Islam elders, so his headhunting was tolerated, if not encouraged.

To fill them with some of his rage, Samudra in July had beckoned his Banten cadre to Bandung. Given his overseas travels, conversant in Arabic, and mastery of things like computers and cell phones, Samudra's hold over his rural acolytes was hypnotic. When he explained the concept of *fa'i* – robbing non-believers to progress the Islamic cause – they bought into the idea without question. Leading by example, Samudra had already dabbled in credit-card fraud, using stolen numbers to purchase jewelry, then reselling it.[223]

Looking for a bigger score, Samudra in early August decided to stage a more risky armed robbery. For this, he took aside five of his apprentices and provided them with three pistols. One of the five had already identified a suitable target: the Elita Indah gold shop in the Banten provincial capital of Serang. Most importantly, the shop was owned by ethnic Chinese non-believers.

As his men set off to stage their robbery, Samudra that same month shifted with his wife and four children to Solo. Joining him, among others, was Mantiqi 1 leader Mukhlas, his brothers Ali Imron and Amrozi, Dul Matin, and, most senior, Jemaah Islamiyah military chieftain Zulkarnaen. Some of the attendees were under the impression that they were being called to organize a demonstration in front of Solo's Lor Inn, where a gathering of Christian leaders was taking place.

Zulkarnaen, however, had more deadly plans in mind. Topping his agenda, again, was the target list discussed with Hambali in Bangkok during February. Though they had agreed in Thailand that the Dumai fueling station held the most promise, the logistics were daunting. The same held true for the Exxon-Mobil site in Aceh.

Dul Matin, meanwhile, gave a mixed report following his reconnaissance in Lombok. The gold mine's office in Mataram, he said, was less than optimal because it largely employed Indonesian Muslims. On his way back to Java, however, he saw plenty of Westerners holidaying in Bali. Better still, any collateral damage to Indonesians would be limited to Balinese Hindus rather than Muslims.[224]

[223] "Bag of Tricks," *Tempo*, 27 January 2003.
[224] *Buku Putih*, p. 225.

Over the course of several more trysts in Solo during the remainder of August and early September, the cabal settled on Bali as its default target. The group also set about dividing tasks. Patterned almost exactly after the bombing of the Filipino ambassador's residence – but with a far larger car bomb – many of the same figures were charged with the same responsibilities. Amrozi, for example, was again to procure the precursor chemicals. Dul Matin would again be jerry-rigging the detonating device. Ali Imron and Mubarok, both of whom had been on the cross-island trek during the Filipino ambassador operation, were charged with coordinating transportation. An operative named Idris was to handle Bali logistics, while Samudra would source foot soldiers. Mukhlas, who was effectively out of a job following the crippling attrition to his Mantiqi 1, would act as overall supervisor.

Such plans, of course, are useless without funding. For the Bali operation, cash would come from several sources. Some would come from Hambali in Bangkok. Over the previous few months, Hambali had been obsessing over the need to procure more convincing documentation for his alternate identities. In this regard, the Spanish passport he had purchased was hardly sufficient. Showing little honor among thieves, the forgers had done a shoddy job, merely substituting an inkjet color copied bio-page that would only stand up to a cursory inspection at a border crossing. Worse, they had committed the amateurish mistake of not perforating the passport number onto the fake page, even though the rest of the pages were perforated.

Returning to the same Bangkok forger, Hambali looked to purchase yet another document. This time, a bit more care was taken in inserting his clean-shaven image into yet another stolen Spanish passport, this one issued in the name of Daniel Suarez Haviera.[225]

Still unsatisfied, Hambali was leaning toward another solution. For the past couple of months, he had been accompanied in Bangkok by Zakaria Ibuhama (alias Maliq), a Thai national and Jemaah Salafi member on loan from Abu Fatah. Maliq's brother-in-law was Abdul Aziz Hajicheming, a Thai Muslim who taught at the Saudi-financed Om al-Qura school in Phnom Penh. According to Maliq, one could purchase a genuine Cambodian passport for the sum of US$1,000.

---

[225] The owner of the second Spanish passport had made a short trip from Thailand to Laos in early December 2001 prior to his passport being stolen; learning of these visa stamps, some journalists erroneously reported that Hambali had spent time in Vientiane.

Deciding that Cambodia was a good bet, Hambali made plans to leave Thailand. In July, he dispatched Maliq and Ibrahim across the border to lay the groundwork for his document procurement mission.

Before leaving, however, he wanted to disburse funds to his colleagues in Indonesia for use as they saw fit. (Bali had not yet been finalized as their target.) By that time, a fresh case infusion had already been sent to him courtesy of KSM.[226] From it, Hambali turned over US$10,000 to his bagman, Wan Min bin Wan Mat. A former lecturer at the Malaysian Technological University, Wan Min had been with Jemaah Islamiyah since its inception. He had also helped found the Luqmanul Haqiem boarding school, serving as its director while concurrently succeeding Mukhlas as head of the wakalah in Johor. After getting the cash from Hambali, Wan Min hand-carried it to Malaysia, then entrusted it to an Indonesian laborer heading for Java. It was passed to Mukhlas later that same month.[227]

Added to this were funds from Serang. On 22 August, Samudra's cell raided Elita Indah and made off with 30 million rupiah in cash and two kilos of gold. From this, 10 million was retained by the cell members for living expenses; the rest was transferred to Mubarok's bank account for use in the Bali strike.

Together, this was deemed enough to get the operation started. On 8 September, six of the conspirators – Amrozi, Mubarok, Dul Matin, Idris, Imam Samudra, and Ali Imron – took a rented Kijang van to Bali to conduct a survey. There they were met by a Bali resident and sympathizer named Masykur Abdul Kadir. Over the course of the next few days, they rented a pair of houses. This included a residence on Jalan Pulau Menjangan in Tabanan district; complete with its own garage, this would be used as the bomb assembly site.

Amrozi, meanwhile, heading back to East Java and on 10 September found a suitable decade-old white Mitsubishi L-300 minivan for sale. Without haggling, he gave the owner 32 million rupiah in cash and then, taking it back to his motorcycle repair shop, removed the back seats and diligently filed off the serial numbers from the chassis and engine block.

---

[226] The US$20,000 channeled by KSM back in November 2001 was almost exhausted, but in April 2002 Hambali had received a windfall from Karachi. An e-mail message from KSM said the al-Qaeda operations chief was prepared to send "rice" – their codeword for money. It is not clear how much money was transferred to Hambali during the second quarter of 2002, or the method of transfer.

[227] This was the second time that Wan Min had given money to Mukhlas. Back in March, Wan Min had turned over US$15,500, some of which was used to defray Mukhlas' return transportation costs from Bangkok and some of which went into a reserve kitty.

Amrozi then headed to Tidar Kimia, the same Surabaya shop where he had obtained the precursors for the Filipino ambassador bomb. This time, however, he was instructed to get five times the amount of potassium chlorate. While this should have raised eyebrows, the proprietor was more than happy to make the 30-million-rupiah sale and did not question Amrozi's cover story that he was a fertilizer salesman in the outer islands. Sacks of sulfur and aluminum powder were also purchased, to be mixed according to Jemaah Islamiyah's proven recipe of one part each for every three parts potassium chlorate.

Others among the conspirators – Mukhlas, Dul Matin, Samudra – were fine-tuning the actual plan. Taking a page from the Palestinian playbook, they wanted to set off a small diversionary explosion that would draw a crowd, and then set off a larger bomb to inflict maximum casualties on the rubbernecking spectators. They also wanted to set off a third bomb at the U.S. consulate in Denpasar; this last device would not be intended to inflict casualties, but merely to leave no doubts about their motives and collective hatred for Washington.

A critical part of the operation was sourcing foot soldiers that would bring the bombs to the targets. During the Christmas Eve 2000 bombings, such local recruits provided a multiplier effect and an organizational buffer, shielding more senior Jemaah Islamiyah members from possible capture at the scene. But Imam Samudra now saw the foot soldiers serving a more profound purpose: he wanted suicide bombers to dramatically demonstrate Jemaah Islamiyah's commitment to the cause. Indeed, he had already promised his fellow planners that he could source five would-be martyrs.

Although it would be a first for Jemaah Islamiyah, Samudra had good reason to be optimistic he could deliver on his promise. After all, he had been patiently coaching his Banten cell for years, and five of his most loyal followers had blindly agreed to rob the Elita Indah gold shop without flinching.

Beckoning those five to Solo on 1 October, Samudra had given his pitch for martyrdom. His recruitment speech was specially tailored for its Indonesian audience. The suicide candidates were told, for example, that they could bring along their parents to Paradise – a benefit that resonated among Samudra's simplistic, impoverished recruits.

Even so, there proved to be limits to Samudra's grip. Digesting the pitch, most of his acolytes saw it as a quantum leap they would rather not take. Just one of the five – a villager named Arnasan – appeared willing to opt for the fast-track to Paradise.

By that time, it was very late in the planning stage, and the fact that Samudra could only produce one of the five promised martyrs sent a wave of angst among the other conspirators. At a bare minimum, they needed two suicide bombers – one for the diversionary explosion, and the second to set off the minivan device.

At that point, bomb expert Dul Matin stepped forward with a fallback candidate. He had been preening his own small cadre of followers in Central Java, among them a highly impressionable country boy named Fer (alias Isa, alias Iqbal). At that late hour, he quickly introduced Fer into the operation and tentatively designated him as the second suicide bomber.

Sourcing foot soldiers was not the only problem being encountered by the conspirators. By mid-September, they had started running low on cash. Anticipating the need for more funds during the final stage of the operation, Mukhlas passed word to Hambali for an emergency transfer. Just days away from departing for Phnom Penh, Hambali readied US$5,000 and passed it to his Jemaah Salafi assistant, Maliq, who carried it to Wan Min in southern Thailand. Once again, Wan Min turned it over to an Indonesian laborer returning to Java. Two days after this handover, on 28 September, the Malaysian authorities caught up with Wan Min and placed Hambali's bagman under arrest, but by that time the cash was already on its way to Mukhlas.[228]

With this new infusion of funds, the remainder of the conspirators began arriving in Bali. On 5 October, Amrozi took the Mitsubishi minivan for the one-hour ferry ride across the Bali Strait. En route, he paused to buy a dozen plastic filing cabinets, each with four drawers. He then drove to Jalan Pulau Menjangan, where a critical mass of terrorists had huddled. Besides Dul Matin, Idris, Mubarok, and Ali Imron, also present were Umar Arab (involved in the Christmas Eve 2000 operation), Sarjiyo (part of the Filipino ambassador attack), Umar Wayan (alias Abdul Ghoni), and Bali resident Masykur.

---

[228] According to the Indonesian National Police, there was an eleventh-hour infusion of cash from another source. After going to Abu Bakar Ba'asyir to receive his blessing for the operation, the cleric handed over two envelopes with US$5,000, and the equivalents of US$17,000 in Singapore dollars and US$15,000 in Malaysian ringgit. *Buku Putih*, p. 222.

They immediately set out for supplies. With a most unusual shopping list in hand, they went to a nearby department store and purchased a scale, welding iron, and voltage meter. They also found a vest popular with security guards and parking attendants; though somewhat heavy for the tropics, it was perfect for concealing explosives.

The conspirators also sourced more transportation. The sole Bali resident among them, Masykur, was charged with renting a sedan. And on 9 October, Idris, Amrozi, and Ali Imron in search of yet another motorcycle. Following standard al-Qaeda practice, they traveled far – an hour east of Denpasar – to find a used red Yamaha and dished out nine million rupiah without haggling. This was taken back to their safe house and, again following al-Qaeda practices taught in Afghanistan, was modified with three toggle switches concealed under the seat: one to isolate the engine so it could not be turned on by another operator, one to turn off the front lights, and one to turn off the rear lights.[229]

Back at the bomb factory, Dul Matin was busy assembling the devices. Assisting was Umar Arab, Sarjiyo, and Umar Wayan. Three different devices were created. The first, for the diversionary explosion, was fitted into six pockets sewn on the inside of the sleeveless vest. Into each of these went a PVC pipe loaded with sticks of dynamite. Wires from the dynamite went to a container bearing two switches, one of which led to a manual trigger over the right chest, the other of which was connected to a timer. In theory, the suicide operator would set off the device via the manual trigger. In the event he got cold feet, however, the timer provided a lethal fallback.

The second bomb was for the U.S. consulate. As this was for symbolic value rather than to inflict any serious damage, it consisted of a five-kilogram dynamite package linked to a remote detonator made from a Nokia cell phone.

The last was the primary car bomb. It was, by far, the largest and most sophisticated device ever created by Jemaah Islamiyah. Weighing portions on the scale, more than a ton of potassium chlorate, sulfur, and aluminum powder was combined according to Jemaah Islamiyah's proven 3/1/1 recipe; this mixture was then scooped into the four drawers in each of the twelve filing cabinets. The drawers were connected with detonation cord topped with commercial Indian-made detonators; both of these latter items, smuggled into Indonesia from

---

[229] The modifications to the motorcycle were more suitable for operations in places like Europe, where, for example, cameras installed at traffic lights might photograph an illuminated license plate.

Mindanao, had been earlier stockpiled by Ali Imron during the Ambon conflict. Several sticks of dynamite were placed around the cabinets to provide a booster for the precursors. These cabinets – roped together for stability – were then placed inside the rear of the van.

The detonators, in turn, were linked back to the most critical part of the device. Mustering all of his electronic skills, Dul Matin had fashioned a sophisticated circuit board that, connected to ten 9-volt batteries, fit inside a lidded container. This could pass an electrical current to the detonators by four different methods: by a signal from a cell phone, by a timer, a manual trigger, or a booby-trapped automatic detonation if the box's lid was removed. Together, these were deemed to offer more than enough fallbacks.

Other conspirators, meanwhile, had been seeking targets. The search was not particularly difficult. Foreign nationals tended to congregate along two roads in the Kuta tourist district: Jalan Pantai Raya that hugged the beach, and Jalan Legian that paralleled the beach one block inland. And along these two roads, they correctly identified the Sari Club nightclub on Legian as the most crowded on any given night. As a clincher, Paddy's Irish Pub was located just twenty meters away – the perfect location for the diversionary explosion.

Better still, dozens of burly Caucasians with crew cuts had been seen strolling down Legian. Noting them, Samudra was excited because he thought they were U.S. sailors on shore leave and relished the thought of inflicting casualties on American servicemen; in fact, they were Australian rugby players in town for a championship series that weekend.

Not all was going to plan, however. For one thing, construction of the circuit board was proving a bit too daunting for Dul Matin. During a trial run using the voltage meter, the electrical current was found to be not properly flowing to the detonators. As a proper explosion hinged on this working as advertised, they had little choice but to seek help from Jemaah Islamiyah's premier bomb maker, Azhari. After tweaking the circuitry, Azhari managed to get a proper electrical reading to the detonators.

For another thing, there were problems with the foot soldiers. Reduced to just two persons – Arnasan from Banten, Fer from Central Java – the plan called for the pair to depart from the safe house in the van. Once at the Sari Club, Fer would walk across the street, enter Paddy's, and set off his explosive vest to become Jemaah Islamiyah's first suicide bomber. Arnasan, meanwhile, would wait until a crowd materialized in the street before taking his own life with the massive van device.[230]

The trouble was, there were indications that the two bombers were waffling in their commitment. To steel their will, Mukhlas delivered a pep talk. Renowned within Jemaah Islamiyah for his charismatic oratory skills, Mukhlas took the two aside and drilled into them the necessity to seek martyrdom; for the time, at least, it seemed to have its desired effect.

But there were some things that encouragement from Mukhlas could not overcome. Both the bombers were unsophisticated village boys, and it was belatedly learned that neither knew how to drive a car around corners or in reverse. This meant that one of the planners would need to expose himself by driving the van close to the Sari Club, pointing it in the right direction, and then letting Arnasan drive it in a straight line along the final stretch to the target. Ali Imron was given this role, despite much complaining on his part.

By Saturday, 12 October, the conspirators were as ready as they would ever be. That evening, Ali Imron at 2030 hours set out from the safe house in the red Yamaha; strapped to the back was the remote-controlled bomb intended for the U.S. consulate. After throwing it across the wall toward the target, he took a circuitous route back to Jalan Pulau Menjangan.

At 2230, Idris sped off in the red Yamaha motorcycle and Ali Imron got behind the wheel of the van. Fer, wearing the vest, was seated on the far left. Sandwiched between them, and cradling the circuit board, was Arnasan. If all went according to plan, just two of the four would return.

---

[230] Both of the suicide bombers took the alias Iqbal. This, plus the fact that the operation was compartmentalized and some of the conspirators never met Fer, led to confusion during the early weeks after the bombing as to how many suicide operatives were involved.

CHAPTER FOURTEEN

CAMBODIAN INTERLUDE

Ali Imron weaved through the Saturday evening traffic, slowed by the congestion as he neared Jalan Legian. The two suicide bombers spoke little, having withdrawn into themselves as their imminent fate hit home. Arriving at the final intersection before the target, Imron pulled to the left side and set the timers on the vest and van bomb. Too nervous to think clearly, he forgot to attach the wires to the cell phone strapped to the circuit board; this remote option for detonating the minivan was no longer available. As the van was now pointed in the same direction as the Sari Club – and within Arnasan's limited steering ability – Ali Imron got out. According to plan, Idris was idling his motorcycle nearby; with Ali Imron getting on the back, they quickly vacated the scene.

Midway to Denpasar, Idris slowed to a stop. Removing a cell phone from his jacket, he placed a call to the Nokia set strapped to the consulate bomb. He immediately redialed and got the automated mailbox recording; this was the signal that the bomb had already exploded.

Shifting to the driver's seat, meanwhile, Arnasan pressed the gasoline pedal on the Kijang and crept forward. Coming abreast of the Sari Club, he stopped the van. Fer immediately disembarked, crossed the street, and entered Paddy's. It was just past 2300 hours; the pub was packed with revelers.

At that point, Fer almost certainly got cold feet. Eyewitnesses would testify that he entered into a heated exchange with a bargirl, apparently because he was attempting to leave behind the explosives-laden shawl. Whether the timer eventually set off the device, or he suddenly garnered enough will to depress the hand trigger, at 2307 hours the five kilos of dynamite detonated in the center of the bar. Human residue from Fer was later found sprayed on the ceiling; his head and legs were recovered elsewhere in the rubble.

In front of the Sari Club, meanwhile, Arnasan had been drawing heat because he had not been able to maneuver the van close to the curb and was partially blocking traffic. Plans called for him to wait several minutes after the Paddy's explosion before setting off his bomb. But whether because he was nervous over the flak he was getting from other motorists, or because he was too pumped full of adrenaline to make an accurate calculation, he depressed the trigger on his device just fifteen seconds after Fer's detonation.

From a purely technical point of view, the resulting minivan explosion was a failure. Although it left a two-feet-deep crater and could be heard five kilometers away, only about a third of the precursor chemicals actually exploded; the rest simply burned in a huge fireball.

But in a sick twist, the poor detonation of the precursors actually worked in favor of the terrorists. This was true for two reasons. First, the concrete shell of a partially-constructed bank building stood across the street from the Sari Club; its back wall had been completed, but the front was open to the street. The Sari Club, meanwhile, had an open dance floor framed by a high concrete wall across its back and sides. When the minivan detonated, the shock waves raced outward – only to be contained, concentrated and reversed by the rear walls of the bank and the Sari Club in a deadly echo effect.

Second, the Sari Club had a relatively weak thatched roof. As the shock waves from the bomb ricocheted back from the rear wall, it sent Sari's roof tumbling down on the packed dance floor.

When the enormous fireball from the burning precursors flamed outward, the intense heat ignited thatch from Sari's collapsed roof, trapping patrons dazed by the blast concussion. A wave of flames rushed down the road, scorching buildings 200 meters away. Bali's fire department was fully overwhelmed by the blaze, not bringing it under control until it consumed structures 400 meters away.

The tally from the twin blasts was horrific. Two hundred and two persons were confirmed dead, including 88 Australians. Some 350 others were wounded. Fifty-eight buildings were damaged; 19 cars and 32 motorcycles were destroyed.

For at least the first two hours, foul play was not confirmed. Early suspicions pointed toward exploding propane tanks used at some of the popular roadside kitchens along Legian. But by 0300 hours, 13 October, initial eyewitness testimony, plus the sheer scale of the damage, pointed toward terrorism.[231]

❦

In the weeks leading up to the Bali bombing, the Indonesian authorities had indications that Jemaah Islamiyah had something in the works. This was the result of a mid-2002 BIN penetration operation which had succeeded in locating Yasir, the extremist who had shuttled the van to Jakarta during the Philippine ambassador bombing. Extended surveillance of Yasir and his closest contacts revealed a scheme to attack an Italian-flagged ship that was headed for Poso, Central Sulawesi, with humanitarian aid. Its mixed crew of Italians and Singaporeans were believed to be in particular danger.

Rather than immediately arrest Yasir, however, BIN elected to keep him under watch in the hope that he would lead them to co-conspirators. Letting him board a vessel from Jakarta, it was not until 2 October 2002 that they swooped in and detained him in Central Sulawesi. Though the plot against the Italian boat was frustrated, the authorities still had reason for concern. Under interrogation, Yasir revealed that Jemaah Islamiyah was in the final stages of an impending operation. Due to compartmentalization he did not know any details – other than it was going to be "big."[232]

Concurrently, a second BIN operation had been ongoing against a cell of extremists in West Java. The back-story to this operation was convoluted. Back in May 2002, BIN Deputy Chief As'at Said had visited counterparts in Yemen and received a list of six phone numbers from known Yemeni militants who had called Indonesia.

---

[231] At 1930 hours on the same night, a pipe bomb detonated outside the Philippine consulate in Manado, North Sulawesi. The main gate was damaged and the windows were shattered. Given the timing, many speculated that the attack was part of a coordinated effort by the same persons that conducted the Bali bombing. An exhaustive investigation by Indonesian and Filipino authorities, however, concluded that the bombing was the result of a business dispute by persons linked to a small gold mine near Manado and a Filipina gold-trader. NICA Report, "Activities of Fact-Finding Team," November 2002; *Tempo*, 25 August 2003, p. 75.

[232] Interview with As'at Said, 22 August 2002.

Back in Indonesia, these numbers were checked. Among them, one was linked to a 42-year-old Indonesian of Arab descent living in West Java. When he was scrutinized over the following month, it was learned that he had made calls to a number associated with Umar Faruq (who had recently been captured in Bogor). Other calls were made to extremists in Ngruki.

All of this led BIN to scrutinize him further. Over the following three months, a telephone tap on his landline found the target to be braggadocio, liberally mixing facts, hearsay, and empty boasts.

On 13 October, the day after the Bali bomb, this subject was in fine form. Bragging to a colleague, he claimed to know with authority that nine persons had conducted the attack. Among them, he said, were Imam Samudra (true) and Abdul Jabar (false). He further claimed that the device had been assembled from high explosives stockpiled in Semarang, and that a Yemeni member of al-Qaeda – allegedly named Syafullah, allegedly traveling on a fake U.S. passport – had provided key technical assistance and had been in Bali during the days immediately before the bombing.

This last detail sent BIN on a tangent that would persist for the next six months. Seeing the massive extent of the damage in Bali, the agency bought into the idea that it was the result of high explosives.[233] They also convinced themselves that a bomb which inflicted that much carnage was beyond the ability of Jemaah Islamiyah, and thus must have been constructed with the assistance of the mysterious Syafullah.[234]

On a parallel track, the Indonesian National Police dedicated some of its best investigators to the Bali case. They were assisted from the earliest days by ten police counterparts from around the world, the most prominent being the Australian Federal Police. As might be expected in such a major undertaking, some

---

[233] On a more infantile level, several so-called Indonesian experts claimed that the Bali blast was the result of a "micro-nuclear" bomb. A former head of the Indonesian intelligence agency, Z.A. Maulani, who was known for his extreme religious beliefs, charged that only the U.S. or the Israelis could have been behind the attack. See *Forum*, 24 November 2002, p. 14, 19; Z.A. Maulani, *Jama'ah Islamiyah dan China Policy* (Jakarta: Daseta, 2004), p. 57.

[234] The mysterious Yemeni connection to the Bali bombing remained a leading BIN theory for years. It was first reported in "The Jihadi's Tale," *Time*, 27 January 2003, p. 18.

of their leads proved to be dead-ends. Weeks, for example, were spent looking for the alleged Yemeni named Syafullah. As it turned out, there were several Yemenis who had been in Kuta during the run-up to 12 October. Some were Yemeni crewmembers from a Spanish fishing vessel which had developed engine trouble in the Bali Strait and briefly came ashore in early October. Others were Indonesian nationals of Yemeni descent – woodworkers from East Java – who had been looking to ply their wares in Bali. And one was a Yemeni tourist found in possession of a fake U.S. driver's license. None had any ties to radical organizations.

Other leads were even more fanciful. Ten Pakistani itinerant preachers were quizzed when it was learned they had been in a Kuta mosque in early October, but an investigation showed they all had sound alibis during the period leading up to the bombing. And in a bigger stretch, the police interrogated the Italian owner of Kuta's Scandal discothèque. The reason: his disco had coincidentally held an "Ultimate Explosion Party" on 12 October, and the police thought that the party fliers might have held a coded message for the terrorists.[235]

But through good forensic work and serendipity, the investigators began to catch some lucky breaks. The first came on 13 October, when a caretaker at a Denpasar mosque reported that a Yamaha motorcycle had been abandoned in the parking lot. What's more, he had seen two men drive it there 40 minutes after the bomb, wipe down its seat with a cloth, and disappear into the night. (This had been used by Imron and Idris, who headed to the mosque for prayers after the bombing, then walked to a rented room used by Imam Samudra.)

One aspect about the motorcycle immediately caught the attention of the police. Under its seat, they noted the toggle switches used for turning off the lights. A counter-terrorism expert from the French police, who had rushed to Bali to provide assistance, quickly recognized this as an al-Qaeda signature modification. Equally damning, explosive residue was found on the handlebars and key.

Focusing on the motorcycle, the authorities soon traced the serial number on its engine to a used motorcycle showroom in Denpasar. Two employees vividly recalled three men – later confirmed as Amrozi, Ali Imron, and Idris – who had purchased his motorcycle on 10 October. What was noteworthy,

---

[235] "Power Plays," *Tempo*, 4 November 2002, p. 25.

they said, was that they had weighed options for about an hour and then paid the sticker price without haggling. What's more, when a police artist sketched three portraits, two were the same as the pair seen by the caretaker at the Denpasar mosque.

More luck followed over the ensuing weeks. After isolating parts of the minivan from the rubble, on 2 November they discovered that an additional serial number had been engraved under a welded plate on the engine block. This was because one of the previous owners of the van had been a Balinese who used it for carrying paying customers – and a local ordinance called for all public transportation vehicles to have an additional serial number engraved on the engine. Amrozi had no way of knowing this, and had thus failed to file it off.

Armed with this serial number, the investigators traced the van to its sixth owner in East Java. That owner, in turn, fingered Amrozi as the seventh.

Arrested on 5 November in Lamongan, Amrozi proved to be a windfall for the police. From the earliest hours of his interrogation, he readily gave up six other conspirators in the bombing: Ali Imron, Dul Matin, Idris, Imam Samudra, Umar Arab, and Umar Wayan. Though he made no mention of older brother Mukhlas, the authorities intuitively added him to the list of suspects.[236]

A massive dragnet ensued. To assist, the Australians provided cutting-edge equipment for triangulating cell phone transmissions. But even with this advanced technology, tracking the Jemaah Islamiyah suspects was a major challenge. Said one investigator from the Australian Federal Police, "They were like Colombian drug lords: they used three cell phones apiece, each with six SIM cards."

And even if the technical surveillance teams could isolate all of the numbers used by a particular terrorist, the tracking technology had limits. In rural areas with few cell phone repeater towers, for example, triangulation could only narrow down the search area to several square kilometers.

Persistence, however, paid off. With one joint Indonesian-Australian team concentrating on Imam Samudra, they tracked his cell phone moving west across Java toward his native Banten. Though the phone then went dead in mid-November, analysis of his call history showed he had been in frequent contact

---

[236] Found buried in the teak forest behind Amrozi's house were six large PVC pipes filled with weapons and ammunition, including two M-16 rifles. "Hunt for the Terror Mastermind," *Tempo*, 25 November 2002, p. 14. Neighbors had been suspicious of Amrozi for months; they noted he had erected spotlights pointing toward the teak forest. *Buku Putih*, p. 213.

with a cell phone in the town of Cilegon. This turned out to be used by Abdul Rauf, one of Samudra's Elita Indah gold robbers. Placed in custody on 20 November, he led investigators to Yudi, an Elita Indah accomplice. Yudi, in turn, gave the police Samudra's new cell phone number. After Rauf was enticed into making e-mail contact with the target, it was learned he was preparing to head for sanctuary in Sumatra.

Realizing that time was of the essence, undercover police officers rushed to the port of Merak. Arriving at 1700 hours, they found a line of buses waiting to board the trans-island ferry. Entering them in turn, at 1745 they spied a man fitting Samudra's description with a cap pulled low over the face. A local police officer, who happened to have been a high school classmate, made a positive identification as the fugitive was placed into custody.[237]

At 2100 hours that night, police visited Samudra's last known address and made some tantalizing discoveries. Topping the list was an Acer laptop computer, whose hard drive dramatically revealed Samudra's hyper-caffeinated activism. Part of it was loaded with secular normality: Japanese anime, photographs of Britney Spears, even pornographic spreads of Caucasian women. There was also evidence of Samudra's dabbling in credit-card fraud.[238]

But part of it was loaded with the blueprint for a radical website Samudra had dubbed istimata.com. Deriving its name from the Arabic word for "martyr," Samudra had built the site "to answer Moslems' questions about the Bali blast." In it, he made clear his hatred for Jews and non-believers, and offered no apologies for targeting Bali because it was a "popular place of sin." He had put the finishing touches on the wording just two days earlier, but had yet to post it on the Internet before his arrest.

At the same time Samudra was being brought to justice, a second Indonesian-Australian technical team was in Central Java pursuing Mukhlas. They did not realize how close they were until 3 December when, in the shadow of the Merapi volcano, they visited a village residence on the trail of another suspected extremist. Entering the house, a glaring Mukhlas – bellowing *Allah Akbar!* – leapt toward the investigators in an attempt to wrestle away a pistol. He was quickly subdued.

---

[237] BIN report, Staf Ahli Bidang Sosial Budaya, Tim Penyelidikan Kejahatan Transnasional, "Tertangkapnya Imam Samudra," 22 November 2002, p. 2.

[238] "Porn Found on Samudra's Computer, Trial Told," *Sydney Morning Herald*, 7 July 2003.

More arrests ensued. By mid-2003, some 83 persons linked to the Bali blasts were in custody. Of them, 15 were directly related to the attack, another 35 were guilty of harboring fugitives or withholding information, and another 30 possessed explosives or firearms. In Australia, meanwhile, raids conducted in late October 2002 effectively closed down Jemaah Islamiyah's embryonic Mantiqi 4.[239]

One key suspect that still eluded the authorities was Hambali. During the months prior to the Bali bombing, most regional intelligence agencies surmised that he was hiding out in Indonesia. Early in the second week of October, in fact, a BIN team had ventured to a small Arab community on the north coast of East Java where an informant had reported the recent presence of a clean-shaven Hambali. Residents identified photographs of the fugitive on 11 October, though the terrorist himself had apparently departed.

Two months later, BIN resumed its search for Hambali. This came after an unsolicited letter from Medan arrived in December; the letter stated that an acquaintance of the writer, who had spent considerable time among the Ngruki exiles in Malaysia, reportedly met Hambali at a market near Medan circa mid-2002. BIN operatives rushed to North Sumatra, located the writer, and then found the acquaintance who allegedly met Hambali. The terrorist was again said to be clean-shaven, just as had been reported in East Java. But as the information was stale – it predated the East Java sighting – the lead went nowhere.

In hindsight, the Indonesia sightings were not grounded in fact.[240] Through

---

[239] Mantiqi 4, created on paper in 1996, theoretically covered Australia and Papua New Guinea. It consisted of 15 individuals, virtually all of them Indonesian-Australians or Indonesian nationals. The mantiqi commander, Abdul Rahim Ayub, had moved from Indonesia to Australia in 1997 and lived in a Perth suburb; he fled back to Indonesia a few days after the Bali bombing. When his Perth house was raided in late October 2002, among the evidence recovered by the authorities was Hambali's old Malaysian bank account number. For the most part, the main role of this mantiqi was to provide financial support for Indonesian operations, but there were exceptions. During a raid at the home of another Jemaah Islamiyah member in Sydney, the authorities found a suspicious letter from an aviation company regarding an inquiry about pilot training. In addition, when Australian national and Muslim convert Jack Roche was arrested and questioned during the same time frame, he revealed that he had trained in Afghanistan and spoke with both Hambali and KSM about attacking the Israeli embassy in Canberra. The authorities found evidence he twice spoke with Hambali via telephone in May 2000, and cased the Israeli embassy the next month. This plot was allegedly called off after infighting between Ayub and Hambali.

[240] It is possible that the Medan witness had in fact seen Hambali, but was off in his reported timing by half a year.

late September 2002, Hambali had not left Thailand. Toward the close of that month, he departed Bangkok for the Cambodian border. His associate, Ibrahim, had already gone ahead and reported that illegal crossings could be easily accomplished at Cambodia's coastal Koh Khong province. Ibrahim had already identified a corrupt border policeman who would arrange an undocumented entry into Koh Khong for a nominal fee of US$35 – no questions asked.

True to Ibrahim's word, the Cambodian police officer was waiting at the Koh Khong crossing in an unmarked vehicle. They drove for a few kilometers, met up with Ibrahim, and continued all the way to the Cambodian capital, Phnom Penh.

Once there, Hambali found an Internet café and sent off a series of e-mail messages to top Jemaah Islamiyah members in Indonesia. A return message from Mukhlas was particularly revealing. Without offering specifics, the Mantiqi 1 boss said that he was working on a major operation that would happen on a weekend in the near future. You will read about it in the news, Mukhlas promised.

That same week, Imam Samudra also sent a message. "I want to *jalan-jalan* [go] to Bali," it read. From Samudra's indiscreet reference, Hambali now knew the target of the upcoming attack.

In the month after the Bali bombing, Hambali and Ibrahim laid low. Making like tourists, they visited the Angkor Wat temple complex in Siem Reap and spent time in Kampot province.

But by mid-November, the pair refocused on their original intention to source Cambodian passports. Helping them was Ismael Smann, a member of Cambodia's Cham ethnic minority. Once proud rulers of Champa – a kingdom covering southern present-day Vietnam – the Cham had forfeited control of their homeland in the mid-fifteenth century and migrated west into Cambodia. Two decades later, while steadily ceding territory to the ethnic Khmer, the Cham converted to Islam en masse.

The Cham had hit upon hard times in recent decades. Singled out for particularly harsh persecution during the reign of the Khmer Rouge, their culture for a time was all but obliterated. But by the mid-nineties, the Cham had made a rebound of sorts. With money flowing in from humanitarian organizations in Malaysia and the Middle East, new mosques and Islamic boarding schools mushroomed for the estimated 120,000 Muslims in predominantly Buddhist Cambodia.

Coming, too, were opportunities for Islamic study outside of Cambodia. This included about 80 scholarships a year to study in the Middle East and Pakistan, many of them at Wahhabi institutions.[241] As of 2002, it was estimated that 6 percent of all Cham subscribed to this ultra-orthodox branch of Islam.

This group included Ismael Smann. A simple village boy, he had not progressed past junior high school in his native Kampot. From there, he had gone to Islamic schools in Kompong Cham and Phnom Penh before getting a scholarship from Abdul Fatah's pesantren in southern Thailand. He had been in Thailand off and on since 1999; his mother sold a cow each year to provide him with spending money.

Based on a referral from Abdul Fatah, Ibrahim had met Ismael when he arrived in Koh Khong prior to Hambali's arrival. Ismael was more than happy to assist, and introduced the pair to a fellow Cham named Hasan. It was through Hasan, and the same corrupt policeman who helped them cross the border, that Hambali and Ibrahim were able to procure false Cambodian resident cards.

Ismael had something else to offer. His sister, a young divorcee named Khat Ti Yah, had caught the eye of Ibrahim. Having been on the run for nearly a year, he was in the market for a second wife. Khat Ti Yah was amenable, and after a hasty ceremony, the two were newlyweds.

For the next month, Hambali, Ibrahim, and his wife stayed in Kampot. On one level, it was perfect because they could lead anonymous lives far from the prying eyes of regional intelligence agencies. But the arrangement soon proved less than ideal because Khat Ti Yah's extended family constantly pressured her Malaysian husband for monetary handouts.

Opting to return to Phnom Penh, the trio was in the capital by December. By that time, Ibrahim had grown tired of Cambodia and was seeking an alternative sanctuary in the Middle East. Compensating his wife with money to buy a cow, he stole out of the kingdom on his own.

For his part, Hambali immersed himself in the life of a budget tourist. Moving into a cheap guesthouse overlooking Phnom Penh's Boeng Kak Lake, he spent most days keeping to himself and reading English-language magazines. He also would occasionally stay at the house of Abdul Aziz Hajicheming, the

---

[241] NBR Analysis, "Funding Terrorism in Southeast Asia: The Financial Network of Al Qaeda and Jemaah Islamiyah," by Zachary Abuza, Vol. 14/No. 5 (December 2003), p. 33.

Thai Muslim who was the brother-in-law of Maliq, his Jemaah Salafi associate in Bangkok.

Under the surface, however, he itched to reengage in the Jemaah Islamiyah struggle. He was not alone: joining him in Cambodia at the opening of 2003 was a member of KSM's Malaysian suicide squad, Zubair.[242] Brainstorming, the pair began to plot future operations. The problem was that Phnom Penh was seemingly bereft of viable targets, however. The U.S. embassy, for one, was surrounded by too much security. The British embassy was slightly more promising; during a reconnaissance mission, Zubair noted that its Cambodian guards tended to drift off to sleep and its open front gate offered an opportunity for a car bomb. But with no ready source of explosives or bomb experts, the plan went nowhere.

Going nowhere, too, was a scheme by Hambali to procure a surface-to-air missile. This plan had been hatched when he was waiting on the beach near Johor Baru in late 2001. During that occasion, he had seen passenger jets pass overhead on their way to Singapore's Changi airport. So low were the jets that Hambali thought it possible to visually identify an Israeli airliner and down it with a missile over Singaporean airspace. He was reminded of the idea in late November 2002, when he read that an al-Qaeda team fired two missiles at an Israeli airliner in Kenya in an unsuccessful bid to bring it down.

Hambali had good reason to think he could procure the necessary weaponry in Cambodia. That kingdom, after all, had experienced almost continuous fighting from the late sixties to the mid-nineties. Not only was the country awash with weapons, but its military had more than its share of corrupt officers willing to sell arms without asking questions.

In this particular instance, however, he was to be disappointed. After sending Zubair to seek out Cambodian arms merchants, his lieutenant returned with nothing more than some photocopies and secondhand information that missiles might be available in Burma for about US$30,000. The idea was soon shelved.

Hambali was disappointed on one other count. He had originally gone to Cambodia to purchase an authentic passport. But despite repeated attempts, he

---

[242] The leader of the suicide squad, Marsan bin Arshad, was captured by Malaysian authorities in mid-2002 when he attempted to re-enter his homeland.

found that the Cambodian authorities were too inquisitive and were suspicious of his inability to speak Khmer.

Frustrated, Hambali decided to return to Thailand. There were other considerations that factored into this decision. For one thing, his name and face were appearing in the regional media with increased regularity, and he was afraid of being recognized in the relatively small Phnom Penh expatriate community. Already, Abdul Aziz Hajicheming, who had come to know his true identify after a January 2003 article in *Time* magazine, was giving him the cold shoulder.

For another thing, he needed to return to Thailand for financial reasons. At the close of 2002, he had gone to a cyber café and downloaded an e-mail from Pakistan. Forwarded by an intermediary, it said that KSM was going to send more "rice" by courier – but only after Hambali was back in Bangkok.

Travel to Thailand was suddenly not an option, however. Following a quick deterioration in Thai-Khmer relations during January 2003, anti-Thai mobs went on the rampage in Phnom Penh and torched the Thai embassy. Thailand retaliated by sealing the border.

Not until February 2003 did bilateral ties edge back toward a state of normalcy. Wasting no time, Hambali and Zubair bade farewell to Boeng Kak and made their way to the Poipet border checkpoint. Waiting until 0730 hours, when hundreds of Cambodians regularly stream across the frontier to procure goods on the Thai side of the border, they paid the equivalent of a quarter apiece and entered with the flow of shoppers to the Thai town of Aranyaprathet. From there, it was a simple bus ride to Bangkok.

Upon reaching the Thai capital, Hambali and Zubair were greeted by a third colleague. Lillie, another member of KSM's Malaysian suicide squad, had arrived a few days earlier, linked up with Hambali's wife, and had a rented apartment waiting for them amidst the Muslim community in Bangkok's On Nut district.

Settling into the apartment, the three terrorists had ample reason for concern. Following the wave of detentions in Indonesia after the Bali bombing, Jemaah Islamiyah was in a state of disarray. Within the markaz, schisms had developed as acting amir Abu Rusdan, who advocated more discreet steps toward achieving an Islamic state, was at increasing odds with several of his peers. One echelon down, the mantiqi leadership had been devastated by arrests. The wakalah leadership was also heavily depleted, leaving many local cells with little command structure to provide guidance or coordination. And on a more symbolic level, spiritual leader Abu Bakar Ba'asyir was among those sitting in a jail cell.

The silver lining, at least for Hambali, was that a handful of Jemaah Islamiyah's most deadly operatives remained on the loose. This included military czar Zulkarnaen, bomb makers Azhari and Dul Matin, and Malaysian fugitive Noordin Top. Avoiding capture, too, was ranking KMM operative Zulkifli Hir, who had fled to Mindanao and was operating alongside the MILF.

Before any of these figures could consider their next major operation, they needed money. A trickle was coming from southern Thailand, where Zubair had gone to collect Jemaah Islamiyah's accumulated profits from its Jemaah Salafi rice-growing investment; this, however, would barely cover living expenses for Hambali and his cohorts in Bangkok.

But as KSM had promised, more of al-Qaeda's brand of "rice" was on the way. So pleased was he with the Bali bombing, the al-Qaeda operations chief had earmarked US$50,000 for both operational purposes and for the families of the imprisoned Bali bombers.

To handle the transfer, KSM back in December 2002 had beckoned his nephew, al-Qaeda facilitator Ammar al-Baluchi. Gathering in a Karachi apartment, KSM had turned over a brick of US$100 bills. Ammar, in turn, had rendezvoused in a nearby park with an al-Qaeda member who intended to travel to Thailand with his wife. The plan was for this operative to carry the money to Bangkok. Once there, he would e-mail Ammar with a time and location to pass the cash to Hambali.

Upon further consideration, however, Ammar changed his mind. Given heightened airport security, he feared that the money might be discovered and the al-Qaeda operator would have a hard time explaining why he was carrying such a large amount of funds.

Instead, he instructed the operative to use a *hawala* transfer. The hawala underground banking system, common in the Muslim world, was based on simplicity itself: a person wishing to transfer funds would find a hawala money changer and turn over the cash plus a modest administrative fee. The money changer would supply the name of a counterpart money changer in the destination city, along with a password. The onus was on the money changers to ensure that the required amount of cash was available for the person providing the password at the other end. In short, it was similar to Western Union, but without the electronic money trail linking back to the party sending the cash or the one retrieving it. What's more, the hawala operators asked no uncomfortable questions.

For the al-Qaeda transfer to Thailand, a hawala money changer in Karachi accepted the US$50,000 and provided the name and phone number of his Bangkok counterpart. He also gave the password "Sohail," a common Pakistani surname.

Upon getting this information, Ammar relayed the details in an e-mail to Hambali after the latter's return from Cambodia. Zubair soon showed up at the stipulated money changer in Bangkok and uttered the password "Sohail." He walked away with US$50,000.

With this infusion of cash, Hambali had to decide on its use. Already, he and his two colleagues had established e-mail contact with some of their key Jemaah Islamiyah brethren. Compartmentalizing this contact, Hambali himself exchanged messages only with Noordin Top, while Zubair handled Azhari. Lillie, meantime, kept in touch with Zulkifli Hir in the Philippines.

Azhari, in particular, was especially eager to go operational. "I want business," pleaded one of his messages, "but have no capital."

Hambali was more than willing to oblige the Malaysian doctor, with certain conditions. He made clear that he favored a single spectacular operation rather than a series of pinpricks. He also told Azhari that, if an embassy attack was not feasible, he still preferred a hit on a major Western economic target like the Dumai oil facility or a tanker in the Malacca Strait. "No McDonald's or Kentucky Fried Chicken," he admonished.

With Azhari amenable to these stipulations, Hambali earmarked half of the amount provided by KSM for Indonesia: US$15,000 for Azhari's living expenses and operational funds, plus US$10,000 for the families of the arrested Bali bombers. In the latter category, he noted that Mukhlas' wife had recently been arrested on lesser charges and needed about US$3,000 to get out of detention.

Then came the mechanics of getting the money to Azhari. A series of hand transfers were to be used. That May, Lillie took the cash to Hat Yai in southern Thailand. There, he turned it over to a Malaysian school friend named Johan, who carried it to Dumai in Sumatra, where a courier from Azhari was waiting. Soon thereafter, Noordin Top sent an e-mail to Hambali confirming the funds arrived safely.

For the other half of KSM's money, Hambali wanted to fund Philippine operations. Thinking aloud, he already talked with Zubair about the possibility of attacking U.S. military facilities in Mindanao. Another option was to hit nightclubs or restaurants frequented by U.S. servicemen.

To do this, Hambali wanted to use the KMM's Zulkifli Hir as a proxy. Just as he had done with Azhari, he was to shift the funds via a series of hand transfers. That June, Lillie's Malaysian friend, Johan, carried the cash to an intermediary named Raymond in Cebu City, who then delivered it to Zulkifli. Lillie soon received an e-mail stating that the funds were in hand. Without giving any specifics, Zulkifli promised that he would use if for an operation "like Chechnya."[243]

⌘

Operations in Indonesia and the Philippines were not the only ones envisioned by Hambali. Closer to home, he very much wanted to lash out in Thailand. He had already sent his lieutenants to case Bangkok's Don Muang International Airport, where they noted that Israeli tourists tended to congregate at a bus stop near the arrival hall after every El Al flight. A suicide bomber using a backpack with explosives, they reasoned, would be guaranteed to inflict significant casualties.

Another possible target was one of the Israeli restaurants in Bangkok's budget tourist district. Again, they envisioned a strike with a backpack stuffed with explosives.

Finally, Hambali contemplated a spoiling attack a week ahead of the Asia-Pacific Economic Cooperation conference slated for Bangkok in mid-October.

To do any these, however, they needed local support, bomb-making materials, and (for at least some of the scenarios) suicide volunteers. But Hambali was being held at arm's length by Jemaah Salafi, he had no ready source for chemical precursors or bomb triggers, and – with Lillie and Zubair too valuable to sacrifice – no martyrs on hand.

---

[243] After a series of arrests in May 2004, the Philippine authorities discovered how the money had actually been spent. Half of the US$25,000 was retained by Zulkifli Hir, ostensibly to fund bombings. The other half was divided, some used as seed money for a money-changing operation that would fund future Jemaah Islamiyah activities in Mindanao, some to rent a safe house in Cotabato City, and some as a dowry for Zulkifli's future wife.

This, it turned out, was the least of his worries. In late May, the Cambodian authorities, acting on intelligence from the U.S., arrested four extremists in Phnom Penh ahead of a visit by Secretary of State Colin Powell. Among them were Abdul Aziz Hajicheming and Ismael Smann, both of whom quickly informed the authorities about their dealings with Hambali through the beginning of the year.

From Pakistan came new information. On 1 March, KSM was captured by the authorities after a fierce gun battle outside Islamabad. Almost immediately, he began providing tantalizing leads to his interrogators, including clues as to the whereabouts of this nephew. Based on these tips, Ammar al-Baluchi was in a prison cell by the following month. Ammar, in turn, revealed details of the US$50,000 transfer to Bangkok.

For Hambali, Lillie, and Zubair, the noose was quickly tightening.

CHAPTER FIFTEEN

THE FOREIGNERS

Hambali no doubt had a premonition the end was near. Local newspapers, after all, had widely covered the May capture of Aziz Hajicheming, Ismael Smann and the other militants in Phnom Penh, and he could only assume they had revealed his recent presence in Cambodia and subsequent move to Thailand.[244]

The news closer to home was equally disturbing. On 16 May, acting on a tip from Singaporean intelligence, Thai police had staged a raid in Bangkok that netted one Singaporean and four Thai extremists. They had been caught with marked maps of the city and were apparently contemplating attacks on five embassies. Though this was a segregated cell that had no links which could lead to Hambali, the heightened vigilance of the Thai authorities offered him little comfort.

All of which led Hambali and his cohorts to fall back on their familiar refrain of sourcing more convincing false identities and seeking more secure sanctuaries. To these ends, Lillie was instructed to make a quick trip to Laos in order to determine whether Vientiane was a good bet. Zubair, meanwhile, was tasked with collecting travel literature to weigh other options. He was also given photographs of Hambali's wife and told to look into the possibility of having them substituted into a stolen Filipino passport.

---

[244] In late December 2004, a Cambodian court sentenced Jemaah Islamiyah members Hambali and Ibrahim, Thai nationals Aziz Hajicheming and Mohammad Yalaludin Mading, Egyptian Rousha Yasser and Cambodian national Ismael Smann to life in prison for plotting terrorist attacks. Egyptian Mohamid Khird Ali was freed on lack of evidence. Only five of the seven were present: Hambali by that time was in U.S. custody and Ibrahim was still a fugitive.

By late June, Hambali's two lieutenants reported back. Vientiane, said Lillie, should be discounted. Not only was the expatriate population far smaller than Phnom Penh – offering them little camouflage – but the government security services were pervasive. The xenophobic governments of Burma and Vietnam, stated Zubair, were equally unappealing. For the time being, they had little choice but to stay in Thailand.

But there was also a question of money. With KSM and Ammar al-Baluchi arrested, they had no assurances of more "rice" transfers. The only other financial resources at their disposal was a bag filled with US$50,000 in al-Qaeda cash that Zubair had earlier couriered from Pakistan – and which they had not been authorized to disburse – as well as their share of the monthly profits from the rice company in Yala. Focusing on the latter, Hambali dispatched Zubair to southern Thailand in mid-July to collect their dividends.

Though Zubair did not realize it, he was already a marked man. His undoing had come from Ammar al-Baluchi, who gave U.S. interrogators Zubair's contact details used during the earlier hawala transaction. These details – including a cell phone number – were passed to Thai intelligence. Monitoring that cell phone, they picked up Zubair's trail during the second half of July as he made his way from Bangkok to the southern border. Fearful that he might slip across the border, they grabbed him shortly before month's end.

A defiant prisoner, Zubair was initially uncooperative with the authorities. What's more, when he missed a scheduled communications check, this prompted Hambali, his wife, and Lillie to hurriedly vacate their On Nut apartment and flee Bangkok. Their destination was 70 kilometers away in the temple city of Ayutthaya. Not coincidentally, Ayutthaya hosted a small but vibrant Muslim community. This dated back to the fifteenth century, when the first group of Persian traders had landed in central Thailand to compete with the Europeans.[245]

For Hambali, the Thai Muslims offered thin but welcome cover. He rented a one-bedroom flat in the six-story Boon Yarak Apartments, a new building that catered to Asian businessmen working in a nearby industrial park. From there, he visited one of the sixty mosques that dotted the cityscape; when he claimed he was a Malaysian businessman contemplating a generous philanthropic donation to the Muslim community, they had no reason to doubt his story.

---

[245] "Arrest Shocks Ayutthaya's Muslims," *The Nation*, 17 August 2003.

Such forays were rare, however. For the most part, Hambali remained sequestered in his apartment. On just a couple of nights, he ventured to the city's
Lotus department store to rent a cell phone; he reportedly racked up extraordinarily large bills in overseas calls. He and Lillie also sought out an Internet café
in an attempt to re-establish contact with their colleagues in Indonesia. But
when they told Noordin Top and Azhari that Zubair had been captured, the
skittish Malaysians unilaterally broke off e-mail contact and did not respond to
further messages from Ayutthaya.

With his world closing in fast, Hambali returned to the issue of his identity
papers. Since his return from Cambodia, he had been making use of his second
fake Spanish passport – like when he rented the apartment – but this required a
valid visa. Months earlier, Lillie had located a Pakistani living in Bangkok who
had connections with corrupt Thai immigration officials at various immigration
posts. For a fee, the Pakistani would take passports to these crossings and get exit
and reentry stamps, thus prolonging the stay of the bearer without that person
actually having to be present. Hambali had already had this done on a couple of
occasions; in early August, Lillie departed for Bangkok to hand off the passport
for another visa run.

By that time, however, the interrogation of Zubair was starting to pay dividends. Under questioning, he gave up details of the Pakistani and his visa services. Canvassing border posts, the Thai police caught up with him at the Nong
Khai crossing opposite Vientiane. To their pleasant surprise, he readily admitted
he had an imminent meeting scheduled in Bangkok with Lillie.

During the late afternoon of Monday, 11 August, members of the Thai
police Special Branch were waiting for Lillie during his promised rendezvous
with the Pakistani. Like Zubair, however, Lillie was initially uncooperative when
placed in custody. This greatly concerned the team from the Special Branch,
who recognized that if Lillie missed a scheduled communication check with his
boss, Hambali would again take to flight.

Lillie, it turned out, did not have to cooperate. When they searched his
pockets, inside was a key for a flat at the Boon Yarak Apartments in Ayutthaya.[246]

---

[246] "Malaysian's Apartment Key Exposed Hambali," *The Nation*, 21 August 2003.

Realizing that quick action was necessary, Police Brigadier General Trithos Ronnaritthiwichai, head of the Special Branch Division 2, placed a call at nightfall to the police headquarters in Ayutthaya. It was already after business hours, and many of the police officers had gone home for the day. Fortunately, Colonel Nares Nanthachote, Ayutthaya's deputy police chief, was still in the office and promised full cooperation.

Packing a mixed assault team from the Special Branch and Armed Forces Security Center into some unmarked sedans, Trithos raced to Ayutthaya, paused to link up with some local officers under Nares, then continued to the Boon Yarak Apartments. At 2230 hours, they quietly entered the lobby.

The assault team now faced a couple of concerns. For one thing, there had been widespread speculation that Hambali had undergone plastic surgery and might not be recognizable. Anticipating this, a member of Special Branch had ventured to Jakarta months earlier when there were indications Hambali entered Thailand from Cambodia. From his Indonesian counterparts, he had requested copies of any and all photographs they had of Hambali. Reasoning that the plastic surgeons would not be able to alter his eyes and eyebrows, the Thai police had made life-size reproductions of only that part of Hambali's portrait. Copies of these were with Trithos in the lobby.

For another thing, they intuitively knew that an assault on a cornered Hambali could be extraordinarily dangerous. Given the relatively easy access criminals in Thailand had to weapons, there was no telling what he had been able to stockpile over the preceding months. With his penchant for violence, he posed a deadly risk to the assault team, other tenants in the apartment building, and anyone else he might have in his flat.

Weighing their options, police officers decided against an assault on the target's unit. After determining which flat was being used by Hambali, they had the apartment manager beckon him to the lobby on the pretext of taking an incoming call. The plan was remarkably successful. A couple of minutes after the summons, a stout, clean-shaven Asian male exited the elevator. When plain-clothes police advanced, he made a fast move under his shirt – but not before an army lieutenant colonel tackled him to the floor. A 9mm pistol was reportedly found tucked into Hambali's waistband; important documents were hidden inside a belly pouch.

Taking an elevator to the sixth floor, ten Special Branch members pounded on the door to Room 601. After no one answered the repeated knocks, they kicked in the door. Noralwizah, Hambali's wife, was escorted out with a towel over her head. Inside the flat, they found an assault rifle, more documents, the bag with al-Qaeda cash, and a photograph of Osama bin Laden.[247]

Counter-terrorism officials from Washington to Southeast Asia were ecstatic over the capture of Hambali.[248] But arguably nobody was happier than the Thai agencies credited with tracking him down. One month later, the U.S. government handed over US$10 million in reward money, divided among ten officers who were instrumental in the capture, their parent units, and a foundation for officials killed or injured in the line of duty.[249]

From his first days in detention, Hambali proved extraordinarily talkative. The result: less than two weeks after being captured, intelligence agencies across Asia received almost daily reports based on his revelations. Not surprising given that he had spent the previous six months in Thailand, much of his initial information concerned scheming in that kingdom. He admitted, for example, to contemplating an attack on the J.W. Marriott hotel in downtown Bangkok – but could not find the required explosives. And because he was fixated on evading the authorities, he claimed not to have advanced any specific plans for spoiling the upcoming Asia-Pacific Economic Cooperation forum set for the Thai capital in October.

---

[247] Among the documents in Hambali's possession was a four-page report in English and Indonesian outlining a paramilitary training curriculum. Part of it involved infiltrating a camp site in Malaysia in order to practice drawing out information from unsuspecting campers. It also advocated watching films such as *Saving Private Ryan* and, for examples of facial disguises, *The Jackal*.

[248] A special U.S.-chartered aircraft whisked Hambali out of Bangkok's military airport on the morning of 13 August. Media reports, initially broken by an Israeli journalist in October 2004, suggest he was taken to an interrogation facility in Jordan's southern Al Jafr desert.

[249] The bulk of the reward money went to the Armed Forces Security Center (a technical surveillance unit that had been tracking Zubair's cell phone communications), the police Special Branch, the Ayutthaya police, and the National Intelligence Agency. Most of the ten officers who received individual awards were from these units. A large chunk of the reward money, however, went to a mysterious "coffee vendor" who allegedly provided a tip to the police; cynics would later claim that the vendor was notional and merely served to pad the reward claim. Mention of the coffee vendor can be found in "Thais Should Help in the War on Terrorism," *The Nation*, 24 August 2003.

Some of Hambali's most startling revelations were not about Thailand, but concerned one of his own brothers half a world away. That brother, Gun Gun Rusman Gunawan, was twelve years Hambali's junior. For more than a decade prior to 1999, the two had barely met apart from Hambali's infrequent trips back to his hometown. Still, aspiring to be like his older brother, Gun Gun in late 1999 ventured to Malaysia and spent a month alongside his elder sibling.

Hambali, it turns out, had big plans for Gun Gun. In December 1999, he sent him packing to Pakistan with two instructions. First, he was to enroll as a student at Abu Bakar Islamic University in Karachi. Second, he was to make contact with Abu Bakar Ba'asyir's son, Abdul Rahim. For the previous several months, Rahim had been diligently laying the groundwork for the student cell he had envisioned with Hambali. A handful of Malaysian students had already been informally identified as sympathetic and trustworthy; all were either students at Abu Bakar Islamic University or Jamia Darasat, a Karachi-based institution known for its strong jihadi curriculum. Every Thursday, they were beckoned to Rahim's guesthouse for dinner; every Friday, they would return for a movie. As Southeast Asians studying in a distant land, Rahim had given them a nickname: al-Ghuraba, Arabic for "The Foreigners."

Now assisted by Gun Gun, Rahim set about formalizing al-Ghuraba in early 2000. About a dozen Malaysians and Singaporeans – as well as a single Indonesian – made the cut. There were several common features among them. For one thing, most were of the right pedigree – meaning that they were the sons of Jemaah Islamiyah members. Malaysian student Abu Dzar had perhaps the most extensive family ties. His father, a longtime associate of Hambali, and two uncles were all trusted Jemaah Islamiyah adherents. One of the uncles was in the Johor wakalah, had attended Camp Hudaibiyah in Mindanao, and would later donate US$1,050 of his own cash for the Christmas Eve 2000 church bombings in Indonesia. Another uncle, who drove a taxi in Singapore, would later attend al-Qaeda training in Kandahar during 2001. And his sister had recently married Masran bin Arshad, the leader of KSM's suicide cell.

Another Malaysian student, Mohammad Ikhwan, was equally well connected. His father, who would attend an al-Qaeda surveillance course in Kabul later in 2000, was a Jemaah Islamiyah member and a lecturer at the Malaysian Technological University, the same institute that spawned several prominent Jemaah Islamiyah personalities. Too, his older sister married a Jemaah Islamiyah member. Likewise, Singaporean student Mohammad Riza had a father who was sent by Mantiqi 1 to attend Camp Hudaibiyah at the opening of 2000.

For another thing, virtually all of the al-Ghuraba students had received their high school education from conservative pesantren back in Southeast Asia. No less than six, for example, counted Luqmanul Haqiem in Johor as their alma mater. The lone Indonesian, Mohammad Saifudin, had graduated from Darus Sya'adah ("Place of Martyrs"), a boarding school in Central Java with strong links to Ngruki. Further burnishing his credentials, Saifudin had attending Camp Hudaibiyah for three months in 1999 before heading to Pakistan.

But perhaps their most striking common denominator was their impossibly young, impressionable ages. Abu Dzar and Mohammad Ikhwan, for instance, were just fifteen when they joined. Some of their conduct, not surprisingly, showed secular proclivities expected of teenagers. One of the Malaysians, Noor ul-Fakri, began spending up to five hours a day at cyber cafés, forcing Rahim and Gun Gun to impose fines if members were caught spending too much time surfing the Internet. Another Malaysian, Faiz Hussein, got grief from Gun Gun over his infatuation with heavy metal.

Most of the members, too, liked rap music. In fact, when they were given an Arabic-language fight song that had been especially written for al-Ghuraba, they promptly adapted the tune to a rap beat. With background music blaring from a boom box, they would half-sing, half-read aloud the verses during their meetings. Translated into English it read:

> He is not a foreigner, he who has left his home,
> But the foreigner is he who finds those around him asleep,
> And follows the path of goodness, while those around him are misguided.
> My comrade tells the truth when he says I am the foreigner,
> Among these sinners, I know this is my path.
> I am the foreigner, foreign from the pessimism among humans,
> With my God on His blessed pedestal.

By the third quarter of 2000, however, not all of al-Ghuraba's activities were so innocent. As originally envisioned, al-Ghuraba was supposed to provide logistical support for Jemaah Islamiyah members traveling to and from al-Qaeda training camps in Afghanistan. Very quickly, however, it turned into something different. During weekly meetings at a safe house rented in Karachi's Johar Square, the al-Ghuraba students were lectured on the need to build their capabilities to defend against the enemies of Islam, including Jews, communists, and the United States and its allies. Defending themselves, they were told, included the need to accept martyrdom.

To prepare for this role, al-Ghuraba members themselves began rotating through Afghanistan during their university breaks. In the second half of 2000, three Malaysians and one Singaporean received basic military instruction at al-Farouq, the al-Qaeda camp on the outskirts of Kandahar.[250] Gun Gun also received basic instruction at al-Farouq during this same time frame.[251]

Early the next year, some changes were in store. During March, Abdul Rahim was reportedly beckoned across the border for duties in Afghanistan, leaving Gun Gun to take over as al-Ghuraba's senior advisor. (Abdul Rahim has publicly and repeatedly denied any affiliation with al-Qaeda, Jemaah Islamiyah or any terrorist activities. He also denies spending time in Afghanistan.) Mohammad Saifudin, the only other Indonesian in the group, was elevated as his deputy.

Gun Gun quickly arranged a second round of al-Qaeda training for al-Ghuraba's most promising members. By that time, brother Hambali had fled Southeast Asia and had taken up residence in Kandahar. Two of the Malaysian students – Abu Dzar and Mohammad Ikhwan – were placed under Hambali's tutelage for four months of intensive lessons in Islamic law. In a heady experience for a pair of sixteen-year-olds, they attended sermons by Osama bin Laden during ten occasions when he was in Kandahar.

Others in the group got advanced paramilitary instruction. During their university breaks, Mohammad Saifudin went to al-Farouq, while Mohammad Uddin was called back to Afghanistan for a course in urban warfare. Gun Gun arrived in June for ten days of advanced bomb-making classes at al-Farouq.[252] Six of them, meantime, traveled to Pakistan-controlled parts of Kashmir. There, *Laskar-e-Tayyiba*, a guerrilla movement affiliated with al-Qaeda, gave them a month of physical and military training.[253]

---

[250] The Singaporean, who was overweight and emotional, washed out of training and was sent home early.

[251] "Gun Gun Rusman Gunawan," *Surat Tuntutan*, (October 2004), p. 4.

[252] *Ibid.*, p. 43.

[253] They were not the only Southeast Asians to be linked to militants in Kashmir. According to al-Qaeda member Umar Faruq, seven Indonesians from Ambon were sent for paramilitary training under Laskar-e-Tayyiba in Pakistan during 2001. As late as April 2003, Western aid workers active near Pakistan-controlled Kashmir reported seeing an armed Southeast Asian tentatively identified as an Indonesian national.

Then came the terrorist attacks of 11 September. Four al-Ghuraba members were in Kandahar at the time. Given the almost immediate saber-rattling out of Washington, none were particularly optimistic about their long-term prospects in Afghanistan. Very quickly, all four made their way back to Karachi.

Ironically, al-Ghuraba was coming to feel the greatest pressure not from the Pakistani government or the United States, but rather from al-Qaeda. In early October 2001, KSM desperately wanted to stage an encore round of terrorist strikes. He had come to know about al-Ghuraba and, in need of potential martyrs, was lobbying to have them ready for deployment under his control. Thinking aloud, he fancifully contemplated using them in more airplane plots, possibly in the United States.

Hambali, who was in Karachi by that time, had other ideas. He had come to see al-Ghuraba as a sleeper cell of future Jemaah Islamiyah leaders, not cannon fodder to be wasted in some act of desperation by KSM. Fending off the advances by al-Qaeda, he successfully argued that they would not be operationally ready for at least another two years.

True to its newfound purpose, the al-Ghuraba sleeper cell went to sleep during much of 2002. As Afghan training was no longer an option, and Laskar-e-Tayyiba was no longer offering training slots, the members did little other than attend university classes and gather for weekly talk-fests at their safe house. When they did get specialized training, the subjects were sufficiently mundane so as not to attract the attention of the authorities. That June, for example, Abdul Rahim offered a one-month computer course. The next month, a middle-aged Pakistani came to the safe house to drill them on emergency medical procedures. They also practiced basic surveillance techniques by surreptitiously following targets around the neighborhood.

Gun Gun, it turns out, had more pressing duties outside of al-Ghuraba. Beginning in late 2002, he took over as the intermediary for e-mail messages between al-Qaeda and Hambali, who at the time was hiding in Cambodia. Gun Gun also passed e-mails to Lillie and Zubair when arranging the hawala transfer to Bangkok.

This role entailed risk. His primary point of contact with al-Qaeda had been KSM, which made him properly concerned when the al-Qaeda's operations chief was captured in March 2003. He was equally concerned when his other al-Qaeda contact, Ammar al-Baluchi, was arrested the following month.

But apparently neither KSM nor Ammar fingered Gun Gun while under interrogation. Without pause, Gun Gun sought out Ammar's successor in Karachi, a youthful al-Qaeda member named Abu Tahla al-Pakistani. Born Mohammad Naeem Noor Khan, 24-year-old Abu Tahla had been a reserved but brilliant computer student in Karachi before moving to the United Kingdom to live with relatives near Heathrow airport. After returning to his native Pakistan during a summer holiday, he had fallen under the influence of a militant cleric; he subsequently made frequent visits to al-Qaeda camps between 1998 and 2001. Inducted into that terrorist organization, he had helped formulate plans for attacks against Heathrow, the London subway system, and financial buildings in the United States.

Just as he was opening channels with Abu Tahla, Gun Gun received word from Indonesia that his al-Ghuraba cell was about to receive an infusion of new members. Four were slated to arrive during mid-2003; another six had applications pending at Abu Bakar Islamic University. All of them, he was told, had been vetted by the Jemaah Islamiyah chain of command.

Two features set this new group apart. First, they were older than the original members of al-Ghuraba, ranging in age between 22 and 27. In theory, they would be more mature and capable of assisting Gun Gun.

Second, all of them were Indonesian nationals who had graduated from the Darus Sya'adah pesantren in Central Java, the school attended by Mohammad Saifudin, the al-Ghuraba deputy advisor.

As promised, two Indonesians arrived in Karachi on 4 July. Mohammad Anwar Siddique, a native of Central Java, and David Pintarto, another Javanese, were greeted at the arrival hall by Gun Gun and Mohammad Saifudin before being whisked off to the al-Ghuraba safe house.

On 24 July, two more Indonesians, Furqon Abdullah and Ilham Sopandi, landed in Karachi. They, too, were escorted to the al-Ghuraba safe house.

Though the newcomers had no way of knowing it, al-Ghuraba was in its dying days. During the second week of August, Gun Gun read newspaper accounts of his brother's capture in Thailand. Two weeks after that, Hambali was informing U.S. authorities about his sibling's activities.

On 1 September, Pakistan's Inter-Service Intelligence (ISI) agency descended on Johar Square. Tracking down Gun Gun, they led him away in handcuffs.

Deprived of its leader, the rest of the al-Ghuraba cell scattered. But after laying low for a week, the remaining members gathered back at the safe house. Perhaps to deflect guilt by association to Indonesians Hambali and Gun Gun, they agreed that, if captured, they should tell the Pakistanis that al-Ghuraba consisted only of Malaysian nationals. On further consideration, they further agreed to keep the name "al-Ghuraba" a secret.

As it turned out, it was another three weeks before ISI finalized plans to move against the remaining Southeast Asians. By that time, Gun Gun had given up his colleagues. Between 20 and 22 September, all remaining eighteen members – thirteen Malaysians and five Indonesians – were arrested on campus.[254] This included the four Indonesians who had arrived just two months earlier.

As the al-Ghuraba members collectively rested their heels in jail, they did not necessarily have much to fear. Aside from Gun Gun, who had knowingly intermediated between al-Qaeda and Hambali, the remaining cell members appeared guilty of little aside from tough talk.

But during a search of the al-Ghuraba safe house, ISI officers were drawn to a number of suspicious items. Strangely out of place, for example, were several yellow pages torn from a Northern Virginia phone book. They also found a Karachi license plate written on a memo pad. To their concern, they learned that the plate was from a Honda Civic registered to a U.S. petroleum company.

This last point hit a raw nerve. After sizable oil reserves were discovered in southwestern Pakistan in the late nineties, several foreign oil companies had set up shop in Karachi. Their presence had long provided ample targets for militants. Back in November 1997, four American auditors working for the Union Texas Petroleum Company, the largest international oil firm in Pakistan, had been gunned down by extremists on their way to the office.[255]

Quizzed about the license plate on the memo pad, most of the al-Ghuraba members feigned ignorance. One of the Malaysians, however, made a critical slip. Admitting that the memo pad was his, he claimed that he was in the habit of jotting down odd figures. When he noticed that license plate, he improbably claimed that he wrote it down in order to later use it as an e-mail address.

---

[254] At least four other Malaysian and two Singaporean members of al-Ghuraba had returned to Southeast Asia during the previous months and years.

[255] These killings were linked to the execution of Mir Aimal Kasi, a Pakistani national who had murdered two CIA employees outside their Langley, Virginia headquarters in 1993.

Such a laughable explanation only piqued the attention of his interrogators. Revisiting the story during the next round of questioning, the Malaysian conjured a different explanation. This time he said that he was dropping off his brother at the airport, and had written down the license plate because he thought it belonged to a police vehicle and he feared he was being followed. But his nervous demeanor, not to mention the continued implausibility of the explanation, suggested this story was also a fabrication.

Not until the third session did the truth begin to emerge. Beginning in mid-August, the Malaysian confessed, al-Ghuraba decided to take revenge for the capture of Hambali. Nine members were taken into confidence and told they were to kidnap a senior U.S. executive. If successful, this was to be the first of many such operations.

Over the course of three planning sessions, which were attended by al-Qaeda's Abu Tahla, the plan was fine-tuned. From Abu Tahla, they were given the license plate for the Honda Civic and told that the driver made airport pickups of expatriates on Saturday evenings between 2000 and 2100 hours. They were further told that the Pakistani driver favored a parking slot in front of a fast food outlet across from the airport's arrival terminal.

Quickly, their kidnapping scheme was fine-tuned. To start, one of al-Ghuraba's Malaysians was to stake out the Honda Civic at the airport. If and when an expatriate approached the vehicle, he would place a call to five other cell members and Abu Tahla, who would be waiting in a Toyota van along the main road outside the airport. They would intercept the Honda, bundle the executive inside the van, and speed off to the western outskirts of Karachi. Abu Tahla had already identified a vacant house that would suffice as a transit point before taking their hostage further outside the city.

By the close of August, the plan was finalized. In order to provide cover for the Malaysian to loiter at the airport on a Saturday night, three al-Ghuraba members (including the Malaysian's brother) were intentionally booked on a flight back to Southeast Asia on the Saturday evening during the second week of September.

At that point, Murphy's Law made an appearance. Before the scheme could be put into effect, Gun Gun was arrested and it was not until 8 September that the rest of al-Ghuraba got up the nerve to regroup at their safe house. Determined to forge ahead, five days later the Malaysian and his three homeward-bound countrymen headed for the airport as scheduled. While they were queuing for the vehicle security check, their targeted Honda Civic tried to squeeze into the line ahead.

As expected, the Pakistani driver parked near the fast food outlet. Also as expected, a short time later a bearded Westerner and a female companion emerged from the arrival terminal and got into the Honda Civic.

Sticking to plan, the Malaysian phoned the telephone number for the kidnapping party. One of the Indonesians answered the phone and instructed him to return to the safe house.

Eager to learn whether the abduction had been a success, the Malaysian sped back to Johar Square. When he went inside, however, he found his fellow cell members sound asleep. A collective case of cold feet had killed the plan.

By that time, a sense of fatalism had consumed the group. Trying to head off the inevitable, the remaining members of al-Ghuraba cancelled their scheduled safe house meeting for the next week. It was to no avail. By 22 September, the ISI had made its move. "The Foreigners" were no more.[256]

---

[256] All of the al-Ghuraba detainees were repatriated from Pakistan to their home countries during December 2003.

CHAPTER SIXTEEN

PHOENIX

The arrests of Hambali and the al-Ghuraba cell members were devastating body blows to Jemaah Islamiyah. After all, Hambali had been the figurative spigot for al-Qaeda funds – monies all the more critical given Jemaah Islamiyah's difficulties in conducting more conventional fundraising activities. The loss of al-Ghuraba, meanwhile, deprived the group of potential future leaders.

Closer to home in Indonesia, the damage being inflicted on Jemaah Islamiyah was no less debilitating. Though the Jemaah Islamiyah markaz was able to secretly call a meeting on 7 April 2003 in the resort area of Puncak, West Java, it would prove to be its last.[257] During the second half of the month, the police arrested nineteen suspects in such far-flung locations as Central Sulawesi, West Sumatra, and the outskirts of Jakarta.[258] Among them was acting amir Abu Rusdan, who was taken into custody in Central Java.

Gaining momentum, the Indonesian authorities made three more arrests in June, then a wave of ten in July. Noteworthy was a raid on a shoe factory in Semarang, which netted the ingredients for another Bali-sized bomb: nearly a ton of potassium chlorate, more than a thousand detonators, and thirty kilos of PETN high explosive.[259] Based on documents found at the same locale, Jemaah

---

[257] The Puncak meeting was attended by wakalah representatives from East Java, Central Java, Solo, and Jakarta. Their talk was not about future operations, but largely about the arrests that had taken place since the Bali bombing.

[258] Media reports claim that telephone records found in Pakistan when KSM was detained on 1 March led to some of the April arrests in Indonesia.

[259] The media incorrectly reported that rocket-propelled grenades were found in the Semarang raid. The PETN (mistakenly identified in the press as dynamite) had been procured through MILF channels and smuggled into Indonesia via East Kalimantan. Nasir Abas interview.

Islamiyah was contemplating attacks against such domestic targets as a Bank Central Asia branch in Semarang, evangelical churches, the Citraland mall in Jakarta (owned by a prominent ethnic Chinese businessman), and four politicians from the ruling Indonesian Democratic Party of Struggle.[260]

Together, these detentions sent a chill across Jemaah Islamiyah. Of the few top members still evading the authorities, several prudently decided to go underground. Zulkarnaen, the group's military czar, presided over a mantiqi meeting in Central Java the week after the Bali bombing, then promptly vanished from the scene; rumors subsequently placed him everywhere from southern Thailand to rural Java to Mindanao. Bomb-makers Dul Matin and Umar Arab, meanwhile, took leave of Indonesia in early 2003 and sought sanctuary among Islamic extremists in the southern Philippines.

But even at a fraction of its former strength, Jemaah Islamiyah was still formidable. This was largely on account of two persons: Noordin Top and Azhari. Over the previous years, these two Malaysian nationals had shared a similar path to extremism. Both were married and each had a pair of children. Both were linked to the Malaysian Technological University: Azhari had served as a lecturer; Noordin was a student. Both had joined Jemaah Islamiyah at roughly the same time and together ventured to Camp Hudaibiyah for a short paramilitary course in 1997. Both, too, were members of the Johor wakalah: Noordin Top was eventually promoted to head a fiah; Azhari, despite being eleven years his senior, was a subordinate.

In terms of personality, the two were worlds apart. Azhari had an outwardly calm and submissive persona; despite his age and academic achievements, he was satisfied with offering technical support from the sidelines rather than taking any leadership role. Noordin, by contrast, was renowned for his wealth of ideas and considerable ambition.

Noordin was also exceedingly patient. Back in 2000, while many of his colleagues mobilized for the Christmas Eve bombing campaign – Azhari, for example, worked on the explosive devices destined for churches in Batam – he stayed behind in Johor to administer the Luqmanul Hakim pesantren. And while Azhari was designing the Bali bombs in 2002, Noordin kept his ambition

---

[260] *Berkas-Perkara, Toriquddin alias Abu Rusdan alias Hamzah*, dated 5 August 2003, testimony of Pranata Yudha alias Mustofa interrogation, pp. 7-8. Media reports later in August 2003 incorrectly stated that a target list captured in Semarang included the J.W. Marriott hotel in Jakarta.

in check and chose the shadows; though already a fugitive in Indonesia by that time, there is no evidence he played any role in the Bali operation.

All of this no doubt contributed to Noordin's longevity. As scores of his higher-profile Jemaah Islamiyah colleagues were detained in the post-Bali drag-net, Noordin's relative anonymity proved his savior. Stepping into the vacuum, it was not until early 2003 that he finally looked to make his mark on the or-ganization. Azhari, as he was wont, assumed the role of resourceful deputy and technical specialist.

For a time, both looked to gain their second wind from Sumatra. There were several reasons for choosing this island. First, the three Jemaah Islamiyah wakalah that stretched across Sumatra had their fair share of Luqmanul Hakim alumni, providing academic common ground with former school administrator Noordin. Moreover, because those wakalah had generally not participated in the Bali bombing – unlike their counterparts from Central and East Java, for instance – they had sidestepped the brunt of the Bali investigation and entered 2003 vigilant but relatively intact.

Second, both Noordin and Azhari had familial links in Sumatra. For his part, Azhari's wife traced roots to Bengkulu, while Noordin had married a girl from Riau. Indeed, one of the first persons sought out by Noordin in early 2003 was his Indonesian brother-in-law, fellow Jemaah Islamiyah member Moham-mad Rais (alias Edi Indra).[261] And it was with suggestions from Rais that the two Malaysians got to work tapping into the Sumatra network to cobble together a small cell of trusted lieutenants and foot soldiers for their next operation.

As the two were to learn, Sumatra was also scene of a complex shell game involv-ing a lethal cache of bomb-making materials. This traced back to August 2000, when Imam Samudra and Malaysian Yazid Sufaat had pooled funds to purchase a massive haul of explosives – almost two tons of precursors, detonation cord,

---

[261] Born in Riau but raised in Malaysia, Rais had near-perfect Jemaah Islamiyah pedigree. Venturing to Indo-nesia to attend Ngruki, he returned to Malaysia after graduation to teach at Lukmanul Hakim. In 2000, he was selected to attend basic al-Qaeda training at Camp al-Farouq. Impressing the camp cadre, he was retained in Afghanistan for another year to act as an instructor for successive student cycles. Eventually, however, the tough camp life caught up with him; sick with jaundice, he spent time convalescing at Hambali's Kandahar house before heading back to Southeast Asia in mid-2001.

dynamite, and 200 detonators – from one of the many Banten quarries that turn out rocks to line roadbeds.[262] Much of this material was eventually used in the Christmas Eve bombs, particularly those destined for churches on Sumatra.

But as it turned out, a significant portion – six boxes of explosives – had not yet been used and remained hidden away near Jakarta. Spooked that the authorities might find the cache, in early 2001 one of the Christmas Eve conspirators had it shipped from Jakarta for safekeeping with fellow sympathizers in Riau.

For more than a year, the boxes were moved frequently, always near Pekanbaru. Those hiding the deadly parcels had reason to be leery. After all, Yazid Sufaat had already been arrested in Malaysia, and he promptly had revealed details of the quarry purchase during his interrogation. But while this information was passed to Indonesia in May 2002, the authorities assumed that the explosives had been exhausted in the Christmas 2000 campaign and did not chase down the lead.[263]

Still, wakalah members in Riau were growing increasingly skittish, especially after the police fully mobilized in the wake of the Bali bombings. Afraid of getting caught with the explosives, the boxes were repeatedly pawned from one location to the next. As of the opening of 2003, they had been divided among three houses on the outskirts of the Caltex oil fields.

By then, Noordin Top and Azhari had arrived on the scene to seek sanctuary. Hearing of the bomb-making materials – and eager to use them – Noordin in early February took custody of the lot and in early February had it shipped to Bengkulu. There, the two arrived at the house of Asmar Latin Sani, a skinny, goateed 26-year-old Ngruki graduate and acquaintance of Noordin's brother-in-law, Mohammad Rais. Sani – described as a "lost soul" who had been wandering over the previous years across the Darul Islam network in search of direction – quickly fell under the spell of the charismatic Noordin and pledged full cooperation for an as-yet unspecified jihad operation.[264]

That jihad operation almost never happened. Hot on the trail of Noordin and Azhari, the police on 26 April caught up with Mohammad Rais in Pekanbaru. Over the next two days, they arrested two more Jemaah Islamiyah

---

[262] While Yazid Sufaat used funds from his own pocket, it has been suggested that Imam Samudra received his money from Zulkarnaen. See ICG report, "Recycling Militants in Indonesia," 22 February 2005, p. 37.

[263] See BIN document provided by a regional counterpart organization, "Penglibatan Yazid bin Sufaat Dalam Kejadian Letupan Bom dan Pembunuhan Paderi di Indonesia," dated 5 May 2002.

[264] "The Mystery Man from Singkarak," *Tempo*, 25 August 2003, p. 78; John MacDougall interview.

members from Sumatra, both of whom had handled the cache of explosives over the previous year. Under interrogation, the detainees surmised that the Malaysians might have sought sanctuary at the Bengkulu house of Asmar Latin Sani. But when the police descended on Bengkulu at month's end, Sani, the Malaysian fugitives, and the explosives were nowhere to be found.

In fact, Noordin and Azhari were constantly on the move. Showing good tradecraft after the April arrests, they had left Bengkulu for alternate sanctuary in Lampung province. Lampung had been chosen with purpose. Not only was it strategically near Jakarta, but the province was renowned as a destination for Javanese and other recent migrants seeking better jobs – or an escape from a shady past. The province also hosted more than its share of religious radicals; indeed, Jemaah Islamiyah had established a wakalah in Lampung to cover Sumatra's southern rump.

From Lampung, Noordin and Azhari finally got around to planning their next operation. Unlike the relatively large scale of the Bali bombing, they envisioned a streamlined plot that – out of necessity – would be conducted on a shoestring budget with a minimum number of participants. Indeed, as of early May they had taken just four Sumatrans into confidence. The first was Asmar Latin Sani, the impressionable photocopy operator who was doing his best to avoid the police in Bengkulu. Two others – Ismail Datam and Tohir – were young Luqmanul Hakim graduates who almost immediately pledged support to former schoolmaster Noordin. Aside from a short stint at Camp Hudaiybiyah by Tohir, all three were novice jihadis.

Only the last, Toni Togar, had any standing in Jemaah Islamiyah. A Ngruki graduate who had spent time as a teacher at Luqmanul Hakim, Togar had made a name for himself as an exceedingly aggressive proponent of jihad in his native Medan. Indeed, he had been active in the church bombings that had plagued Medan since mid-2000.

With support from these four, Noordin and Azhari next tackled the issue of funding. They had gotten lucky in a sense, as they had incurred considerable savings by inheriting the six boxes of explosives for free. Still, they were short of cash for renting safe houses and purchasing vehicles. They had requested funds from Hambali, but they had been on hold pending the hawala transfer from Pakistan.

Toni Togar had a more immediate, if not violent, solution. Displaying a flash of his trademark aggression, during the first week of May he walked into a Medan bank with a pistol, shot dead three employees, and walked out with 113 million in rupiah. He next went to the town of Dumai and robbed a money-changer at gunpoint. He would later boast that, with Allah on his side, he had seen no need to use a mask.

On 12 May, Noordin went to an ATM in the city of Bandar Lampung and, using Togar's identification number, withdrew part of the robbery proceeds. While helpful, it proved unnecessary. A week later, e-mails from Hambali confirmed that US$25,000 was en route via a courier; of this, US$15,000 was available for operational expenses and the rest was earmarked to help the families of the Bali bombers.

To collect the money, Noordin sent an e-mail to Ismail. A 24-year-old former auto mechanic, Ismail proceeded to Dumai at month's end, rendezvoused with Hambali's courier, and took possession of a black parcel stuffed with foreign currency. Heading to Lampung, he met up with Noordin and Azhari in a dormitory near the local university and turned over the cash.

By 4 June, Tohir and Sani had also made their way from Bengkulu to Lampung. They had not come empty-handed: with them were four plastic crates stuffed with 120 kilos of the bomb-making materials.

Noordin quickly set about assigning tasks. As expected, he named himself overall head of the operation; Azhari would function as field coordinator. As he revealed the upcoming operation would take place in Jakarta, Sani, Tohir, and Ismail headed for the capital to find safe houses. Noordin had one other critical bit of information: turning to Sani, he announced that the Bengkulu resident had been selected to gloriously serve as suicide bomber.

Toni Togar was not present at this meeting, and for good reason. Every since his deadly bank heist – for which he had seen no need to wear a mask – the police had been hot on his trail. On 11 June, they finally caught up with him in Medan and placed him under arrest.

Significantly, word of the Togar arrest was not immediately released. This soon provided important, and chilling, dividends. Ever since he was nominated to act as suicide bomber, Sani had been agonizing over the decision. He had since made his way to Jakarta and, along with Tohir, rented a room in East Jakarta. It was from there, on 18 June, that he finally accepted his fate and decided to inform his co-conspirator back in Sumatra. Finding an internet café, he sent a simple message to Togar's e-mail account: "I wish to marry." This, the police learned, was terrorist double-speak for accepting martyrdom.

The police now had several crucial pieces of the puzzle. From all of their Sumatra arrests to date, they knew that Noordin and Azhari were planning another bombing and had the necessary bomb-making materials on hand. Adding to their sense of frustration, from the e-mail to Togar they even knew the name of the suicide bomber. They did not know with certainty, however, the targeted city, much less the target.

Unfazed by the loss of Togar, Noordin in early July directed his Sumatran accomplices to rent a second room in Jakarta. He then beckoned Ismail and Tohir back to Lampung. There they broke open the plastic crates and inventoried the contents. It was literally a mixed bag – black powder, several kilos of dynamite, ten meters of detonation cord, two dozen detonators – but Azhari was satisfied it was enough to get the job done. With the bulk of this load in hand, the group boarded buses for the capital.[265]

Once in Jakarta, Noordin began handing out tasks at a dizzying pace. Thinking two steps ahead, a pair of members were dispatched to Bandung on 9 July to find a safe house in that city. Others rented yet another safe house in South Jakarta on Jalan Kemuning Raya; ironically, it was just 500 meters from the headquarters of the country's State Intelligence Agency. Next, some 26 million rupiah was handed over to Tohir and Sani, who on 21 July purchased a used blue Toyota Kijang van. The seller would later recall that the two spoke with Sumatran accents and had remained anonymous; they claimed that the vehicle was going to be taken back to Lampung.

More money was handed out to buy a Honda motorcycle. With this, Azhari and Tohir began touring the capital in search of targets. Keeping in mind Hambali's directive – "No McDonald's or Kentucky Fried Chicken" – they looked for sites where an attack would have a profound impact. After discounting embassies due to high security, they reduced the choices down to a pair of international schools, the Citibank branch in the posh suburb of Pondok Indah, and the J.W. Marriott hotel.[266]

From this shortlist, Noordin harkened back to Osama bin Laden's 1998 fatwa calling for jihad against the United States. Both Citibank and the J.W. Marriott, he reasoned, were suitable American targets. Of these, he chose the latter. Significantly, the J.W. Marriott was one of the few luxury hotels in Jakarta

---

[265] On 18-19 July, Ismail and Tohir returned to Lampung to bring the remainder of the explosives to Jakarta.
[266] "Gun Gun Rusman Gunawan," *Surat Tuntutan*, (October 2004), p. 14.

that had a busy – and easily visible – coffee shop just a few meters from the entrance ramp to the lobby.

With these decisions made, all that remained was for Azhari to construct the bomb. It is apparent that he had learned from the shortcomings of the previous car bomb in Bali. During that earlier occasion, most of the precursors had burned rather than exploded. "It was like a firecracker that was not properly packed," said one security advisor in Indonesia. "It sizzled and popped, but didn't have the intended blast."[267]

This time around, the doctor took extra care in wiring together the components to ensure a simultaneous detonation of the individual parts. If successful, it would theoretically pack a punch as big as at the Sari Club, despite being only a fraction of the size. And as with Bali, Azhari provided the Marriott bomb with multiple methods of detonation: a timer, a manual switch, and probably a booby-trapped lid. In the end, the entire assembly was packed into three plastic drums and, with the rear seats removed, placed in the back of the Kijang.

To inflict maximum casualties, the conspirators looked to time the attack for noon during the middle of the work week. At that hour, they reasoned, the Marriott's coffee shop would be teeming with foreign guests.

Keeping to this plan, at 1145 on 5 August, Azhari and Sani departed the Jalan Kemuning Raya house in the Kijang. Behind them, Ismail trailed in the Honda motorcycle. Navigating through the lunch traffic, the two vehicles turned west onto Jalan Casablanca. There, in front of a small mosque, the Kijang pulled to the curb. As Sani went inside to say a final prayer, Azhari activated the timer on the bomb.

A few minutes later, Sani emerged and got in the driver's seat. Azhari, meantime, walked to the motorcycle 200 meters to the rear and took a seat behind Ismail. The Honda then sped in front, leading the Kijang toward the hotel. Two hundred meters before the target, the Kijang overtook them and Ismail peeled back toward Jalan Casablanca.[268]

At 1244 hours, Sani slowed the Kijang near the Marriott's U-shaped entrance ramp. Whether because of this hesitation, or because the battered Kijang looked out of place among the higher-class vehicles that normally frequented the venue, a hotel security guard posted at roadside approached the van. His

---

[267] Interview with Philip Taulelei, 25 July 2005.
[268] *Surat Tuntutan*, p. 15.

judgment no doubt clouded knowing that he only had seconds to live, Sani was still near the curb when he activated the manual trigger.

By that time, Azhari and Ismail had reversed direction and paused in front of the Carrefour department store. With an unimpeded view of the hotel, they watched as an enormous black plume engulfed the front of the Marriott. Ismail's only comment: "God is great."

What he was celebrating was an explosion that claimed a dozen lives and wounded nearly 150, the vast majority of them Indonesians. Among the fatalities was a Dutch banker; most of the remaining victims were chauffeurs and taxi drivers that congregated near the entrance. It might have been far worse. Although the bomb left behind a two-meter wide crater that penetrated 32 centimeters, much of the blast had been absorbed downward as the entrance ramp gave way into the parking basement. Too, the lobby had been spared far greater damage because Sani had set off the device too close to the road.

The conspirators had not remained behind long enough to gloat. By day's end, the four had reached the room they had earlier rented in Bandung. With Noordin passing himself off as a student and Azhari as a handbag salesman, they struck neighbors as quiet and polite. The only complaints were registered by a local maid, who noted that the group refused her entreaties and insisted on doing their own cooking and laundry. When the four suddenly vacated the room a month later, most barely even noticed their departure.

⋖◈⋗

Using lessons learned from Bali, the Indonesian National Police immediately delved into the Marriott investigation. The trouble was that one of their greatest challenges came from within, however. This was because not one, but two, police formations were competing over the counter-terrorist mandate.

The first was an ad hoc formation known as the National Bomb Task Force. This was headed by the dynamic Brigadier General Gregorius "Gories" Mere, whose sole faults were that he was of the wrong pedigree (a Catholic from Flores) and he constantly irritated rivals because of his aggressive drive for fast results. Formed in the immediate wake of the Bali bombing, Mere's task force had made exceptional headway alongside counterparts from the Australian Federal Police. Helping this was the fact that the Australians had generously provided his unit with advanced communications intercept technology.

The other unit, formally founded on 30 June 2003, was known as Special Detachment (*Detasemen Khusus*, or Densus) 88. Funded by the U.S. Department of State and headed by Brigadier General Pranowo Dahlan, this detachment was envisioned as a combination of counter-terrorist investigators, explosive ordnance specialists, and hostage rescue teams that would eventually replace Mere's ad hoc task force.[269]

As might be expected, there was immediate competition between both units. In particular, some in Densus 88 were openly jealous of the task force's coddling by the Australians and easy access to the chief of police.

At the time of the Marriott bombing, however, such inter-unit competition was moot. Densus 88, after all, was still untested and largely on paper. By default, Mere's task force was again in the forefront of the case.

With his normal flair, Mere made fast progress. Though an effort had been made to scratch off the Kijang's serial number on the engine block, the police were able to image those digits with chemicals and a powerful electro-magnet. This allowed them to locate the car's previous owner, who in turn helped them sketch portraits of the two buyers.

On a more macabre level, investigators found a hand and several fingers in the wreckage of the Kijang. On the fifth floor of the ravaged hotel, meanwhile, they found a severed head. DNA testing matched all to the same body. Though the head was in bad shape, the jailed Mohammad Rais identified it as belonging to Sani. This identification was echoed by Sani's sister, who recognized a scar and birthmark on the neck. The police now knew the identity of the person who had sent the e-mail to Togar back in June.

Belatedly tracing the exact path of the explosives in Sumatra, over the following week the police arrested four persons in Riau. All of them had safeguarded the boxes at some point over the previous two years.

---

[269] Densus 88 was funded via the U.S. Department of State's Anti-Terrorist Assistance (ATA) program. The way it received its name was a humorous tale of miscommunication. During a briefing for a senior police official on the ATA program, this police official – hearing the constant references to "A-T-A" – thought the briefing officers were saying "Eighty-Eight." As the number eight is considered lucky in some Asian cultures, the official stated that a double reference to eight would be especially auspicious and concurred that it was an excellent title for the new unit. As his subordinates were unwilling to correct their superior, the name stuck.

Back in Jakarta, meanwhile, all three of the safe houses were quickly located. At Jalan Kemuning Raya, little was found except a newspaper in the trash. In the margins, in Noordin's own handwriting, was the shortlist of possible targets.

Two months later, a tip led police to one of two safe houses the fugitives had been using in Bandung. Late in responding, the police arrived just hours after the four had vacated the locale.

Two of them, it turned out, had not gone far. Tracking Ismail and Tohir to the West Java town of Cirebon, they arrested the pair on 29 October as they were at a roadside stall eating a pre-dawn meal during the Islamic fasting month. As for Noordin and Azhari, the trail had grown cold, leaving both free to plan their next project.

CHAPTER SEVENTEEN

PROGENY

If one looked long and hard, there was a thin silver lining to the Marriott bombing in that the government's counter-terrorism units appeared increasingly capable. Within the Indonesian National Police, after all, Gories Mere's task force had spearheaded the arrest of those responsible in short order – save for Noordin Top and Azhari.

And though still untested in the field, Densus 88 was making fast progress in the classroom thanks to U.S. largesse. Under the watchful eye of foreign training specialists – including several former members of the U.S. Army Special Forces – the initial Densus assault teams began rotating through an impressive counter-terrorism school built at a former tea plantation set amidst the scenic hills of Megamendung, Bogor district. After a national-level reserve force completed instruction, plans called for provincial-level teams to start rotating through Megamendung, beginning with candidates from the Jakarta metropolitan police.

At BIN, meanwhile, a special team had been formed in early 2003 for the express purpose of penetrating extremist groups. Staffed with a mix of Arab linguists, religious experts, surveillance teams, and analysts, the team quickly earned kudos from regional intelligence counterparts. In several cases, elements of the team had even deployed overseas, including a Pakistan assignment to work with the ISI in the immediate wake of the al-Ghuraba arrests.

Better still, the police and BIN had set aside turf wars and begun to meaningfully cooperate in the field. This was largely the result of a decision by the chief of intelligence to co-opt a cadre of police generals to head BIN's upgraded provincial-level posts, thus giving the police a direct stake in BIN's intelligence-collection efforts.

Still, there was reason for serious concern among the authorities. First, there was the dark realization that Noordin and Azhari had been able to inflict significant material damage and loss of life – not to mention tremendous harm to Indonesia's overseas reputation, which undoubtedly had a negative ripple effect on foreign investment – with just a handful of operatives. Indeed, had Sani detonated the bomb further up the hotel's driveway, the results might have been just as catastrophic as Bali.

Second, the suicide element to the Bali bombings proved not to be a fluke. In fact, Jemaah Islamiyah, or what was left of it, had yet again proven its ability to identify and motivate a martyr with dizzying speed. There was every reason to think that Noordin and Azhari would be able to recruit more candidates willing to give their lives, if and when needed.

But perhaps the greatest factor that concerned the authorities was that, despite the fact that Jemaah Islamiyah's formal structure had largely been dismantled, the extremist threat was hardly receding. This was true because, following a power struggle within the Darul Islam network in December 1998, it was left with no overall leader. As an underground movement during the New Order regime, Darul Islam never had a highly articulated chain of command that extended across the archipelago; now that it was deprived of a supreme leader, its nationwide structure further devolved into an often chaotic shifting of alliances among like-minded radicals. Fractured in this manner, it was harder to map their structure and plot their direction. And in some cases, these disparate cells and individuals found appeal in Jemaah Islamiyah's outrage at the West.

Nowhere was this trend better illustrated than in the so-called Ring Banten. Though a Darul Islam presence in Banten traced back to the Kartosuwirjo era, the ring was synonymous since the eighties with the aggressive, resourceful Kang Jaja. An avid subscriber to jihad, he had arranged paramilitary training for a handful of Bantenese back in 1996. Three years later, he sent an initial group of nine recruits to Camp Hudaibiyah, then dispatched a steam of members to the battlefield in Ambon.

A turning point for the ring came in mid-2000. Darul Islam was already in a state of chaos, but as some of the more senior cadre leader in West Java opted to forgo violence and adopt a more passive, defensive interpretation of jihad, Kang Jaja was infuriated. Severing his ties with what passed as the Darul Islam mainstream, his Ring Banten effectively became an autonomous network.

In striking out on his own, Kang Jaja redoubled the focus on his aggressive brand of jihad. More of his men soon headed to Mindanao and the local jihads brewing in Central Sulawesi and Maluku. He also took steps to found an Islamic commune – what he termed Wisma Palem – in Saketi, Pandeglang. A pragmatist, he forged cordial ties with Laskar Jundullah in Poso, and with Jemaah Islamiyah through the one local boy who had achieved stature in that organization, Imam Samudra.

Such cross-pollination, of course, carried risks. When the August 2001 Atrium bombing had failed, the following month the authorities had descended on Wisma Palem. Although Kang Jaja for a time was forced to go underground, almost immediately he began shopping for an alternate site for a jihadi training ground.

He did not have to look far. Across Banten's border in Sukabumi district, the southern reaches near Java's coast were dotted with villages populated by aging Darul Islam members from the pre-1962 generation. It also happened to be a rather impoverished part of West Java, and Kang Jaja had astutely courted favor by sponsoring the construction of fish ponds around a village known as Gunung Batu.

At the close of 2001, Kang Jaja returned to Gunung Batu. Reasoning that it was sufficiently desolate to restart the paramilitary training earlier offered in Pandeglang, he purchased some land and announced plans to establish a new camp.

To head the effort, Kang Jaja appointed a especially abrasive Javanese radical named Harun. Previously a platoon commander in the so-called Abu Bakar Battalion that went to Ambon in late 1999, Harun had a long history of burning bridges among his fellow extremists. Indeed, a year earlier he had repeatedly scuffled in Poso with Kang Jaja's own jihadists deployed from Banten.[270]

Now allied with Kang Jaja, Harun spent the next three years tutoring a flow of young recruits from Sukabumi and Banten, including the Bali bomber recruited by Imam Samudra. Other classes, to include instructions on bomb-making, were conducted in and around Jakarta. Said one observer: "Harun took students with the right inclination, then pushed them the extra three degrees to make them dangerous."[271]

---

[270] John MacDougall interview.
[271] *Ibid.*

In hindsight, none of this should have been a surprise to the Indonesian authorities. After all, they had come dramatically close to crushing Ring Banten during the September 2001 Pandeglang arrests. But not realizing what they had stumbled across, the lead was not pursued to the fullest and Kang Jaja remained free.

The following year, the police had another chance to bring Ring Banten to a close when they received a copy of the suicide note penned by Bali bomber Arnasan. In the note, he addressed his comments to twenty-one of his colleagues from Malingping (his hometown) and Gunung Batu. Had this clue been pursued, the police could well have uncovered Kang Jaja's Sukabumi camp in the midst of one of Harun's training cycles.

A third and final opportunity came on 31 March 2004. After Harun had given a class in bomb-making to a congregation from Depok district just south of Jakarta, his students blew the roof off of a house while they were trying to practice their newfound art. The police promptly arrested eight men and one women, who this time pointed a finger at Harun. But by the time they got around to tracking him, both Harun and his sponsor, Kang Jaja, had fled Java for sanctuary near Poso.

Remarkably, while the authorities had yet to make any links to Gunung Batu, fugitives Noordin Top and Azhari had. Learning of the training site while they were on the run in West Java, Noordin personally visited the locale in June 2004. Though Harun was long gone, the camp was being run by Rois (alias Iwan Darmawan), the 29-year-old nephew of Kang Jaja by marriage. Brash and relatively wealthy, Rois had been among the nine Bantenese who had ventured to Mindanao for training back in 1999, then had headed a contingent that fought in Poso the following year.

What came next was a unique convergence of interests. Rois had on hand a band of jihadis from Ring Banten that were in search of a jihad. Noordin, by contrast, was fixated on his anti-Western crusade, but was in need of foot soldiers and a local support network. It was a perfect match.

From that point forward, Noordin's next terrorist strike took shape at a rapid clip. Rois, given his contacts across Banten and Sukabumi, would assist with logistics. He would be assisted by two lieutenants drawn from Jemaah Islamiyah: 34-year-old Ahmad Hasan and 24-year-old Jabir. The latter, who had briefly attended Ngruki in 1995, then was in the inaugural class at Darus

Sya'adah that same year, was the first cousin of the late Jemaah Islamiyah bomb-er al-Ghozi. Jabir had briefly returned to take up a teaching position at Darus Sya'adah in May 2004, but had gone absent without leave that same month to answer Noordin's call for assistance.

There was also the need to identify a suicide operative. Several impression-able recruits had been present at Gunung Batu earlier in the year, but the most promising of the lot had taken to flight after the accidental Depok bombing in March. The best of the remaining students was 26-year-old Heri Gulon. A for-mer delinquent, he had been placed under Harun's tutelage in an effort to instill him with discipline and direction. Alternately bombarded with praise and pleas by Rois and a second Gunung Batu trainer named Irun Hidayat, Heri in short order appeared sufficiently malleable to accept martyrdom.

Next, the conspirators had to address the issue of funding. For the Bali and Marriott operations, key cash infusions had come from Hambali via Bangkok. This was no longer an option, nor did Jemaah Islamiyah have access to a dona-tion network for domestic funds. But Noordin and Azhari had caught a lucky break during their previous operation. Not only had they been able to stage the Marriott strike on the cheap, but there is no evidence that they ever disbursed the US$10,000 that had been earmarked for the families of the Bali bombers. As a result, there was more than enough to cover living expenses for the pair over the previous months, as well as a sufficient reserves to underwrite another strike.

Dipping into this savings, Noordin handed Rois a wad of cash and in-structed him to rent a safe house in Cengkareng, West Jakarta. This was done by 20 July, after which several of the conspirators – Noordin, Azhari, Rois, Hasan – took up residence. Azhari quickly took stock of six boxes of dynamite; these he had reportedly acquired from Jemaah Islamiyah sources on Java that had been storing the material since the Ambon jihad. The doctor also began to piece together the circuitry for the detonator.

Rois and Heri, meanwhile, took leave of Cengkareng to venture across Ja-karta and purchase a used Daihatsu box truck. They then headed down to Suka-bumi, where the pair procured 500 kilos of potassium chlorate and 200 kilos of sulfur from a chemical supply store.

Constantly on the move, by 24 July most of the group converged at a sec-ond safe house established in Cisuren, Sukabumi. There they waited until early

August, when the group moved to yet another safe house, this one in Serang, Banten. It was at this last locale that Azhari got down to the business of building the bomb. Following a familiar script, he packed the precursor chemicals in three plastic filing cabinets, the same type of container that had been used in Bali. Once more, he arranged for alternate means of detonation, including a timer and an automatic switch connected to a rope leading into the truck's cabin.

All that remained was for the cell to pick its target. Although it was known that Jemaah Islamiyah had considered strikes against the American, British, and Australian embassies in Jakarta as far back as 1999, more recent evidence – including testimony from Hambali – suggested Jemaah Islamiyah no longer entertained embassy strikes because they were too hardened. This was especially true of the Australian embassy, which had taken additional counter-measures in September 2003 after documents uncovered during a raid at a terrorist compound in Afghanistan indicated possible planning for a truck bombing at its Indonesian diplomatic post.

Noordin and Azhari, it seems, were determined to go against the conventional wisdom. During the second half of August, the cell began a series of surveys of the Australian compound on Jalan Rasuna Said. These trials were not without risk: while Azhari was conducting a rehearsal during the final days of the month, he was stopped by police officers conducting a vehicle document search. (Such police vehicle searches for infractions real or imagined are not uncommon in Jakarta.) The fugitive went unrecognized and reportedly was sent speeding on his way after slipping the officers a 50,000 rupiah bill.

The conspirators, meantime, had to contend with other headaches. It was fast becoming apparent that the Australian embassy was going to be a tough nut to crack. On their last trial run, Rois attempted to estimate the width of the front gate to see if their truck could squeeze inside while an authorized vehicle was gaining entry. As a fallback, they considered smashing through the gate. Though they had no way of knowing it, neither option was viable.

Just as problematic was the fact that – shades of Arnasan in Bali – Heri Gulon could not drive. At nearly the eleventh hour, Rois took him aside and tried to impart in him the basics of steering a truck.

By 8 September, all was set. In the garage of their Serang safe house, Azhari assembled the bomb and placed it in the rear of the box truck. That same night, the group headed for yet another safe house, this one in West Jakarta. Barring unforeseen circumstances, their attack would take place the next afternoon.

⋘⊙⋙

For its part, the Indonesian authorities were clueless as to Jemaah Islamiyah's imminent intentions. Not that they were short of theories; rather, they were being whipsawed by too many. Back in early June, there had been a scare that extremists were going to strike at a Canadian nickel-mining operation in South Sulawesi. These fears were sparked by dozens of graphic threats that were being sent to the company's executives – including the Canadian president director – via text messaging over their cell phones.

On that occasion, Gories Mere and BIN had deployed personnel to the scene. Using sophisticated electronics gear to triangulate the signals, Mere and his team apprehended the culprit within 72 hours. Ironically, the perpetrator was not an Islamic radical, but a Catholic dentist from Mere's own island of Flores. The reason for the threats: the dentist was afraid that a company audit would uncover his more corrupt medical practices, so he had concocted the threatening messages to divert attention and send expatriates fleeing.

Later that same month, the authorities received information that Jemaah Islamiyah might be planning a strike during a police anniversary set for Jogjakarta on 3 July. A few weeks after that, there were hints that Jemaah Islamiyah might be reconsidering a bombing at the U.S.-operated gold mine on Sumbawa. To guard against this contingency, Mere visited Sumbawa with a new set of computer-generated mug shots showing Noordin Top and Azhari with various hair lengths and styles. Later still, by the beginning of September, several Western embassies issued warnings about the possible targeting of luxury hotels.

There were also fears that Jemaah Islamiyah might try to disrupt Indonesia's first direct presidential elections, set for the third week of September. Late on the morning of 9 September, the chief of the Indonesian National Police, Da'i Bachtiar, testified in front of the House of Representatives as to the state of security ahead of the polls. He assured the legislators that all was secure.

At the precise moment that Bachtiar was uttering those words, Azhari, Ahmad Hasan, and Heri Gulon had left their West Jakarta safe house and reached the Central Business District. Stopping at a street-side stall near a mosque, the trio got out for a quick prayer. After that, Azhari got in the driver's seat and departed with Heri. Hasan, meanwhile, got on a black motorcycle that had been delivered by a sympathizer named Sapta.

Following the same script used at the Marriott, the truck and motorcycle headed north along Jalan Rasuna Said. After continuing past the Australian embassy for a couple of kilometers, they exited and circled below the thoroughfare along an underpass. Pausing near the Italian Cultural Center, Azhari got out to set the bomb's timer for twenty minutes. Even in the event of heavy traffic, that would allow more than sufficient time to reach their target.

Now heading south, the two vehicles next paused at a bus stop fifty meters from the embassy. There Azhari got out and got on the rear of the motorcycle being driven by Hasan. They sped ahead, leaving Heri to navigate the final stretch.

After following a slight bend in Jalan Rasuna Said, Hasan slowed by the curb. Almost as soon as he did so, a massive blast reverberated down the road. "We're successful," Azhari muttered.

On several levels, Azhari was speaking the truth. The box truck had disintegrated in a massive blast near the embassy's front entrance, killing ten and wounding 180. This time, the bomb had exactly exploded as advertised – rather than burned, as had been in the case of Bali – indicating that Azhari was getting better at his craft. It was only due to the strategic placement of an earthen berm, some enlightened architecture that diverted the pressure wave away from the building, and pure luck that no Australian nationals were killed or seriously wounded.

⋘⋙

Always thinking several moves ahead, the bombers immediately converged at a safe house in Cikampek to the east of Jakarta. After staying there for only a few days, they departed for another safe house rented in Purwakarta, West Java. Over the following month, Noordin and Azhari discreetly passed messages to Jemaah Islamiyah sympathizers in Central Java. Help, they were told, was on the way.

Meanwhile, Azhari took steps to pass on his bomb-making knowledge to other cell members hiding with him in Purwakarta. He also constructed a series of belt bombs fitted inside Tupperware containers. Strapped to the stomach, these were equipped with two fuses: one allowed for an instant detonation in the event that the wearer wanted to commit suicide, the other provided for a delay of several seconds in order to use it as a makeshift hand grenade. Each cell member was provided with one.

At that point, the cell split. Noordin, Azhari, and Jabir headed for Central Java. Meantime, Rois, Hasan, Apuy (a Gunung Batu graduate), and another radical named Ashori shifted to Cicurug, West Java. The latter group promptly ran into hard times. On 14 October, while attempting to follow Azhari's bomb-making instructions, there was an accidental explosion in their safe house. Panicking, the four fled Cicurug for Bogor.[272] On 5 November, they were eventually apprehended while chatting at an Internet café.

Although Noordin, Azhari, and Jabir remained on the loose, there was some reason for cheer. The police had once again shown added capabilities in the investigation phase of the Australian embassy bombing. In particular, Densus 88 had shown its ability to assume added responsibilities after Gories Mere was discharged on 6 October.[273]

But there were many more reasons to see the glass as half empty. For one thing, 1,800 students continued to study at the Ngruki pesantren, despite the fact that nearly three dozen accused and convicted Jemaah Islamiyah terrorists count it as their alma mater.

For another thing, arguably the five most dangerous members of Jemaah Islamiyah – Noordin, Azhari, the shadowy Zulkarnaen, Dul Matin, and Umar Arab – have proven remarkably elusive. In the case of Zulkarnaen, he dropped off the radar screen in 2002. In the cases of Dul Matin and Umar Arab, they are reportedly trekking the Mindanao jungles between camps run by the MILF and Abu Sayyaf Group.

There were also renewed concerns over terrorist financing. There had been hopes that the spigot of funds from the Middle East would close following the August 2003 capture of Hambali. But in December 2004, this assumption

---

[272] In Cicurug, the police found Azhari's lecture notes on bomb construction, as well as some of the Tupperware devices.

[273] Mere had come under intense pressure in the days immediately before the Australian embassy bombing after he was caught escorting convicted Bali bomber Ali Imron to a Starbuck's in downtown Jakarta. In his defense, the general said he was treating the repentant Imron in an attempt to glean information about the possible whereabouts of Noordin and Azhari. On 6 October, Mere was discharged and replaced by his deputy, Bekto Suprapto. Shortly thereafter, the bomb task force was officially disbanded and Bekto was named the new commander of Densus 88.

came under fire following the arrest by Philippine authorities in Zamboanga City of a 26-year old Indonesian named Mohammad Yusuf Karim Faiz (alias Saifuddin). Faiz told investigators that he had recently rendezvoused with a Middle Eastern benefactor in a Jakarta restaurant and reportedly received more than US$20,000 in cash. On orders from Noordin Top, he was couriering those funds to Dul Matin before being captured by the Philippine police. Evidently, Jemaah Islamiyah had been able to compensate for the loss of Hambali and open new avenues of foreign funding.

By mid-2005, the Indonesian government of President Susilo Bambang Yudhoyono, who had taken the oath of office the previous October, was growing understandably concerned. Promises by some of his top security officials to capture Noordin Top and Azhari during the first one-hundred days of his administration had long since passed with no firm leads as to the whereabouts of the two Malaysians. And with the anniversaries of the 11 September attacks in the U.S. and 12 October bombing in Bali looming, the president saw fit to issue a general warning at the opening of September. Jakarta, he said, might be due for an encore strike some during the coming two months.

In terms of timing, at least, he was deadly accurate. During the early evening hours of Saturday, 1 October, three young suicide bombers set off bombs inside backpacks and killed themselves – as well as nearly two dozen others – at a trio of crowded restaurants on Bali. For obvious reason, Noordin Top and Azhari were fingered as the masterminds.

There was an uneasy feeling of déjà vu with what was soon dubbed by the Indonesian press as *Bom* Bali II. There was little mystery as to why the terrorists would revisit Bali. Their October 2002 attack, after all, was seen within Jemaah Islamiyah as their only clear-cut previous success because they had been able to inflict heavy casualties on Western nationals far in excess of what even they themselves had predicted.

Too, the reports of shrapnel injuries from ball bearings had precedent. Almost a year earlier, the Tupperware belt-bombs captured in Cicurug had been encrusted with ball bearings to add to their lethality. Azhari, it seems, had merely reconfigured these devices for backpacks.

As the dust settled in Bali, the sense of frustration among Indonesia's security officials was palatable. If their previous annual operations were any indicator, Noordin Top and Azhari had already mapped out a string of safe houses and were lying low as the initial dragnet passed overhead. The pair was also likely receiving sanctuary from pockets of sympathizers strung across the Java heartland. To be sure, nobody has come forward to collect the bounty that has been posted on their heads for the previous two years.

Frustration, too, was being expressed by the authorities over the fact that, while the formal Jemaah Islamiyah ranks may have been heavily attrited since late 2002, the remaining radicals were proving adaptable and pragmatic. Since the Marriott operation, for example, Noordin Top and Azhari had successfully forged common cause with a range of Darul Islam cells, injecting into them a violent anti-West direction that previously was absent from the Darul Islam mainstream. Such ad hoc alliances made it that much more difficult to identify the extremists and map their next move.

All of which gave little reason for optimism looking ahead. Still, Indonesia's intelligence chief, General Syamsir Siregar, tried his best to put his best spin on events. "If the top five – Noordin Top, Azhari, Dul Matin, Zulkarnaen, and Umar Arab – can be stopped," he said, "Jemaah Islamiyah can be managed."[274]

Or at least until Darul Islam's next violent progeny takes root.

---

[274] Interview with Sjamsir Siregar, 10 August 2005. In October 2005, the U.S. government offered a reward of US$10 million for assistance in the capture of Dul Matin, and another US$1 million was placed on the head of Umar Arab.

INDEX

also from EQUINOX PUBLISHING

LaVergne, TN USA
22 March 2011
221128LV00002B/140/A